VISUAL QUICKSTART GUIDE

Final Cut Pro X

LISA BRENNEIS • MICHAEL W

 Peachpit Press

Visual QuickStart Guide
Final Cut Pro X
Lisa Brenneis and Michael Wohl

Peachpit Press
1249 Eighth Street
Berkeley, CA 94710
(510) 524-2178
Fax: (510) 524-2221

Find us on the Web at www.peachpit.com
To report errors, please send a note to errata@peachpit.com
Peachpit is a division of Pearson Education

Senior Editor: Karyn Johnson
Development Editor: Stephen Nathans-Kelly
Copy Editor: Kimberly Wimpsett
Production Editor: Cory Borman
Proofreader: Elizabeth Welch
Composition: Danielle Foster
Indexer: Emily Glossbrenner
Interior Design: Peachpit Press
Cover design: RHDG / Riezebos Hozbaur Design Group, Peachpit Press
Logo Design: MINE™ www.minesf.com

ISBN-13: 978-0-321-77466-8
ISBN-10:   0-321-77466-3

9 8 7 6 5 4 3 2 1

Printed and bound in the United States of America

Contents at a Glance

Table of Contents

Introduction

When the two Steves started Apple back in 1976, they dreamed of making a computer that people could use as a tool to change the world. Final Cut Pro, launched in 1999, has been an Apple program worthy of the founders' vision.

Final Cut Pro attracted a worldwide community of users, ranging from award-winning icons of cinema to people you never heard of who were suddenly able to make movies. Twelve years is a long time—you might recognize their names now.

Apple has had a busy and insanely successful decade. It's a very different company now, with different ambitions, but it's still resolutely and always facing forward, not backward. With this release, Final Cut Pro X, Apple pushed the big reset button. This is an all-new application.

FCP X, launched in June 2011, has dramatically divided the Final Cut Pro community. Reviews have ranged from "revolutionary and visionary" to "I want my money back."

FCP, once part of the Final Cut Studio application suite, is a stand-alone application once more and available (only as an Apple App Store download) at a much lower price.

The changes in this latest edition of Final Cut Pro include, well, everything: power and performance gains, a completely redesigned editing interface that works differently, a different (and smaller) feature set, and different names for many features and functions.

This book, *Final Cut Pro X: Visual Quick-Start Guide*, is the first QuickStart Guide for Final Cut Pro, but its authors have been with FCP since before the beginning. This is our first collaboration.

This edition describes the operation of FCP X. If you're using FCP 4, HD, 5, 6, or 7, you'll need an earlier edition of *Final Cut Pro: Visual QuickPro Guide*.

Who Should Use This Book

Final Cut Pro X: Visual QuickStart Guide is designed to be used by Mac users with a little basic knowledge of video-editing terms and procedures and the Mac operating system; explaining basic video production and editing is beyond the scope of this book. Final Cut Pro is designed to be easy to use, but it's still a professional-level video-editing and compositing program. If you're familiar with the Macintosh but you're completely new to video editing, consider some basic training in video-editing fundamentals before you plunge into this program.

Or try Apple's free iMovie program. It's a great way to get a taste of basic video editing in a stripped-down program that's a little easier for beginners to use.

What's in This Book

This book starts with a quick feature overview of the entire program, followed by hardware setup and program installation.

Next you'll find four chapters devoted to FCP's clip handling, media marking and organization, and project structure.

Chapter 6 introduces the Import window—the Final Cut Pro tool you use for importing and organizing media in preparation for an edit.

The next part of the book details the variety of ways you can use FCP's editing tools to assemble and refine an edited project.

These chapters cover basic editing procedures and the operation of the Timeline, Viewer, and Precision Edit windows for editing, with a couple of chapters devoted to audio editing and effects.

The next nine chapters are devoted to using the program's special effects and compositing tools. You'll find chapters devoted to creating motion effects, using filters, and creating titles and other generator effects.

The final chapter lays out your options for outputting a final product.

How to Use This Book

This guide is designed to be a Final Cut Pro user's companion, a reference guide with an emphasis on step-by-step descriptions of specific tasks. You'll encounter the following features:

- "Anatomy" sections introduce the major program windows with large annotated illustrations identifying interface features and operation. If you're not a step-by-step kind of person, you can pick up quite a bit of information just by browsing these illustrations.

- Sidebars throughout the book highlight production techniques, FCP protocol rules, and suggestions for streamlining your workflow.

- Tips are short bits that call your attention to a neat trick or a cool feature or warn you of a potential pitfall in the task at hand.

Learning Final Cut Pro

Here are some tips to help you get up and running in Final Cut Pro ASAP.

Basic Theory

"Secrets of Nondestructive Digital Editing," a sidebar in Chapter 1, "Welcome to Final Cut Pro," explains how nondestructive editing works and how it affects the operation of Final Cut Pro. You don't absolutely have to read it to operate Final Cut Pro, but understanding some of the basic concepts underlying the design of the program will make FCP much easier to learn.

Test, Test, Test

Many times, what you're able to produce with Final Cut Pro depends on the capabilities of your external video hardware and the video format you're working in. So, before you rush out and submit a budget or sign a contract, take your entire Final Cut Pro system, including your external video gear, for a test-drive.

Keyboard Commands

Final Cut Pro was designed to support a wide variety of working styles ranging from heavy pointing, clicking, and dragging to entirely keyboard-based editing. More keyboard commands are available than those listed in the individual tasks in this book; you can find complete keyboard shortcut info here:

http://help.apple.com/finalcutpro/mac/10.0.1/#ver90ba5929

Shortcut Menus

Final Cut Pro makes extensive use of shortcut menus. As you explore the program, right-clicking items and interface elements is a quick way to see your options in many areas of the FCP interface, and it can speed up the learning process.

Buy a Two-Button Mouse

You'll be amazed how much a two-button mouse with a scroll wheel will improve your Final Cut Pro editing experience. The FCP interface is quite scroll-friendly; everything from major program windows to the parameter controls on the Viewer's effects tabs respond to the scroll wheel. Right-clicking a two-button mouse is equivalent to a Control-click, so FCP's shortcut menus are never more than a single click away.

Touching

If your computer has a multi-touch trackpad, you can interact with FCP using its repertoire of multi-touch gestures. Final Cut Pro Help has details.

Refer to the Manual

The official Final Cut Pro Help documentation can come in handy. The latest edition has shrunk dramatically from the days of FCP 7, but the official word from Apple is available on Apple's website and from your Mac's Help menu. Final Cut Pro's manual is no longer available as a printed document, but you can (and should) download the PDF version from Apple's website: *http://help.apple.com/finalcutpro/mac/10.0.1.*

The Help Viewer and online versions of the manual do not offer page numbers. Use the FCP Help search field to look up the section by name, or create a PDF version of the FCP manual on Apple's website. For more information on how to make your own PDF, see "On-screen Help" in Chapter 1, "Welcome to Final Cut Pro."

Check Out Apple Support

Apple posts a steady stream of valuable Final Cut Pro articles and updates on its online Apple Support site: *www.apple.com/support/finalcutpro/*.

Apple Support is also the place to go for program update info, user manuals, and user forums. The company also posts information about FCP "known issues" (that's corporate-speak for bugs) as technical articles on the site.

The Web Is Your Friend

Using the World Wide Web is an essential part of using Final Cut Pro. Apple, as well as the manufacturers of the video hardware you'll be using with Final Cut Pro, relies on the Web to inform users of the latest developments and program updates and to provide technical support. You'll find a starter list of online resources on the Apple FCP Resources page (*www.apple.com/finalcutpro/resources/*) and specific URLs sprinkled in this book. There are some great sources of information, technical help, and camaraderie out there. If you get stuck or encounter difficulties getting started, go online and ask questions. After you've learned the program, go online and answer questions. Helping other people is a great way to learn.

Thank You

Program interfaces may come and go, but the people in this community tend to stick around. It's been an adventure and a privilege to explore this world and meet so many of you. We look forward to our further adventures together.

Special thanks to Kira Ryder of *www.lulubandhas.com*, the very real yoga instructor who appears in this book.

Heartfelt thanks to Cupertino, Los Angeles, San Francisco, Berkeley, Ojai, Irvine, West Hollywood, Seattle, Chicago, New York, London, and Sydney.

Can't wait to see your movie.

Welcome to Final Cut Pro X

Welcome to Apple's Final Cut Pro—a combination digital video editing, compositing, and special effects program.

Final Cut Pro is tightly integrated with Apple's Intel processors, high-speed data transfer technology, and QuickTime multimedia format. It supports a wide variety of digital video formats, including AVCHD, DV, HDV, and DVCPRO HD, along with the latest high-definition (HD) digital formats. Final Cut Pro also supports nonbroadcast formats, streaming formats such as H.264, and all QuickTime formats.

Final Cut Pro provides professional editing functionality in a variety of styles, from strictly drag-and-drop edits to entirely keyboard-based editing.

Soon you'll be spending plenty of time working with clips, audio levels, and other editing minutiae, so let's start with the big picture. In this chapter, you'll find a brief overview of Final Cut Pro workflow and features. You'll be introduced to the main interface windows used for editing and for creating effects. You'll also learn about Final Cut Pro's import and export options and its functions for undoing changes.

In This Chapter

Your First Final Cut Pro Project: Start to Finish

Here's a road map you can use to chart a course through your first FCP project. This flowchart describes the production pathway of a typical project from media import through output of the finished program. At each step, you'll find pointers to sections in this book that describe that part of the process in more detail.

- **Import media:** Use the controls in the Import window to transfer video and audio from tape or file-based camcorders—or from another hard drive—and save them to a folder in FCP's Event Library. For more information, see Chapter 6, "Importing Footage."

- **Import other media elements:** Add music or sound effects or graphics elements such as digital stills or graphics. See the "Importing Files" section of Chapter 6, "Importing Footage."

- **Rough assembly:** Review your raw video in the Viewer, and select the portions you want to use by marking In and Out points. Assemble the selected portions into a "rough cut" in an empty project in the Timeline. If your project includes narration, be sure to edit a "draft" narration into your rough cut. If you plan to base the rhythm of your cut on a piece of music, you should edit the music into the rough cut as well. See Chapter 7, "Basic Editing."

- **Fine cut:** Revisit your rough cut, and make fine adjustments to edit points directly by using the Precision Editor in the Timeline or by opening sequence clips and making adjustments in the Viewer. See Chapter 9, "Fine-Tuning."

- **Finishing:** When your fine cut is complete, use FCP's text generators (or the Motion application) to add titles, use the color correction tools to tweak the video's color balance, and fill out the audio tracks with effects and music. See Chapters 11 through 21.

- **Output:** Select an output option from FCP's Share window to export your finished project. FCP's Share feature can produce finished Blu-ray Discs, upload your day's work to YouTube, and do much more. If you need batch export options or more control over format settings, use Apple's companion video-encoding utility, Compressor (sold separately). See Chapter 22, "Creating Output: Sharing and Exporting."

Secrets of Nondestructive Digital Editing

Nondestructive editing is a basic Final Cut Pro concept. Digitally arranging and editing your footage in FCP means constructing a playlist, much like a playlist you would create in iTunes.

In iTunes, your archive of song files is stored in the iTunes Library; an iTunes playlist is just a set of instructions telling the iTunes jukebox how to sequence the playback of songs you select. A single song file can appear in multiple playlists, and deleting a song from a playlist doesn't delete the actual song file from the Library. In Final Cut Pro X, projects operate like iTunes playlists.

An FCP project (or storyline) is a collection of instructions to the program to play a certain bit of Media File A, then cut to a bit of Media File B, then play a later bit of Media File A, and so on. The full length of each file is available to the editor from within the edited project. That's because in Final Cut Pro, the *clip*—the basic media element used to construct edited projects—is only a set of instructions referring to an underlying media file.

When you play back an edited project, it only looks as though it's been spliced together; in fact, Final Cut Pro has assembled it on-the-fly. Since you're viewing a simulation of an edited project and the full length of each captured file is available at the edit point, extending a shot is simply a matter of rewriting the editing program's playlist to play a little more of Media File A before switching to Media File B. In Final Cut Pro, you do this by modifying the clip's length in your edited project.

Nondestructive editing is key to editing in a program like Final Cut Pro, which allows you to use media source files multiple times across multiple projects or to access the same source file but process it in a number of different ways. Having many instances of a clip (which, in Final Cut Pro, is just a set of instructions) all referring to the same media file saves disk space and offers flexibility throughout your editing process.

A final warning: Nondestructive editing rules do not apply in FCP's Event Library. Copying, moving, and deleting clips within the Event Library *does* copy, move, or delete your actual source media files on disk. So, treat Event Library files with the same respect and care as your original files.

Touring Your Desktop Postproduction Facility

Three program windows in a single stream-lined interface form the heart of the Final Cut Pro interface: the Event Browser, the Viewer, and the Timeline **A**.

Because the program combines so many editing and effects creation capabilities in a single application, each of these windows performs multiple functions; additional program windows are hidden from view until you reveal them—making maximum use of your screen real estate.

The tools arrayed on the interface's center strip can be used to make selections, navigate your footage, and perform edits in the Timeline.

Access and sort your source clips in the Event Browser.

Assemble your edit in the Timeline.

Play back your source clips and your edited project in the Viewer.

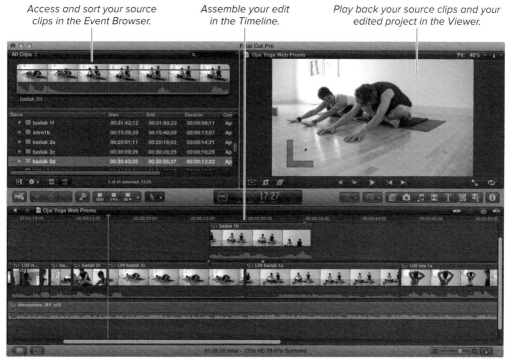

A The three main program windows in Final Cut Pro X

Useful Features

The following are a few useful features that apply throughout the program:

- **Hidden program windows:** Final Cut Pro makes maximum use of interface space by hiding the program windows you don't need to access continuously **B**. When you need access to the Event Library, the Project Library, the Inspector, or one of FCP's stack of media and effects libraries, a single mouse click calls up the window you need.

TIP You can see a full list of FCP's interface windows in the View menu.

TIP When a hidden window is displayed, its control button turns blue to indicate that the window is displayed. The Event Library button's blue status light surely will be fixed in the next version....

Click to show or hide
the Event Library window.

Event Library

Inspector

Click to show or hide
the Inspector window.

Click to show or hide
the Project Library window.

Project Library

Effects Browser

The Media Browser and
Effects Browser display is
controlled by this row of
buttons. Click one to show
the corresponding Media
Browser or Effects Browser.

B This is the FCP interface with its hidden windows displayed.

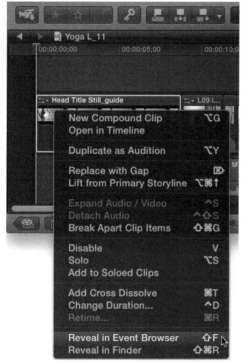

C Rest the pointer over a button, and a *tooltip*—a label with the tool's name—will appear. Tooltips also display keyboard shortcuts for tools and buttons.

D Right-clicking a project clip in the Timeline calls up a shortcut menu with a list of functions related to that clip.

- **Tooltips:** You can use tooltips to identify most of the controls in the Viewer window and on the Tool palette **C**. Tooltips also display the keyboard shortcut for a tool or button. Rest the pointer over the button and wait a moment, and a label will appear.

Menus, Shortcuts, and Controls

Final Cut Pro offers several methods for performing video-editing tasks. Some people work fastest using keyboard shortcuts; others prefer to use the menu bar or shortcut menus as much as possible. Apart from the menu bar and window buttons, you can use several other means to access Final Cut Pro's functions; experiment to find out which control methods work best for you:

- **Shortcut menus:** Shortcut menus can speed your work and help you learn Final Cut Pro. Right-click an item in one of the main interface windows, and select from a list of common functions specific to that item **D**. Right-click often as you learn your way around the program just to see your options in a particular area of the FCP interface.

- **Keyboard shortcuts:** You may find that these shortcut keys help you work more efficiently. See "Customizing Your Workspace" later in this chapter to learn how to reassign FCP's default keyboard shortcuts to keys that please you.

- **Timecode entry shortcuts:** Final Cut Pro provides a number of time-saving shortcuts for timecode entry. See "Navigating with Timecode in the Timeline" in Chapter 8, "Editing Tools."

Customizable Interface

FCP's flexible interface can be custom-tailored to suit your needs. Within the integrated interface, you can adjust the overall size of the main program window and the proportions between program windows.

You can also elect to display the Viewer window or the Event Browser on a second computer display and build custom keyboard configurations. See "Customizing Your Workspace" later in this chapter.

On-screen Help

The on-screen help for FCP is also the official Final Cut Pro User Manual. The Help Viewer version has certain disadvantages over the PDF manual offered with previous versions: there's no index, no chapter or page numbers, no Boolean word search, and limited printing access. An online version of the same manual is available on Apple's website: *http://help.apple.com/finalcutpro/mac/10.0.1.*

The online manual has a couple of advantages: You can bookmark manual pages for later reference, and you can use the Left and Right Arrow keys to page through the online text.

To access on-screen help:

- Choose Help > Final Cut Pro X Help.

TIP The FCP X manual you find on Apple's website features a Print button **E**. You can use that Print command to save a fully text-searchable PDF version of the Apple manual.

E Apple offers Final Cut Pro X's manual on its website. To make a PDF version of the official manual, click the Print button, and then choose Save As PDF in the Print dialog window.

FCP X Alert: Event Library and Event Browser Actions Affect Source Media Files

Every FCP user should read this alert. It's a bit tricky, but it's vital to remember.

When you copy, move, and delete files in FCP's Event *Library*, FCP will copy, move, or delete your *actual source media files* on disk.

Copying or moving a clip from inside the Event *Browser* does not affect its source media file on disk, but deleting an Event Browser clip will move its source media file to your Mac's Trash. Don't accidentally delete the last copy of your original media.

Editing and Effects Windows

The following brief descriptions of the features and functions of the main program windows are simplified summaries of the full list of features. Final Cut Pro's designers went all out to support a wide variety of editing styles, and they have produced a very flexible editing system.

The Event Library and Event Browser

The Event Library displays all the clips, audio, and graphics you've imported into FCP organized into *events*—FCP's name for a folder containing clips.

Clicking an event's icon in the Event Library displays its contents—the clips contained in that event—in the Event Browser.

The Event Browser is the window you use to organize and access individual clips, audio files, graphics, and offline clips—all the media elements you use in your project **Ⓐ**.

In list view, the Event Browser displays a filmstrip view of the selected clip. Other clips are displayed in a sortable, searchable list.

Click an event's icon to display all its clips in the Browser

Click to display Event Browser in List view

Click to display Event Browser in Filmstrip view

Click to display or hide the Event Library

Event Library

Event Browser

Enter a search term in the Filter field or click the field to open the Filter window

Drag range-selection handles to select a section of clip. Selected range can be edited into a project, tagged with a keyword, rated Favorite or Reject.

Set Action pop-up menu options to control sort order and date display in the Event Library and Browser

Ⓐ Use the Event Library and Event Browser windows to organize the media elements in your projects.

The Viewer

The Viewer is bursting with functions. When you're editing, the Viewer acts as your source monitor; you can review individual video and audio clips and mark edit points **B**. You also use the Viewer to play back your project as you edit it in the Timeline. Load clips from the current project into the Viewer to refine your edits, apply effects, create titles—and, as they say, much, much more.

Filmstrip indicates first (or last) frame of source media

Clip or Project Name

Viewer Display Options menu

Viewer Zoom menu

Compositing controls

Use these on-screen playback controls—or keyboard commands or timecode entry—to move around in your clips.

Full-Screen Playback button

Loop Playback button

B Use the Viewer window to play back your source clips and your edited project.

The Timeline

The Timeline displays your edited project as clips arrayed on multiple video and audio tracks along a time axis 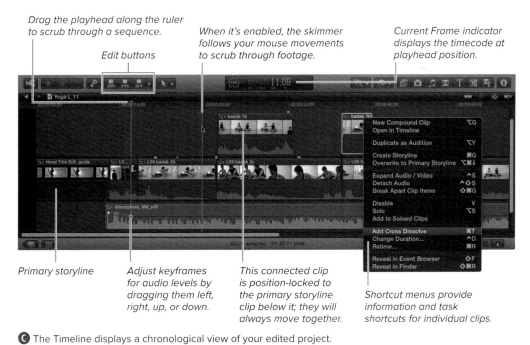 **C**. You view Timeline playback in the Viewer. You can edit by using keyboard commands, by using the editing buttons on the Tool Strip just above the Timeline, or by dragging clips directly from the Event Browser and dropping them in the Timeline; see Chapter 7, "Basic Editing."

The middle row (or *track*) contains your *primary storyline*, where you place most of the clips that make up your movie. These clips can contain both audio and video. You can *connect* additional clips above or below the primary storyline to synchronize them with a particular frame in one of the primary clips.

In the Timeline, a connected clip is indicated by a connection line that extends from the first frame of the connected clip to the sync point in the primary storyline.

Drag the playhead along the ruler to scrub through a sequence.

Edit buttons

When it's enabled, the skimmer follows your mouse movements to scrub through footage.

Current Frame indicator displays the timecode at playhead position.

Primary storyline

Adjust keyframes for audio levels by dragging them left, right, up, or down.

This connected clip is position-locked to the primary storyline clip below it; they will always move together.

Shortcut menus provide information and task shortcuts for individual clips.

C The Timeline displays a chronological view of your edited project.

Media and Effects Browsers

A strip of buttons above the Timeline on the right side of the FCP interface controls access to FCP's various Effects Browsers—video and audio effects, generators, titles, and transitions. Media Browsers—which display the contents of your iTunes and iPhoto libraries—are accessed from the same button strip **D**. You use the Effects Browsers to apply effects to your clips and the Media Browsers to import audio and stills into your FCP project from your other Apple apps.

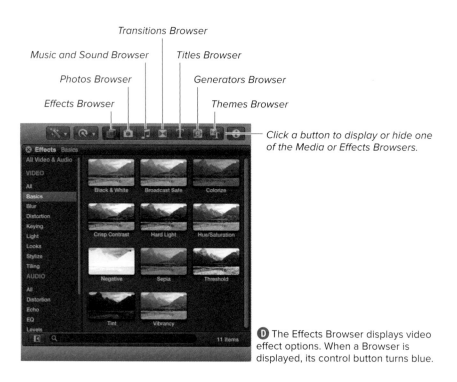

Transitions Browser

Music and Sound Browser *Titles Browser*

Photos Browser *Generators Browser*

Effects Browser *Themes Browser*

Click a button to display or hide one of the Media or Effects Browsers.

D The Effects Browser displays video effect options. When a Browser is displayed, its control button turns blue.

The Inspector

You can select a clip in the Event Library or Timeline and click the Inspector button to open the Inspector window ⓔ. A wealth of clip information is displayed in the Inspector window's Video, Audio, and Info panes. You can review and modify a clip's settings or effects, and much more. For more information, see Chapter 4, "Marking Clips."

The Inspector window's Video pane displays controls for all the effects applied to the selected clip. You can review or modify effect settings.

Click this button to display or hide the Inspector window.

ⓔ Select a clip, and then click the control button to display the Inspector window.

Input and Output Windows

Although you perform most editing tasks in Final Cut Pro's main editing and effects windows, you'll need to use a couple of other windows to shape your program's input and output.

Import Window

FCP supports a range of capturing options, from live video capture on-the-fly to automated transfer from a hard drive archive.

Use the Import window to import video and audio media from your file-based camera or from a hard drive **A**. FCP is compatible with a wide variety of file-based formats, including files recorded with Advanced Video Codec High Definition (AVCHD), a highly compressed non-tape-based video format.

Import functions are explained in detail in Chapter 6, "Importing Footage."

A The Import window supports a wide variety of file-based formats. In this example, the Import window is transferring video footage from an iPhone.

Import and Export Options

Final Cut Pro's media handling is based on Apple's QuickTime, and that means you have a lot of import and export format options. If QuickTime can handle it, so can Final Cut Pro.

- You can import QuickTime-compatible media files into a Final Cut Pro project.

- You can import audio directly from your iTunes library.

- You can import still images in a full range of formats.

- You can import an Adobe Photoshop file, although Final Cut Pro will flatten Photoshop layers on import.

- You can use the Share feature to create and deliver output media files for a wide variety of uses **B**. Share menu options include file export to many QuickTime formats. You can also use Share to burn DVDs and Blu-ray Discs, or process and upload files to online sites like YouTube in a single automated operation.

- You can use the Export Media option to export clips or projects either as Quick-Time movies or in a variety of image and sound formats.

- You can organize your production audio using FCP's Roles tagging feature and then export audio *stems*—dialogue, effects, or music-only tracks for post-production sound work.

- You can use Compressor, FCP's affiliate compression application, to perform high-quality batch transcoding and export operations.

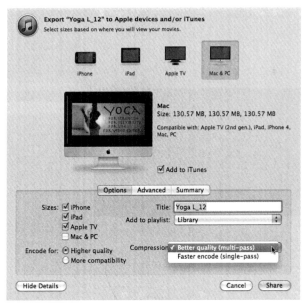

B The Share window offers a streamlined automated way to output and deliver your media. This example shows the options available in the Share > Apple Devices window.

Installing and Setting Up FCP X

This section summarizes the process of assembling the necessary hardware, hooking everything up, and installing Final Cut Pro. Topics include Final Cut Pro system requirements as well as hardware selection and configuration for both a basic setup and a more full-featured system.

The perfect time to get the latest news on Final Cut Pro and your hardware options is before you commit to a particular system. There's a bustling community of resources for Final Cut Pro. The FCP website, FCP user group meetings, and reputable vendors are our favorite sources.

It's possible to do great work on a simple, low-cost Final Cut Pro system, but if that money is just burning a hole in your pocket, there are a number of ways to spend your dough and upgrade your FCP system.

System Requirements

Final Cut Pro 1.0 was conceived as a DV postproduction system that would run on a Macintosh G3 computer. Each new version of Final Cut Pro stiffens the minimum system requirements a bit more (FCP X requires a minimum Intel Core Duo, plus an OpenCL-capable graphics card), but because fast CPUs, graphics cards, and high-speed data transfer ports have spread throughout the Mac product line, FCP wanna-bes can keep pace on just about any recent Intel Mac. If you're unsure whether your machine makes the grade, go to the Specifications page on Apple's website, and look up its complete specifications at *www.apple.com/finalcutpro/specs/*.

Apple is continuously testing and qualifying third-party software and third-party external devices for compatibility with Final Cut Pro. To review the latest list of Apple-approved video hardware and software, go to Apple's Final Cut Pro Technical Specification page at the URL listed above.

TIP FCP X's official minimum RAM requirement is 2GB, but you would be strongly advised to go with Apple's "recommended" 4GB RAM requirement if you want the program to work properly.

Hardware Selection and Connection

You'll need a few additional items to transform your Mac into a video production studio. This section describes two possible setups. The basic system is the bare minimum required; the recommended setup is, well, highly recommended for anyone with more than a passing interest in making movies.

A basic hardware configuration includes an AVCHD camcorder and a FCP-qualified Mac equipped with a high-resolution computer monitor **A**. The beauty of the basic system is its simplicity—an AVCHD camcorder connected to your Mac with a USB cable. That's all there is to it. Here's a rundown of the function of each piece of the system.

- **AVCHD camcorder:** The AVCHD camera transfers your digital video and audio files into the computer via USB. During footage import, you must monitor audio through your camera's or deck's audio outputs; computer speakers are muted.

- **Computer:** Final Cut Pro, installed on the Mac, imports and then stores digital video files from the AVCHD camera in your Event Library on its internal hard drive; no additional video-digitizing card is needed. You view the results of your work on the computer's monitor, and you use your computer's speakers to monitor your audio. You edit your footage with Final Cut Pro and then export it to a format of your choice using the Share feature.

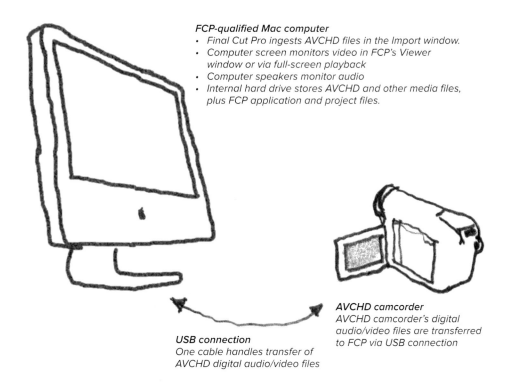

FCP-qualified Mac computer
- *Final Cut Pro ingests AVCHD files in the Import window.*
- *Computer screen monitors video in FCP's Viewer window or via full-screen playback*
- *Computer speakers monitor audio*
- *Internal hard drive stores AVCHD and other media files, plus FCP application and project files.*

AVCHD camcorder
AVCHD camcorder's digital audio/video files are transferred to FCP via USB connection

USB connection
One cable handles transfer of AVCHD digital audio/video files

A A basic FCP hardware setup

A recommended AVCHD setup adds a dedicated hard drive to store your media and enhances your monitoring capabilities with the addition of a second computer display and external speakers ⓑ.

- **Dedicated hard drive:** Adding a dedicated drive for your media improves the performance as well as the storage capacity of your system.

- **Second computer display:** If you're producing video to be projected or viewed on television, you should preview your video output on a full-screen monitor as you edit. A real studio monitor would be best, but until FCP X supports output to a true broadcast monitor, even a mid-range second display will give a more accurate idea of how your program looks and sounds. See "Customizing Your Workspace" later in this chapter for more information on connecting a second display.

- **External speakers:** Monitoring audio output from your computer with external speakers provides higher-quality audio output. External speakers are not expensive, and you'll be surprised how much better you can hear your production audio—I hope it's a pleasant surprise.

FCP-qualified Mac computer
- *Final Cut Pro ingests AVCHD files in the Import window*
- *The computer screen monitors video in FCP's Viewer window or shows full-screen video playback*
- *Internal hard drive stores AVCHD and other media files, plus FCP application and project files*

Second computer display
- *Second computer display can be used as dedicated video monitor to display FCP's Viewer or Event Browser*

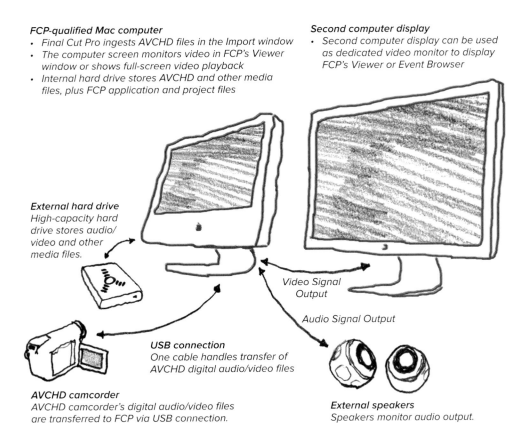

External hard drive
High-capacity hard drive stores audio/ video and other media files.

Video Signal Output

Audio Signal Output

USB connection
One cable handles transfer of AVCHD digital audio/video files

AVCHD camcorder
AVCHD camcorder's digital audio/video files are transferred to FCP via USB connection.

External speakers
Speakers monitor audio output.

B Recommended FCP hardware configuration

Installing Final Cut Pro from the App Store

Final Cut Pro X is available only as a $299 download from Apple's App Store, which is accessible from your Mac's Apple menu **C**.

Apple's App Store controls the installation process, so just follow the on-screen prompts and then plan enough time for a 1GB-plus application download **D**.

TIP Purchasing FCP X from the App Store entitles you to two installations. If you have a workstation and a laptop, you can install FCP X on both machines. Once your first installation is complete, return to the App Store on your second machine and navigate the Apple authorization process to obtain your second download. If things don't go perfectly for you, know you are not alone. Courage.

C Choose App Store from your Mac's Apple menu to launch the App Store.

D The Final Cut Pro X page in Apple's App Store

Customizing Your Workspace

This latest version of Final Cut Pro has traded in its fabled array of customization options for a simplified, streamlined operation. Custom column layouts, custom screen layouts, and custom shortcut buttons are gone, but there are still a couple of useful customizing features worth mentioning:

- You can connect a second display to your Mac and use it as a dedicated full-screen playback monitor for the Viewer or to display your Event Browser's clips and data on a big screen.

- You can create and save custom keyboard command setups.

Viewing Full-Screen Playback on a Second Display

FCP's full-screen playback option is a terrifically useful option for enhanced video playback, especially for FCP users working on a laptop. Attach a second computer display to your Mac, and it gets even better:

- You can use the second display as a dedicated video monitor for the Viewer window. If you plan to project your movie or show it on a large TV, you're strongly advised to get a bigger, better look at the quality of your footage as you edit it.

- You can expand your FCP workspace by using the second display to display your Event Browser's clips and data on a big screen.

TIP If your second display is lower quality than your Mac's screen, shifting the Event Browser to that second display will recapture video playback space for the Viewer on your higher-quality main screen.

To switch video playback to full-screen view:

1. *Do one of the following*:

▶ Choose View > Playback > Play Full Screen, or press Command-Shift-F.

▶ Click the Play Full Screen button to the right of the Viewer playback controls.

Your selected video plays in full-screen view starting at the playhead position.

2. To exit full-screen view, press Escape.

To show the Viewer on a second display:

1. Choose Window > Show Viewer on Second Display Ⓐ.

The Viewer window appears on your second display. Viewer on-screen controls will still be operational on the second display.

2. Choose Window > Show Viewer in the main window to return the Viewer to the main FCP interface.

To show the Event Library and the Event Browser on a second display:

1. Choose Window > Show Events on Second Display.

The Event Library and Event Browser appear on your second display. Event window on-screen controls will be operational on the second display.

2. Choose Window > Show Events in the main window to return events to the main FCP interface.

Creating Custom Keyboard Layouts

Editors with experience on other professional nonlinear editing systems rely on custom keyboard layouts; customizing keyboard shortcuts to match the editing

Window	Help	
Minimize		⌘M
Minimize All		
Zoom		
Go to Event Browser		⌘1
Go to Viewer		⌘3
Go to Timeline		⌘2
Go to Inspector		⌥⌘4
Show Project Library		⌘0
Hide Event Library		⇧⌘1
Hide Timeline Index		⇧⌘2
Show Inspector		⌘4
Show Color Board		⌘6
Show Video Scopes		⌘7
Show Audio Enhancements		⌘8
Show Audio Meters		⇧⌘8
Media Browser		▶
Record Audio		
Background Tasks		⌘9
Next Tab		^→।
Previous Tab		^⇧→।
Show Events on Second Display		
Show Viewer on Second Display		
Revert to Original Layout		
Bring All to Front		
◆ Final Cut Pro		

Ⓐ Choose Window > Show Viewer on Second Display to move the Viewer window display to a second monitor.

system you know best is a lot faster and easier than rewiring your nervous system to tap unfamiliar keys.

You can do the following:

- Completely reconfigure your keyboard layout.

- Reassign an existing shortcut to a different key.

- Create an entirely new keyboard shortcut.

- Save multiple keyboard layouts, and import and export layouts from other sources.

The Command Editor window makes it dangerously easy to completely rewire your keyboard shortcuts **B**. For a complete rundown on custom keyboard layouts, see Apple's Final Cut Pro Help.

Create and select custom keyboard layouts from the Command Editor's pop-up menu.

Each button accesses the keyboard diagram for a different modifier key combo. Click its button to access that keyboard diagram.

Find a command by entering its name or a keyword in the Search field.

Modifier keys and reserved keys are marked with diagonal shading and won't accept commands.

Use tooltips to identify which command is assigned to the key.

Click a column header to sort the Command list alphabetically, by modifier, or by key.

Drag a command from the list to the keyboard and drop it onto the desired key.

Commands matching the search text replace the Command list.

Click the Keyboard Highlight button to highlight keys that match items displayed in the Command list.

B The Command Editor window

TIP This may be the hottest tip in the book: The Command Editor contains a complete list of FCP's commands—including hidden commands you won't find in anywhere else in the interface. When you're wondering whether it's possible to do something in FCP, browsing the Command Editor's Command list should be your first move.

To create a custom keyboard shortcut:

1. Choose Final Cut Pro > Commands > Customize, or press Command-Option-K .

   The Command Editor appears. Keyboard layout diagrams are arranged by shortcut modifier key and appear on multiple panes. A complete list of commands, sorted by command group, appears at the bottom of the window.

2. To find the command you want to assign to the keyboard, *do one of the following*:

   ▸ Select the command's menu group from the Command Groups list to filter the Command list display to show only commands from that menu group.

   ▸ Enter the command's name or a keyword in the search field, and the Command list will automatically display only commands matching the search term .

   ▸ Click the Command List's Command column header to view the command list alphabetically.

3. FCP's default keyboard layout is locked by default. To customize the keyboard layout, you must first create a copy of the default layout by choosing Duplicate from the pop-up menu in the top-left corner of the Command Editor .

C Choose Final Cut Pro > Commands > Customize to open the Command Editor. Note that a list of previously created custom *command sets* (keyboard layouts) is available for direct selection in the lower-right corner of this submenu.

D Enter the command's name or a keyword in the search field. The Command list will automatically display only commands matching the search term. The search field's submenu options let you refine your search further.

E Before customizing the keyboard layout, you must first create a copy of the default layout by choosing Duplicate from the pop-up menu in the top-left corner of the Command Editor. The default command set is locked by default.

F Drag a command from the list to the keyboard and drop it onto the desired key.

G Click the Save button in the lower-right corner of the Command Editor to save your changes, and then click Close.

4. In the dialog, type a name for your custom command set, and click OK.

   Your custom keyboard layout becomes the active layout and is added to the Command Editor's pop-up menu.

5. To assign the command to a key, select the command in the list, and *do one of the following*:

   ▸ Press the key or key combo you want to assign as the new shortcut for that command. If the shortcut is already in use, a dialog appears asking you to confirm your choice. If you want your new command choice to replace the key's current assignment, click Reassign.

   ▸ If your new keyboard shortcut uses no modifier key, drag the command from the list and drop it on the appropriate key in the keyboard diagram.

   ▸ If your new keyboard shortcut is a key combined with a modifier key, select the keyboard diagram for that modifier key by clicking its tab, and then drag the command from the list and drop it on the appropriate key **F**.

6. To save your changes, click the Save button in the lower-right corner of the Command Editor, and then click Close **G**.

TIP You can reassign a keyboard shortcut by dragging it from one key to another in the keyboard layout diagram.

TIP Heads up: When you reassign a keyboard shortcut by dragging it to a key on the keyboard layout diagram, the change takes effect without any confirming dialog.

TIP You can't assign more than a single command to a key.

Undoing Changes

You can undo almost every type of action you perform in your projects, sequences, and clips, as well as redo actions that you have undone. Starting in FCP X, you can undo every action you've taken up to the last time you quit and reopened Final Cut Pro. That's because Final Cut Pro's default behavior is now to save your project automatically every time you make a change.

You never have to remember to save your project manually, but the only way to revert your project to an earlier state is by using the Undo feature to step back through your actions.

TIP Another way to restore a heavily manipulated clip to its original state and get a fresh start is by adding a new copy of the clip to your project directly from its Event Library folder.

TIP There are a few actions that you can't undo in FCP X. You can't undo an import; you can't undo certain Media Management operations. FCP will warn you if you're about to commit an action that cannot be undone.

To undo your last action:

- Choose Edit > Undo (the name of your last action) **Ⓐ**. Or press Command-Z.

To redo the last undone action:

- Choose Edit > Redo (the name of your last action) **Ⓑ**. Or press Command-Shift-Z.

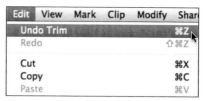

Ⓐ Choose Edit > Undo to undo your last action. FCP specifies the name of your last action in the menu.

Ⓑ Choose Edit > Redo to redo your last undo. FCP specifies the name of your last action in the menu. (Surely an FCP Project History feature must be just around the corner....)

Hate Your Edit?
Undo Can Rescue You

Automatic saving is great as long as you remember this: The *only* way to revert your edited project after you've done something brilliant but basically bad is to use the Undo feature.

Undo is particularly useful when you've just performed an unsuccessful overwrite edit and replaced some clips in your edited project. Deleting the clips that wiped out part of your sequence won't restore your original footage, but if you use Undo (Command-Z) on your overwrite edit, your footage will be restored.

If you're interested in seriously experimenting with your edit, you'll need to duplicate your project file to create an archive copy of your project that won't change as you continue to edit.

So, go forth and be bold. Experiment with your edit. You can always use Undo.

You Need Backup

Automatic saving should not be used as a substitute for your own systematic archiving of your project files.

- Be consistent about where you store your project files. Make sure that all files relating to a project are stored in the same place.

- Back up project files on your FCP system and again on a removable disk or in another safe location to avoid losing files in case of a power outage or another technical problem. Project files contain all your time and hard work. Without the editing information in the project files, your media files have no sequencing information. Protect it. OK—end of lecture.

Stay Out of Trouble, Get Out of Trouble

The best way to stay out of trouble using FCP is to read and heed these performance tips. If you do run into snags when using Final Cut Pro, read the sidebar "How to 'Trash Your Prefs'"—it may help.

- **Latest version of FCP:** Make sure you're running the latest version of Final Cut Pro by checking in Apple's website.

- **Settings:** Avoid running processor-intensive operations in other open applications while you're working in Final Cut Pro (especially when transcoding video for input or output).

- **Clean out your old projects and events:** Move your unused events and projects out of the Final Cut directories in the Finder so they are not "seen." This will free up memory and improve performance.

continues on next page

- **Disk space:** Maintain 10 percent free space on each disk drive. If you fill your disk to the last gigabyte, your performance will take a dive—and that's the best-case scenario.

- **Work locally:** Final Cut Pro performs poorly if you try to work with remote media files over a network connection. Copy files from the network to a local disk before importing them.

- **Display:** Make sure the entire image area is visible in windows playing video. If you see scroll bars on the edge of the Viewer, you're zoomed in too far for optimal performance 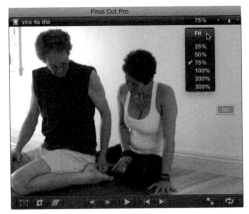.

A If you see this red icon on the right edge of the Viewer's image area, you're zoomed in too far for optimal playback performance. Choose Fit from the Viewer's pop-up menu to bring the entire frame back into view.

How to "Trash Your Prefs"

There are still times when FCP will mysteriously hang up or act strangely. Quitting and then relaunching FCP X would be the first thing to try, but if that does not solve your problem, those of you seeking a solution may be advised to delete your FCP preferences files (or "trash your prefs") to force FCP to restore all your program settings to their default values.

1. Quit Final Cut Pro.
2. Go to User/Library/Preferences/ and remove two files: com.apple.FinalCut.plist and com.apple. FinalCut.LSShared.Filelist.plist.
3. After deleting the files, relaunch Final Cut Pro with your external hardware on and connected. You will have to reset your preferences; however, FCP X has so few preference settings now that it's no big deal.

If you'd like an easier way to back up, restore, and trash your FCP preference files, you could try Digital Rebellion's Preference Manager. You can download it free at *www.digitalrebellion.com/prefman/*.

Update: We've just learned that Mac OS Lion hides the Library folder from you.

Here's a cool workaround that reveals your Library folder:

In the Finder, choose Finder > Go menu > click the control key while holding the mouse button down.

The hidden Library menu item is revealed, so you can get on with navigating to your preferences files and trashing them.

2

Managing Events

iMovie users, Final Cut Pro's Event Library and Event Browser will look familiar to you: The Event Library displays all the clips, audio, and graphics you've imported into FCP organized into *events*—FCP's name for a folder containing clips.

Clicking an event folder in the Event Library displays its contents—the clips contained in that event—in the Event Browser.

The Event Browser is the window you use to organize and access individual clips, audio files, graphics, and offline clips—all the media elements you use in your project. The Event Browser performs these organizing tasks on your project's virtual clips and sequences. Although browser items look like files on your computer desktop, browser items are references to media files, not the files themselves. The "Secrets of Nondestructive Digital Editing" section of Chapter 1 is key to understanding how FCP works.

For more information on organizing your clips and their metadata, see Chapter 4, "Organizing Clips."

In This Chapter

Anatomy of the Event Library

FCP's Event Library is one part of its structure for storing and retrieving clips. The Event Library displays a list of folders, called *events*, containing all the clips, audio, and graphics you have imported into FCP.

Clicking an event folder in the Event Library displays its contents—the clips contained in that event—in the *Event Browser*. For details on the Event Browser, see "Anatomy of the Event Browser," later in this chapter.

The Event Library also displays icons representing other types of data. Mixed into the Event Library you'll see icons that represent keyword collections and smart collections, which are FCP–generated footage analysis data. Click a keyword collection icon in the Event Library, and the Event Browser will display only those clips tagged with a matching keyword. For more information, see "Searching for Clips in the Event Browser."

Events in the Events Library are displayed chronologically by default, but you're free to reorganize your clips into event folders that are useful to you. You can create new event folders, split events, combine multiple event folders into a single new event, and more.

You can use clips from multiple events in a single project.

To display the Event Library:

- Click the Event Library button in the lower-left corner of the Event Browser to display the Event Library pane **A**. Click again to hide it.

FCP X Alert: Event Library and Event Browser Actions Affect Source Media Files

When you copy, move, and delete files in the Event Library, FCP will copy, move, or delete your actual source media files on disk. So, treat Event Library files with the same respect and care as your original files.

Copying, moving, or deleting clips from inside the Event Browser does not affect the source media file on disk, but deleting an Event Browser clip will move its source media file to your Mac's Trash. Don't accidentally delete the last copy of your original media.

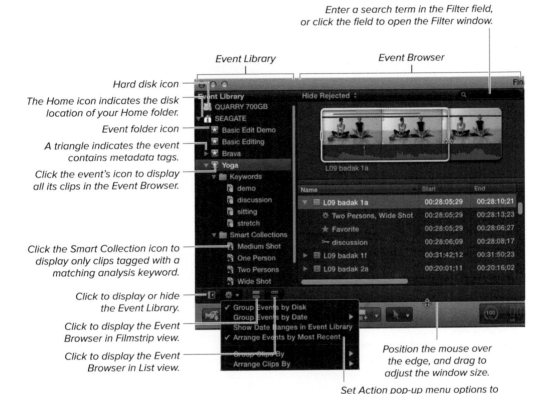

Enter a search term in the Filter field, or click the field to open the Filter window.

Event Library   Event Browser

Hard disk icon

The Home icon indicates the disk location of your Home folder.

Event folder icon

A triangle indicates the event contains metadata tags.

Click the event's icon to display all its clips in the Event Browser.

Click the Smart Collection icon to display only clips tagged with a matching analysis keyword.

Click to display or hide the Event Library.

Click to display the Event Browser in Filmstrip view.

Click to display the Event Browser in List view.

Position the mouse over the edge, and drag to adjust the window size.

Set Action pop-up menu options to control sort order and date display in the Event Library and Event Browser.

A The Event Library and Event Browser windows

Creating Events

Each time you import clips, FCP offers you the option of importing them into an existing event folder or importing into a new event. You can also create new event folders in the Event Library, which is useful for organizing great gobs of clips into neat little groups.

> **TIP** FCP offers other tools to help organize your clips without creating new event folders: keywords, ratings, and favorites. For more information, see Chapter 4, "Marking Clips."

To create a new event in the Event Library:

1. In the Event Browser, if the Event Library is not visible, click the Event Library button to reveal it .

2. Choose File > New Event 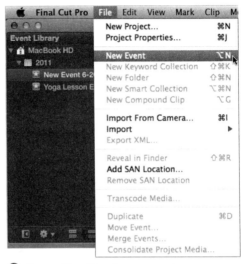, or press Option-N.

   Your new event folder appears in the Event Library with its name field selected.

3. Type a new name, and then press Enter (or Return) .

> **TIP** When you're organizing stuff in the Event Library, use event folders to hold clips, audio, photos, and the like. The other kind of FCP folder (known as a *folder*) holds keyword collections and other kinds of metadata—but it doesn't hold clips.

A Click the Event Library button to toggle the display of the Event Library.

B Choose File > New Event to create a new event folder.

C Type a new name in the name field, and press Return.

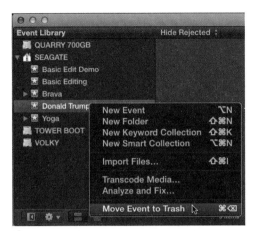

D Right-click the event you want to delete and choose Move Event to Trash from the shortcut menu.

To rename an event:

- In the Event Library, click the name of the event you want to rename to select it, type a new name, and press Return.

To delete an event:

- In the Event Library, right-click the event you want to delete and choose Move Event to Trash from the shortcut menu **D**, or press Command-Delete.

  FCP moves that event folder and all the clips it contains into the Trash.

Working with Event Folders

You can customize your FCP event folder setup to match your working style. You might want to organize your footage by event, with each event folder gathering the footage shot at a graduation, birthday, conference keynote, or intervention into a single event folder.

Editors who draw from stock footage or news clip libraries may prefer to configure their Event Library differently, creating permanent subject- or date-based event folders and filing clips as they acquire them.

You can merge multiple events into a single event folder.

You can create a set of new, empty events and sort clips from a single event into multiple folders by copying or moving them.

FCP's indexes of your clip *metadata*—all the camera information that is imported along with your footage, plus any notes and identifiers you add later—are organized into Keyword Collection and Smart Collection folders, which also reside in the Event Library. Learn more about organizing your metadata in "Working with Keywords and Favorites" in Chapter 4.

TIP Whenever you copy or move a clip between event folders, the clip's source media file is moved to the disk location you select.

TIP You can also tag footage with keywords and build virtual collections without moving your clips from their original import folders. See "Tagging Clips with Keywords" in Chapter 4.

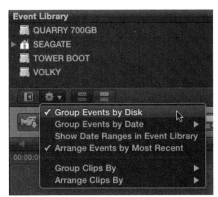

(A) Choose Group Events by Disk from the Action pop-up menu to sort event folders by their hard disk location.

(B) Choose Don't Group Events by Date in the Action pop-up's submenu to sort and display Event Library folders by name rather than by date.

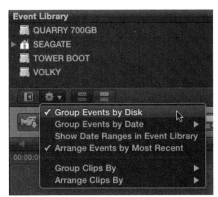

(C) Hide Event Library date display by unchecking Show Date Ranges in the Action pop-up menu.

To sort event folder listings in the Event Library:

1. To control the sort order of your event folders, open the Event Library's Action pop-up menu, and *do one of the following*:

   ▶ Choose Group Events by Disk to sort event folders by their hard disk location (A).

   ▶ Choose Group Events by Date, and then choose an option from the submenu:

   • Choose Don't Group Events by Date to sort and display Event Library folders by name rather than by date (B).

   • Choosing Group Events by Year or Group Events by Year and Month will sort your Event Library by recording date.

2. Choose Arrange Events by Most Recent to sort your newest material to the top of the Event Library list.

TIP FCP users who don't want to be reminded that their four-year-old vacation video is still sitting uncut in the Event Library will be relieved to know that displaying dates in the Event Library is optional. You can hide date display by unchecking **Show Date Ranges** in the Event Library's Action pop-up menu (C).

To merge multiple events:

1. In the Event Library, select all the event folders you want to merge, and then choose File > Merge Events **D**.

   The Merge Events window appears.

2. Type a name for your new event, choose a disk location for the merged events' media files from the Location pop-up menu, and click OK **E**.

   FCP replaces the event folders you selected with a new event folder that contains all the clips from the selected events **F**. The source media files for those clips are moved into a single folder at the disk location you selected in step 2.

To split an event into multiple event folders:

1. Create new, empty event folders by choosing File > New Event, or press Option-N.

2. Name your new event folders.

3. Follow the steps in "To copy clips into a different event" to sort your clips by copying or moving them from their original event folder into the new event folders you created.

   Each clip's source media file is copied or moved into the folder destination at the disk location you select.

D Select the event folders you want to merge, and then choose File > Merge Events.

E In the Merge Events window, name your new event, and choose a disk location for the merged events' media files.

F A new event folder containing all the clips from the selected events replaces the event folders you selected.

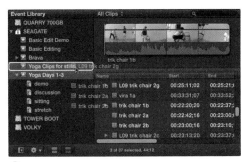

G Select the event folder that contains the clips you want to copy.

H Option-drag the selected clips to copy them into an event folder located on the same hard disk as the source event.

To copy clips into a different event:

1. In the Event Library, select the event folder that contains the clips you want to copy **G**.

   The event folder's contents are displayed in the Event Browser.

2. In the Event Browser, select the clips you want to copy, and then *do one of the following*:

   ▸ If the destination folder is located on the same hard disk, Option-drag the selected clips to an event's icon in the Event Library to copy them into that event **H**.

   ▸ If the destination folder is located on a different hard disk, drag the selected clips to an event's icon in the Event Library to copy them into that event.

   Each clip's source media file is copied into the folder destination at the disk location you select.

TIP **Option-dragging to copy clips only works when the Browser is in List View.**

To move clips into a different event:

1. In the Event Library, select the event folder that contains the clips you want to move.

   The event folder's contents are displayed in the Event Browser window.

2. In the Event Browser window, select the clips you want to move, and then *do one of the following*:

   ▸ If the destination folder is located on the same hard disk, drag the selected clips to an event's icon in the Event Library to move them into that event.

   ▸ If the destination folder is located on a different hard disk, Command-drag the selected clips to an event's icon in the Event Library to move them into that event **I**.

   Each clip's source media file is moved into the destination folder at the disk location you select **J**.

I Command-drag the selected clips to move them into an event folder located on a different hard disk as the source event.

J The selected clips are moved into the destination event folder.

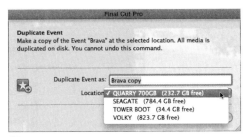

Select the event folder you want to copy, and then choose File > Duplicate Event.

L In the Duplicate Event window, select the destination hard drive for your copy, and enter a name for the duplicated event.

To copy an entire event to a different hard disk:

1. If you haven't already, connect the destination hard disk to your computer, and then choose Group Events by Disk from the Event Library's pop-up menu.

   The destination hard disk is added to the list of disks in the Event Library window.

2. In the Event Library, select the event folder you want to copy, and then *do one of the following*:

   ▶ Choose File > Duplicate Event **K**.

   ▶ Drag the event to the external drive's icon in the Event Library window.

3. In the Duplicate Event window, select the destination hard drive for your copy, enter a name for the duplicated Event, and then click OK **L**.

   FCP copies all the source media files contained in the selected event into the duplicate event folder at the disk location you selected. Copying large video files can take a few minutes.

Working with Clips in the Event Browser

The Event Browser has three primary functions:

- You use the Event Browser to organize and access individual clips, audio files, graphics, and offline clips—all the media elements you use in your project.

- You also use the Event Browser to preview, or *skim*, a filmstrip-sized playback of your clips. The filmstrip icons in the Event Browser are all "live" and play back any time you move your mouse over them.

- You use the Event Browser range selection and marking tools to select the section of a clip you want to include in your edit and to tag clips or parts of clips. Keyword tagging allows you to create custom categories and annotate your clips in a way that makes sense to you. FCP's two rating tools—Favorite and Reject—help you keep track of the best and worst parts of your footage. For details, see "Working with Keywords and Favorites" in Chapter 4.

The Event Browser performs these organizing and marking tasks on your project's virtual clips and sequences. Although Event Browser items look like files on your computer desktop, Event Browser items are references to media files, not the files themselves. File storage is independent of Event Browser organization, so you can place the same clip in several FCP projects, and each instance of the clip will include a reference to the same media file on your hard drive.

See "Secrets of Nondestructive Editing" in Chapter 1 for more background on digital editing technology.

FCP X Update: Sequences Are Now Called Projects and Are Stored in a Separate Library

In previous versions of FCP, the Browser's Project tab displayed all the elements of an FCP project. A single FCP project could contain multiple *sequences*—documents that contain your edit decisions—as well as clip elements.

In FCP X, a sequence is now called a *project*. FCP X projects—your list of edit decisions—are stored in the Project Library, separate from the Event Library's clip information archive.

Keeping clip data separate from any particular edited sequence allows you to build an archive of clip information over time and keep your notes intact. As you move from project to project, your notes stay attached to your clips in the Event Library.

Anatomy of the Event Browser

Clicking an event folder in the Event Library displays its contents—the clips contained in that event—in the *Event Browser.*

FCP opens the Event Browser in Filmstrip view by default **A**. Filmstrip view is useful for tracking down a clip visually by skimming through the live clip icons but doesn't provide the sorting capabilities or wealth of clip data available from the Event Browser columns in List view **B**.

To learn how to switch between List and Filmstrip views (and much more), see "Customizing the Event Browser Display," later in this chapter.

Clip sections marked with rating, keyword, or analysis tags display horizontal color-coded lines:
Green: Favorite
Red: Reject
Blue: Keyword tag
Purple: Analysis Keyword tag

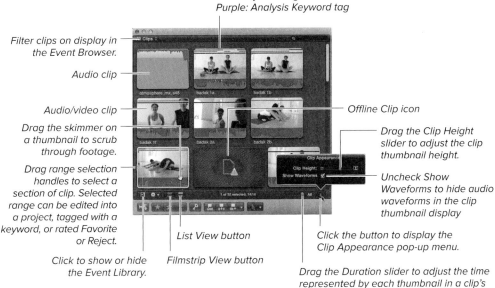

Filter clips on display in the Event Browser.

Audio clip

Audio/video clip

Drag the skimmer on a thumbnail to scrub through footage.

Drag range selection handles to select a section of clip. Selected range can be edited into a project, tagged with a keyword, or rated Favorite or Reject.

Click to show or hide the Event Library.

List View button

Filmstrip View button

Offline Clip icon

Drag the Clip Height slider to adjust the clip thumbnail height.

Uncheck Show Waveforms to hide audio waveforms in the clip thumbnail display

Click the button to display the Clip Appearance pop-up menu.

Drag the Duration slider to adjust the time represented by each thumbnail in a clip's filmstrip.

A The Browser window in Filmstrip view

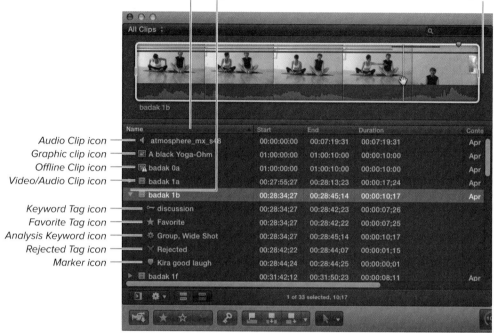

Browser data columns; click to sort data by selected column.
The triangle indicates the clip contains metadata tags or markers.
Drag the range selection handles to select a section of clip. Selected range can be edited into a project, tagged with a keyword, or rated Favorite or Reject
Audio Clip icon
Graphic clip icon
Offline Clip icon
Video/Audio Clip icon
Keyword Tag icon
Favorite Tag icon
Analysis Keyword icon
Rejected Tag icon
Marker icon
All Clips
badak 1b
Name
Start
End
Duration
atmosphere_mx_s48
A black Yoga-Ohm
badak 0a
badak 1a
badak 1b
discussion
Favorite
Group, Wide Shot
Rejected
Kira good laugh
badak 1f
1 of 33 selected, 10:17

B The Browser window in List view

Browser Window Icons

Along the left side of the window, you'll notice icons that accompany each item listed in the Event Browser.

These icons represent file types in FCP:

Clip: A media file; can represent audio, video, graphics, or other media imported into FCP.

Audio Clip: A media clip composed of audio samples.

Graphic: A clip in a single-layer graphic file format.

Offline Clip: Yellow caution icon indicates a placeholder clip referencing media not currently on the local hard drive.

Compound Clip: An FCP clip type that can contain multiple other clips. A compound clip can also contain other compound clips, such as audition clips (not pictured).

Audition Clip: An FCP compound clip type containing selected alternate takes (not pictured).

These icons represent types of information applied to a clip—keyword tags, rating tags, or markers—and appear below a clip when you click the triangle to the left of the clip icon:

Marker: A reference point in a clip

Favorite: A clip or clip section marked as a Favorite

Reject: A clip or clip section marked as Rejected

Keyword: A clip or clip section marked with Keyword tag

Analysis Keyword: A clip or clip section marked with an Analysis Keyword tag

For more information on FCP's system of tagging and metadata tools, see Chapter 3.

Customizing the Event Browser Display

The Event Browser offers two different display modes: List view and Filmstrip view. Each mode offers distinct features, and you'll find yourself using both modes as you edit.

You can use the options in FCP's View menu to switch between views and to show or hide a variety of clip info overlays in the Event Browser.

To display the Event Browser in Filmstrip view:

- In the Event Browser, click the Filmstrip View button at the bottom of the Event Browser pane, or press Command-Option-1  **A**.

To display the Event Browser in List view:

- In the Event Browser, click the List View button at the bottom of the Browser pane, or press Command-Option-2.

To show or hide clip information overlays in the Event Browser:

- *Do one of the following:*
  - ▸ Choose View > Show (or Hide) Clip Names to toggle the display of clip names under Event Browser clips **B**.

> **TIP** View menu options are context-sensitive. For example, you'll see Hide Clip Names in the menu only if names are currently showing. Tricky.

  - ▸ Choose View > Show (or Hide) Waveforms to toggle the display of audio waveforms on filmstrip icons.

A Click the Filmstrip View button at the bottom of the Browser pane to display the Event Browser.

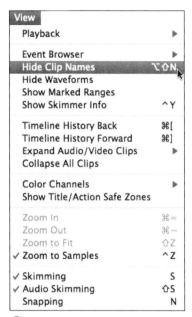

B Toggle the display of clip names under Event Browser clips by choosing View > Show (or Hide) Clip Names.

C Choose View > Show (or Hide) Skimmer Info to toggle the display of this floating data palette that overlays a filmstrip when you pause the skimmer.

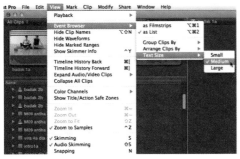
D Choose View > Event Browser > Text Size, and then select a Event Browser text size display option from the shortcut menu.

E Display option controls are located at the bottom of the Event Browser pane. The controls are visible only when the Event Browser is set to display Filmstrip view.

▶ Choose View > Show (or Hide) Marked Ranges to toggle the display of horizontal color-coded lines on filmstrip icons.

▶ Choose View > Show (or Hide) Skimmer Info to toggle the display of the floating data palette that overlays a filmstrip when you pause the skimmer **C**. For more information on using the skimmer, see "Skimming Clips" in Chapter 3.

To change text display size:

- Choose View > Event Browser > Text Size, and then select a text size display option from the shortcut menu **D**.

Filmstrip View Display Options

FCP's filmstrip display options feature scrubbable, "live" filmstrip icons you use to preview and mark footage.

- You can adjust the playback time interval each thumbnail represents, ranging from one thumbnail frame per half second up to several minutes per thumbnail frame. The highest setting—All—fits all clips displayed in the Event Browser into the window.

- You can also adjust the filmstrip icon's height. Larger filmstrips offer a better view of the footage you're scanning; compact filmstrips save space in the Event Browser window.

- You can opt to show or hide audio waveforms in the filmstrip icon display.

TIP The Filmstrip View display option controls at the bottom of the Event Browser pane are visible only when the Event Browser is set to display Filmstrip view **E**.

To expand and contract the number of thumbnail frames in a clip's filmstrip:

- *Do one of the following*:
  - ▸ Drag the Duration slider at the bottom of the Event Browser pane to the right to increase the number of frames represented per thumbnail displayed (and create more compact filmstrips) **F**.
  - ▸ Drag the Duration slider to the left to decrease the number of frames represented per thumbnail displayed and create longer, more detailed filmstrips.

TIP Pressing Shift-Z automatically sets the Duration slider to All and fits all clips displayed into the Event Browser window.

To adjust the clip's filmstrip height:

- In the Event Browser, click the Clip Appearance button to display its pop-up menu, and then drag the Clip Height slider **G**.

To hide audio waveforms in the filmstrip icon display:

- In the Event Browser, click the Clip Appearance button to display its pop-up menu, and then uncheck the Show Waveforms checkbox **H**.

F Drag the Duration slider to the right to create more compact filmstrips.

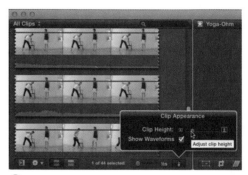

G Drag the Clip Height slider to adjust the filmstrip height.

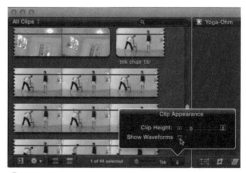

H Uncheck Show Waveforms to hide the Filmstrip Waveform display and make more room to adjust filmstrip height.

I Enter search terms in the Event Browser's Filter field (located in the upper-right corner), and FCP will filter the Event Browser's display, showing only clips that match your search parameters.

J You can add or modify a clip's logging information directly by double-clicking an Event Browser column entry.

List View Display Options

The Event Browser's List view displays your clips in a text list. The selected clip appears across the top of the window as a live filmstrip you can skim, play back, and mark up.

The power of List view lies in the searchable, sortable data available in List view's Event Browser columns. Some columns accommodate notes and other types of logging information that help you track and sort your clips.

Any keyword tags or markers you've placed in a clip will appear under that clip's disclosure triangle in the Event Browser's Name column.

You can enter search terms in the Event Browser's Filter field to search for your clips based on selected clip properties, and FCP will filter the Event Browser's display showing only clips that match your search parameters **I**.

You can customize the Event Browser's List view in the following ways:

- Rearrange, resize, hide, or show as many columns as you like. (You can't hide the Name column.)

- Sort Event Browser items by most columns.

- Add or modify a clip's logging information directly by double-clicking a Event Browser column entry **J**.

TIP When the Event Browser is set to List view, the filmstrip icon displayed above the list automatically adjusts its height and length to fit the window size. Increase the Event Browser window size to create a bigger, more detailed filmstrip.

Working with Browser Columns

When you work with columns in the Event Browser window, you have a number of options, including hiding, rearranging, and resizing them.

To hide a column:

1. In the Event Browser window, right-click the column header.

2. From the shortcut menu, choose Hide Column .

To display a hidden column:

1. In the Event Browser window, right-click the column header to the right of the place you want the hidden column to be displayed.

2. From the shortcut menu, choose the name of the column you want to display 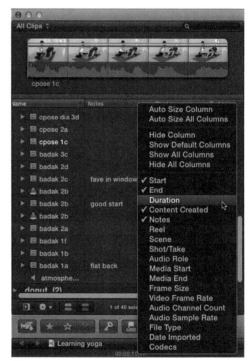.

TIP FCP initially hides some Event Browser columns by default. Check the shortcut menu in the Event Browser's column header for a complete list of available columns.

TIP You can keep your Event Browser columns narrow and still see a full-length entry in every column. Hover your pointer over a column entry to view a tooltip displaying the complete contents of the column.

To rearrange columns:

- Drag the column header to the new location .

To resize columns:

- Drag the right edge of the column header to the new width.

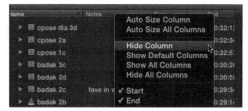

A Right-click the column header, and then choose Hide Column from the shortcut menu.

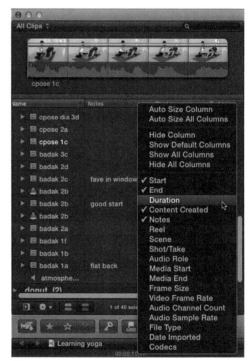

B Right-click the column header to the right of the place you want the hidden column to be displayed, and then choose the name of the column you want to display from the shortcut menu.

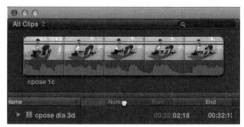

C Drag a column to its new location.

A Command-click to select multiple Event Browser items individually.

Selecting and Sorting Browser Items

FCP offers two types of item sorting in the Event Library and Event Browser:

- **Group:** This item-sorting method categorizes Event Browser items into groups and displays clip groups in the order you select.

- **Arrange:** This item-sorting method determines the sort order of individual Event Browser items and displays clips in the order you select.

Grouping and arranging can be used together or independently. You can choose to group clips into categories and select a sort order for clips within each group, or you can arrange clips into a preferred sort order without grouping them.

To select an item in the Event Browser:

- *Do one of the following:*
  - ▶ Click the item you want to select.
  - ▶ Use the arrow keys to step through the item list until you arrive at the item you want.

TIP Multiple-item selection in FCP's Event Browser works in the same way as it does in the Mac OS X Finder: Command-click to select multiple items individually **A**, Shift-click to select a range of items. In Filmstrip view, you can drag a bounding box around a group of list items or icons.

To group Event Browser items:

- *Do one of the following*:
  - ▸ Choose View > Event Browser > Group Clips By, and then choose one of the submenu options to group your Event Browser clips into an available category 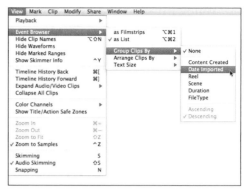.
  - ▸ Choose View > Event Browser > Group Clips By > None to turn off clip grouping.

To arrange Event Browser items:

- Choose View > Event Browser > Arrange Clips By, and then choose one of the sort order options available in the submenu.

Using Event Browser Columns to Sort Event Browser Items

FCP allows you to sort by almost every column you see in the Event Browser.

To sort items in the Event Browser:

1. Click a column header to select the column you want to sort by **C**. The sort column is indicated by a black arrow in the column header.

2. Click again to reverse the sort order.

B Choose View > Event Browser > Group Clips By, and then choose one of the submenu options to group your Event Browser clips into an available category.

C Click in the column header to sort by name. The direction of the tiny arrow to the right of the column name here indicates ascending order. Click again to reverse the sort order.

3

Viewing Clips

The more time you spend watching your source video, the better an editor you'll be. You'd be surprised how many times we see people trying to edit video without really thoroughly watching and taking in the nuances of the footage they're editing.

Sure, watching the clips takes time, but if you're asking your potential viewers to sit through whatever it is you're creating, the least you can do is take the time to watch it yourself, over and over again, to make sure you're showing them only the best, most necessary, most illustrative, most essential bits.

Final Cut Pro X even provides a short-cut for this tedious task: *skimming*. Now you can quickly skim through your shots to find those critical bits, but we can't stress strongly enough that skimming isn't enough. You must watch your video—all of it. Then, later, you can skim to find the moments that stood out to you.

Anatomy of the Viewer

FCP X contains a single, context-sensitive Viewer where the content of your video is displayed Ⓐ. When you're looking at source clips in the Event Browser, the Viewer shows those clips. When you examine the clips in your project, the Viewer shows those clips.

The upper-left corner of the Viewer shows the name of the item displayed within. For a clip it displays the clip name, for a project it displays the project name, and so on.

The upper-right corner contains the Zoom and Viewer Display Options menus. These controls allow you to customize the appearance of the Viewer. They are described in the "Zoom and Display Options" section.

The lower-left corner contains three buttons to enable clip effects such as scaling, cropping, or distorting your clips. For more on these controls, see Chapter 13, "Basic Compositing."

The lower-right corner contains a button to enable full-screen playback and a button to enable looping. Both of these controls are described in more detail in the "Playing Back Video" section.

The filmstrip indicates the first (or last) frame of source media.

Clip or project name

Viewer Display Options menu

Viewer Zoom menu

Folding Pose shots

Fit: 56%

Compositing controls

Playback controls

Full-Screen Playback button

Loop Playback button

A The Viewer window

Playing Back Video

Directly beneath the video, the Viewer contains five playback control buttons. These can be used to navigate the video 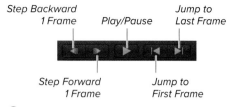.

Step Backward 1 Frame   Play/Pause   Jump to Last Frame

Step Forward 1 Frame   Jump to First Frame

A Navigation controls appear under the main Viewer area.

There are also keyboard shortcuts for all the different playback controls and methods, and most users prefer to use the shortcuts than click the buttons on the screen (see the "Playback Shortcuts" table).

Playing from the Keyboard

Far more varied and flexible playback controls are available if you use keyboard shortcuts. Most important is the J-K-L combination **B**:

- Press J to play backward.
- Press K to stop playback.
- Press L to play forward.
- Press J or L multiple times to play forward or backward at high speed. Pressing twice will play at 2X speed, pressing three times will play at 4X speed, and so on.
- Press J+K together to play backward in slow motion.
- Press K+L together to play forward in slow motion.

B The J, K, and L keys sit comfortably beside each other and enable easy and intuitive playback control.

These three keys sit side by side on the keyboard so you can rest your fingers on them all at once and easily navigate your clips.

Once you get comfortable using these keys, it will quickly become second nature, and you'll be able to use them adeptly without thinking.

Full-Screen Playback button

C Click the Full-Screen Playback button to enter full-screen playback mode.

Loop Playback button

D Click the Loop Playback button to enable or disable playback looping.

TABLE 3.1 **Playback Shortcuts**

Play Mode	Keyboard Shortcut
Play forward	Spacebar or L
Play backward	Shift-Spacebar or J
Pause playback	Spacebar or K
Play slow motion backwards	J+K
Play slow motion forwards	K+L
Step backward one frame	Left Arrow key
Step forward one frame	Right Arrow key
Jump to first frame	Up Arrow key
Jump to last frame	Down Arrow key
Play full-screen	Shift-Command-F
Loop playback	Command-L

Playing Full-Screen

Viewing your video without the distraction of the busy FCP interface can be very helpful, especially if you want to share your video with friends or clients.

To play video full-screen:

- Click the Full-Screen Playback button, or press Shift-Command-F **C**.

  The screen switches into full-screen playback mode, and playback begins immediately.

  Keyboard playback commands still operate.

To exit full-screen playback mode:

- Press Escape.

Looping Playback

Sometimes you may want to watch a section of video play over and over again in a continuous loop.

To loop playback:

- Click the Loop Playback button, or press Command-L **D**.

  The button turns blue to indicate that playback looping is enabled.

TIP Press the Loop Playback button (or press Command-L) again to disable looping.

Skimming Video

Once you've become familiar with your footage, you can use the skimming feature to quickly navigate to a particular frame or section within your clips.

Skimming simply means floating your mouse across a video clip and causing the video frames to display in the Viewer. No clicking is required. As you move your pointer from one clip to another, the new clips automatically load into the Viewer, creating a quick and seamless (if occasionally disorienting) workflow.

When skimming is enabled, you get two separate lines in the clip filmstrip; the white line is the playhead, and the red one is the skimmer .

Skimming can be done with or without audio skimming enabled. Skimming with audio can be very helpful for finding a particular section, but hearing audio skimming when you don't want to can be very annoying, so it's important to know how to turn it off quickly.

Skimming's main disadvantage is that it is imprecise. As you skim across a clip, you may find the frame you're looking for but accidentally skim right past it, which means you waste a lot of time going back and forth.

As you get more adept with skimming, you'll get comfortable toggling it on and off frequently, which can enable you to skim to find a frame and then turn off the skimmer and click in order to move the playhead to the desired frame.

Skimmer   *Playhead*

Ⓐ When enabled, the skimmer appears as a red vertical line in the clip filmstrip.

Enable/Disable Skimming button

B Turn skimming on and off
by clicking the Enable/Disable
Skimming button or by pressing S.

Enable/Disable Audio Skimming

C Turn audio skimming on and off
by clicking the Enable/Disable Audio
Skimming button or by pressing Shift-S.

D Use the
skimmer
to quickly
locate the
frame you're
seeking.

E With
skimming
disabled, click
the mouse
to move the
playhead to
the selected
frame.

To enable skimming:

- Click the Enable/Disable Skimming button, or press S **B**.

  Skimming is enabled.

Note that although skimming can be done
without a project being open, the Enable/
Disable Skimming button is visible only
when a project is open in the Timeline.
The S key works at anytime.

To disable audio skimming:

- Click the Enable/Disable Audio Skimming button, or press Shift-S **C**.

  Audio skimming is disabled.

TIP Disabling video skimming automatically
disables audio skimming as well.

To find a frame using the skimmer:

1. Press S to enable skimming.

2. Skim across a clip filmstrip to find the
   frame you're looking for **D**.

3. As soon as you find the desired frame,
   move your hand off the mouse so you
   don't accidentally move it.

4. Press S to disable skimming.

5. Click the mouse to move the playhead
   to the frame under the pointer **E**.

   The playhead moves to the selected
   frame.

Zoom and Display Options

The upper-right corner of the Viewer contains the Zoom and Viewer Display Options menus. These controls allow you to customize the appearance of the Viewer.

Zoom Controls

In general, you'll want to see the whole video image in the Viewer, but sometimes—especially when designing multilayer compositions, applying filters, or performing other precision tasks—you may want to zoom in on the Viewer.

FCP provides a variety of ways to zoom in and out, including a special command called Fit that guarantees that the image is as large as possible based on the current Viewer size.

To change the Viewer zoom level:

- *Do one of the following*:
  - ▸ Click the Viewer Zoom menu, and select a zoom level from the pop-up menu that appears 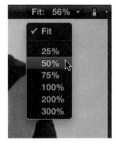.

> **TIP** Choose Fit to set the zoom level to fill the Viewer as much as possible. When set to Fit, the control displays the actual zoom level. In this example, it's set to 56 percent.

  - ▸ Press Command-+ (plus) to zoom in, or press Command-– (minus) to zoom out .
  - ▸ Press Shift-Z to set the window to Fit.
  - ▸ Select the Zoom tool from the Tools pop-up menu in the toolbar, and click in the Viewer to zoom in. Option-click to zoom out .

A The Viewer Zoom pop-up menu

B When zoomed out, a gray border appears around the visible area.

C Choose the Zoom tool from the Tools pop-up in the toolbar, and click the Viewer to zoom. Option-click to zoom out.

D Drag the red box to change the view of a zoomed-in image. The inset image here shows a zoomed-in view of the Zoom Scroll handle.

E Select the Hand tool from the Tools pop-up menu in the toolbar, and drag around the zoomed-in Viewer.

To scroll a zoomed image:

When zoomed in to a level where the entire image is not visible in the Viewer, you may want to control which part of the zoomed-in image is showing.

Whenever you're zoomed in, a Zoom Scroll handle appears on the right side of the Viewer **D**. The white outer box represents the entire image, and the red inner box represents the viewable area. The more zoomed in you are, the smaller the red box will be relative to the white box.

To scroll around a zoomed-in Viewer:

- *Do one of the following*:
  - ▸ Drag the red box in the Zoom Scroll handle to choose a different portion of the zoomed-in image to display in the Viewer.
  - ▸ Select the Hand tool (H) from the Tools pop-up in the toolbar, and drag around the Viewer **E**.

Display Options

The Viewer Display Options menu contains a variety of mostly unrelated controls to change how the Viewer displays the video image .

Least useful of all are the controls for limiting the Viewer's display to one of the four video channels (alpha, red, green, or blue). Ordinarily, the Viewer displays all four channels simultaneously, showing you a full-color image along with any transparency (if it exists).

Selecting one of the individual channels will display a monochromatic version of your image containing just the values in one of those four channels .

If you have no idea when or why you would want to enable this option, you're not alone. The vast majority of editors will never have any need to perform this task. Primarily, it is useful for highly specific color correction tasks or occasionally for verifying the transparency boundaries of imported graphics.

You can also use this menu to display video scopes (used primarily when doing color correction), both video fields (used to detect interlacing issues on nonprogressive video), and title/action-safe zones (used to help position the placement of titles and otherwise account for the convex, *underscanned* displays found on televisions manufactured before 1990). For more on video scopes, see the "Video Scopes" section in Chapter 15, "Color Correction."

F You will rarely need to click the Viewer Display Options menu to modify the appearance of the Viewer.

G Although it may look cool, there is very little practical use for limiting your display to only one channel.

🄷 Yellow lines appear on top of the video. The inner line is intended to indicate the boundary where titles should be kept, and the outer line indicates where some TVs may crop the image.

🄸 Interlacing is normal and desirable when the final video is going to be displayed on an interlaced (that is, traditional television) monitor. Showing both fields allows you to see two fields overlaid on top of one another, which sometimes appears as a comblike artifact.

To display title/action-safe zones:

- Click the Viewer Display Options menu, and choose Show Title/Action Safe Zones.

  Yellow lines are overlaid near the edges of the Viewer to indicate where some televisions will crop or distort the image 🄷.

To display both video fields:

- Click the Viewer Display Options menu, and choose Show Both Fields.

  Both video fields (present only on interlaced source footage) are displayed simultaneously. Fast horizontal movement of objects in the frame may result in a comblike effect 🄸.

  This is normal and desirable, because it indicates smooth motion that will appear correctly on a traditional television.

Marking Clips

One of the most fundamental aspects of the editing process is identifying the portions of your source clips you want to use in your final edit. Think of this concept as *marking* an area of a clip.

In addition to marking the areas you want to use in your edit, you will also frequently do the opposite: mark the sections you definitely *don't* want to use.

Furthermore, there are many occasions where you're not quite sure which parts you will want to use (or not use), so you'll want to mark those with more descriptive information than just "yes" or "no."

Finally, you may want to highlight a particular frame or section of a clip to alert yourself (or your fellow editors) of some bit of important information about the clip.

This chapter will cover all of these different ways of identifying, selecting, and highlighting bits of clips.

Making a Selection

The most straightforward and essential aspect of any sort of clip marking is the idea of selecting the portion of the clip you want to mark. You can use such a selection to add a clip *rating* or a *keyword*. Most importantly, you'll used it to identify what portion of the source clip to edit into the project.

You can make selections with the mouse, which provides instant visual feedback but tends to be imprecise. You can also make them from the keyboard.

This latter method is especially useful in that it allows you to identify the desired selection *while the clip is playing*. Such on-the-fly clip marking allows you to simulate the experience of your viewers (who never get to step through the shots or stare at any individual frame) and make more accurate and effective decisions.

To make a selection with the mouse:

1. If it's not already enabled, press S to activate skimming, then skim the clip to find the frame where you want the selection to begin **Ⓐ**.

2. Click that frame and drag to the right until you reach the frame where you want the selection to end **Ⓑ**.

   A selection is made and illustrated with a thick yellow border.

> **TIP** If you click the clip's filmstrip without dragging, FCP will select the entire clip. You could deselect and try again, or simply click and drag the adjustment handles (located about halfway up the clip's yellow selection border) to fine tune your selection.

Ⓐ Use the skimmer to find the frame where you want the selection to start.

Ⓑ Drag to the last frame you want to include in the selection.

C Pressing I creates an In point and automatically adds an Out point at the end of the media.

D Press O to indicate the frame where the selection should end.

To make a selection from the keyboard:

1. Press the Spacebar or L to play the clip.

2. When you reach the frame where you want the selection to begin, press I.

   The beginning of the selection is marked. By default, the selection extends to the end of the clip media **C**.

TIP For best results, make selection marks while the video continues to play.

TIP You can press I (or O) repeatedly to reset the selection range.

3. When you reach the frame where you want the selection to end **D**, press O.

TIP You can also play in reverse and set the Out point before choosing to set the In point.

TIP You can also combine these methods, using the mouse or keyboard interchangeably during the selection process.

Rating Clips

You can *rate* any selection (including a whole clip) in one of two ways: You can rate it as a Favorite or you can rate it as Rejected. While this "in or out" system may seem overly simplistic, it's a great way to quickly identify the most fundamental identity of your footage.

TIP Footage can be rated a Favorite or Rejected. You cannot rate a portion of a clip as both. If a clip is currently rated as a Favorite, and you reject it, the Favorite rating is removed and replaced with a Rejected rating (and vice versa).

To mark a clip as a Favorite:

1. Select a clip or a portion of a clip .
2. Click the Mark Favorite button , or press F.

   The selection is marked as a Favorite, and a green bar is added to the clip's filmstrip .

A Select the range you want to rate.

Mark Favorite button

B Click the Mark Favorite button to rate the clip favorably.

Favorite item appears

Green bar appears

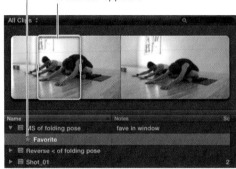

C The rated section is marked with a green bar in the filmstrip, and a Favorite item is added to the clip in list view.

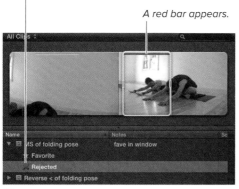

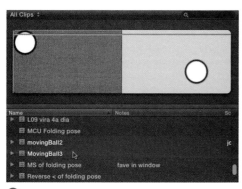

D Mark the area you want to reject.

Mark Rejected button

E Click the Reject button in the toolbar.

The rejected item appears in list.

A red bar appears.

F The rejected section of the filmstrip is marked in red.

G Select the items you want to delete.

To reject a clip:

1. Select a clip or portion of a clip **D**.

2. Click the Reject button **E**, or press Delete.

   The selection is marked as Rejected, and a red bar is added to the clip's filmstrip **F**.

TIP **If the Browser is set to view Favorites and Unrated clips only (as it is by default), rejecting a clip will make that clip seem to disappear. To view it again, see the "Restricting the View" section.**

Rejecting a clip doesn't delete it from the event. It merely marks it with the Rejected tag. You can, of course, also delete a clip, which will remove it from the event, and if it's the only instance of that clip (in other words, it doesn't appear in another folder or project), the source file is moved to the trash.

To delete a clip from an event:

1. Select a clip or a range of a clip (or a group of clips) **G**.

2. Press Command-Delete.

   The clip is removed from the event.

   If the clip being deleted is the last remaining instance in that event, a warning will appear **H**.

3. Click OK.

   The clip is removed from the event, and the file on disk is moved to the trash.

Media Moving to Trash

One or more media files will be moved to the trash since the last reference to them is being deleted. External files remain where they are.

Cancel   OK

H A warning will appear if you're deleting the only instance of the clip.

To select a rated area:

- Click directly on the colored bar in the clip's filmstrip .

  The marked range becomes selected **J**.

TIP This technique works for any colored bar in the filmstrip, which could be ratings, keywords, or analysis keywords.

Unrating Clips

Sometimes you may change your mind about a clip's rating, or you may find you've accidentally rated the wrong portion of a clip. Fortunately, you can unrate a clip as easily as you can rate it.

TIP If only a portion of a clip is rated, you cannot unrate part of that range. You can unrate the entire clip, which will unrate any rated sections, or you can select a range that contains the rated section entirely and unrate that.

To unrate a clip:

1. Select the rated clip, or select a range equal to or greater than the rated range **K**.

2. Click the Unrate button **L**, or press U.

   Any ratings within the selection are removed **M**.

I You can select a marked range by clicking the colored bar.

J Click the bar to select the specific area.

K To unrate a clip, you must select a range equal to or longer than the range you're unrating.

Unrate button

L Click the Unrate button in the toolbar.

M Any rated section within the selected area is unrated.

 Choose a filter from the Filter pop-up menu.

Restricting the View

One of the most powerful aspects of the clip rating system is that the Event Browser view can be filtered to hide clips marked Rejected, to show only those marked as Favorites, and so on.

When such a filter is applied, Clip view is updated dynamically. For example, if your view is set to Hide Rejected, rejecting a clip (or a portion of a clip) makes that rejected bit disappear from the window.

It's not gone forever—you can get it back by changing the filter setting. But often hiding it automatically that way is a great, quick way to weed out the junk and limit your Event Browser view to show just the good stuff.

To restrict the Event Browser view by rating:

- Click the Filter pop-up menu, and choose one of the following settings:
    - All Clips (Control-C)
    - Hide Rejected (Control-H)
    - No Ratings or Keywords (Control-X)
    - Favorites (Control-F)
    - Rejected (Control-Delete)

    The Event Browser is filtered to show only the clips described in the filter setting.

    These filters are saved with the event, collection, or folder in the Event Library. Selecting a different item in the Library will potentially switch the filter setting.

TIP You can also filter the view on a wide range of other criteria. For more, see "Searching for Clips" later in this chapter.

Adding Keywords

Although clip ratings are extremely helpful, they're also quite limited. Fortunately, FCP allows you to add far more nuanced identifiers to clips or clip ranges. You can add your own custom *keywords* to any selection. This means you can choose your own descriptive text to identify the contents of a particular selection.

You might choose keywords that describe the content, such as the name of the person or subject, the location where the scene is shot, or the particular action that's taking place. You could also use keywords to identify how the footage was filmed. For example, is it a *moving camera? Wide shot? Handheld?* Or *out of focus?* You could add keywords judging the quality of the shot: Is it a *good take? No good? Director's favorite?*

You can combine all of these ideas and add as many keywords as you desire. Multiple keywords can overlap, and later you'll be able to find clips based on any or all of these identifiers whenever you need them.

To add one or more keywords:

1. Select a clip or a range within a clip **A**.

2. Click the Show Keyword Editor button in the toolbar **B** (or press Command-K).

   The Keyword Editor opens **C**.

3. Type the keyword in the Keyword Editor **D**, and press Enter.

A Select the area you want to keyword.

Show Keyword Editor button

B Click the Show Keyword Editor button in the toolbar.

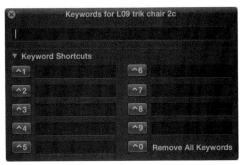

C The Keyword Editor

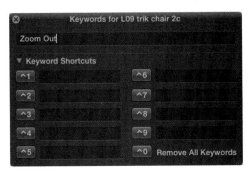

D Type a keyword into the textbox at the top of the Keyword Editor.

E When you press Enter, the keyword is added to the selected range. The range is marked with a blue bar.

F When you add a keyword, it's also automatically added to one of the preset slots, making it easy to consistently add the same keyword to multiple clips.

Disclosure triangle

G To see the keywords listed in the Event Browser, expand the clip's disclosure triangle.

The keyword is added to the selected range. A blue bar appears in the clip's filmstrip **E**.

Additionally, the keyword is added to one of the Preset Keyword slots in the Keyword Editor **F**. This makes it easy to add the same keyword to multiple clips.

TIP Once you assign keywords to the Preset Keyword slots in the Keyword Editor, you can apply those keywords to other clips by pressing the associated shortcut key without even opening the Keyword Editor.

4. To add additional keywords, type additional text in the Keyword Editor, and press Enter.

TIP Only one blue bar appears in a clip regardless of how many keyframes are applied.

5. To add keywords that have already been saved as presets in the Keyword Editor, click the shortcut key button (or press the shortcut on the keyboard).

   The keyword is added to the selected range.

When you expand a clip containing a keyword by clicking the disclosure triangle to the left of the clip icon in the Event Browser in list view, keywords appear in a list beneath the clip **G**.

TIP The Skimmer Info window (opened by pressing Control-Y) also identifies any markers under the current skimmer position.

Notice that Ratings, Analysis Keywords, and Markers also appear in this list. Ratings and markers are also described in this chapter. Analysis keywords are described in Chapter 6, "Importing Footage."

TIP If more than one keyword covers the same range in time, both keywords are listed on a single line in the list. If they cover separate ranges, they are listed separately.

Selecting any of the items in the list automatically selects the range associated with the item in the filmstrip .

To remove a keyword from a clip:

1. Select the keyword in the Event Browser by clicking its name in the list or by clicking the colored bar associated with that keyword in Filmstrip view **I**.

2. Choose Mark > Remove All Keywords **J**, or press Control-0 (zero).

   The keyword is removed.

To remove all keywords from a clip:

- Right-click a clip in the Event Browser, select a keyword, and then choose Mark > Remove All Keywords from the shortcut menu **K**; or press Control-0 (zero).

   All keywords for the selected clip are removed.

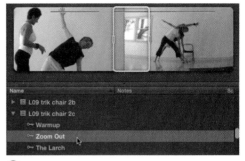

H Selecting a keyword in the list selects the range of the clip covered by the keyword in the filmstrip.

I Select the keyword you want to remove.

J From the Mark menu, choose Remove All Keywords.

K Right-click a clip, and choose Remove All Keywords.

L You can copy a keyword from one slot to another in the Keyword Editor.

M You can also add multiple keywords to the same slot.

N To delete a keyword from the Keyword Editor, select the text and press Delete.

To copy a keyword to a different slot in the Keyword Editor:

- Drag the text of the keyword to a new position L.

TIP You can drag multiple keywords to a single preset slot M. Pressing that shortcut will add all the keywords at once.

To remove a keyword from the Keyword Editor:

- Select the text of the keyword you want to remove, and press Delete.

  The selected text is deleted N.

Keyword Collections

Whenever you add a keyword to a clip in an event, a Keyword Collection is automatically created.

Clicking a Keyword Collection in the Event Library displays a list of all the clips containing that keyword in the Event Browser.

Dragging a clip onto an existing Keyword Collection automatically adds that keyword to the clip. This allows you to effectively use Keyword Collections like folders to organize your clips.

To manually create a Keyword Collection:

1. Right-click an event in the Event Library, and choose New Keyword Collection **O**; or press Shift-Command-K.

   An untitled Keyword Collection appears **P**.

2. Type a keyword as the name of the collection and press Enter **Q**.

3. Drag clips or clip ranges from the Event Browser onto the Keyword Collection to add that keyword to the selection **R**.

To delete a Keyword Collection:

- Select the Keyword Collection in the Event Library, and press Command-Delete.

   The Keyword Collection is deleted, and the keyword is removed from any clips that previously contained it.

O Right-click an event, and choose New Keyword Collection.

P A new Keyword Collection is added.

Q Rename the Keyword Collection with the new keyword.

R Drag clips to the Keyword Collection to add the keyword to that clip.

Marker acting as snap point

Ⓐ Use markers and Timeline snapping to help you align your clip elements and make precision editing easy. In this example, the first frame of the audio clip is snapping to the marker in Shot_01.

TIP You can add markers either in the Event Browser or in the Timeline. In either case, the procedure is the same.

Using Markers

Markers are reference pointers you attach to a clip, and they have a variety of uses. Over the course of your work, you may find that you need to identify specific moments in your footage. You might want to mark an area of a clip that is out of focus, or you might want to mark the specific frame where a car door closes and a sound effect is required. Any time you want to add a note for yourself or your collaborators, you can simply add a marker. And markers can contain text, so you can explain why you put it there.

Markers appear both in the Event Browser and the Timeline and can be one of three colors:

Blue Marker: Normal markers

Red Marker: Uncompleted To Do Item

Green Marker: Completed To Do Item

Markers act as snap points. By adding a marker on a specific frame, you make it very easy to align another clip right to that frame. For example, if you add a marker exactly where you want a title to appear, when you connect the title, you can snap it right to that marker and ensure the precise placement you desire **Ⓐ**.

Markers stay locked to the specific frame where you place them. As you insert or delete other clips in your edited project, any clip markers you've placed will ripple along with the clip they're attached to—moving earlier or later in time to stay aligned with the marked frame.

If you delete a clip that contains a marker, Final Cut Pro will delete that marker as well.

Markers are just tools to aid in your editing work. They have no impact on the playback of your video. They do not appear in the Viewer or when you export or share your finished work.

To add a marker:

1. Move the playhead to the frame you want to mark **B**; then press M.

   A marker appears at the specified frame. If skimming is on, the marker will be placed at the skimmer's position, not the playhead's.

2. To add comments to the marker, press M a second time to open the Modify Marker window **C**.

> **TIP** Any markers you add to a clip in the Event Browser will be edited into the Timeline along with the clip—even if you use the clip more than once.

> **TIP** You can add markers on-the-fly by pressing M while the video is playing. Pressing M twice will open the Modify Marker window.

To add or modify marker text:

1. Move the playhead to the marker you want to modify **D**. Then press Shift-M.

   The Modify Marker window opens.

2. Type descriptive text in the Marker name field **E**. Then click Done.

   The text is saved with the marker.

> **TIP** Once you've created a marker, it's a good idea to add some text to clarify why you put it there. Later you can search for that text in the Event Browser or in the Timeline Index and quickly find the marker.

Skimmer position

B Position the playhead or skimmer on the frame where you want the marker to appear.

C Press M a second time to open the Modify Marker window and add marker text.

D Move the playhead to the marker. Markers get a little bit bigger when you position the pointer directly over them.

E The Modify Marker window points to the marker that it controls.

(F) To delete a marker, you can also right-click it and choose Delete Marker from the shortcut menu.

(G) Select the markers you want to delete.

(H) You can select a whole clip, a portion of a clip, or multiple clips as shown here.

To delete a marker:

1. Position the playhead or skimmer directly over the marker you want to delete; then press Shift-M.

   The Modify Marker window opens.

2. Click Delete **(F)**.

   The Modify Marker window closes, and the marker is deleted.

TIP You can also delete a marker under the playhead without opening the Modify Marker window by pressing Control-M.

To delete all markers in a selection:

- Select a clip or range in which you want to delete all markers **(G)**, and then *do one of the following*:

  ▸ Press Control-Shift-M.

  ▸ Choose Mark > Markers > Delete Markers in Selection.

  All markers within the selection are removed **(H)**.

TIP To delete all markers in a project, press Command-A to select all of them, and then press Control-Shift-M to delete the markers. Wait until your client has departed before you do this.

To Do Items

One of the most common uses for markers is to identify tasks that need to be completed. Editors often go through a project and mark each location where a sound effect (or an audio fix) is needed. You can use markers to take notes during a screening, adding markers at edit points that need finessing. FCP offers a special type of marker called a To Do Item.

To Do Items act just like regular markers except they appear red. To Do Items you've marked as *completed* appear green, so you can see, at a glance, which tasks have been addressed and which are still outstanding. This can be especially helpful when collaborating with another editor.

To add a To Do Item:

1. Position the playhead or skimmer over the frame where you want to mark a To Do Item ⓘ.

2. Press Option-M to add a marker and simultaneously open the Modify Marker window.

   The Modify Marker window opens.

3. Add text to explain what task needs completing ⓙ.

4. Click the Make To Do Item button on the left side of the window; then click Done.

   The button turns into a Completed checkbox and the marker turns red ⓚ.

5. Click Done.

   The Modify Marker window closes.

ⓘ Identify a spot where some work still needs to be done.

ⓙ Type your To Do Item in the text field. Any existing marker can be converted into a To Do Item in the Modify Marker window.

ⓚ To Do Item markers are indicated by their red color.

The marker turns red.

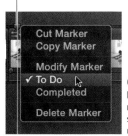

L To turn a To Do Item back into a regular marker, open the shortcut menu and uncheck To Do.

The marker turns green.

M Quickly mark a To Do Item as completed using the shortcut menu.

N This figure shows the blue marker before and after being nudged. Note that you can't nudge a marker across clip boundaries, but you could cut and paste it in a new location.

To convert a regular marker to a To Do Item:

- Right-click the marker, and choose To Do from the shortcut menu **L**.

To mark a To Do Item as completed:

- Right-click the marker, and choose Completed from the shortcut menu **M**.

  Completed To Do Items appear as green markers.

TIP You can also mark To Do Items as complete in the Timeline Index.

Moving Markers

Markers can be moved frame by frame, or they can be relocated from one place to another. You can also copy a marker to create a duplicate in a new location.

TIP If you were setting markers to indicate where footstep sounds should go, rather than having to type *footstep* in a dozen different markers, you could type it once, copy that marker, and just paste a new marker for each successive footfall.

To nudge a marker:

1. Position the playhead or skimmer directly over the marker you want to move.

2. Press Control-< to nudge the marker to the left or Control-> to nudge the marker to the right.

   The marker is moved one frame at a time **N**.

TIP You can hold down Control-< or Control-> to move the marker multiple frames.

TIP You cannot nudge a marker across clip boundaries.

To move a marker to a new location:

1. Right-click the marker, and choose Cut Marker from the shortcut menu **O**.

2. Position the playhead or skimmer on the frame where you want the marker to be moved.

3. Press Command-V.

    The marker is pasted in the new location **P**.

To duplicate a marker:

1. Right-click the marker, and choose Copy Marker from the shortcut menu **Q**.

2. Position the playhead or skimmer at the frame where you want to place your duplicate marker; then press Command-V.

    The duplicate marker appears at the new location **R**.

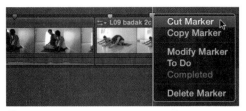

O Choose Cut Marker from the marker's shortcut menu. Cutting a marker copies it to the clipboard and replaces any other data currently stored there.

P The marker is pasted in the new location. Cut and paste is the only way to move a marker across a clip boundary.

Q Choose Copy Marker from the shortcut menu. Copy a marker when you want to duplicate it.

R Press Command-V, and the duplicate marker appears at the new location. In this example, a To Do Item marker has been copied and then pasted several times.

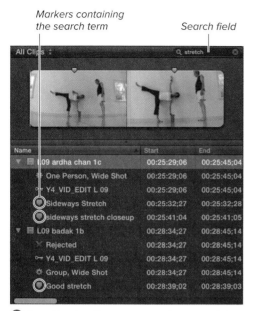

Markers containing the search term

Search field

S Searching for clips, tags, or markers containing the word *stretch*. FCP filters the view so that only items with the search term appear in the Event Browser list. Clips that don't match your search are hidden until you reset the search field.

Selected marker   Selected marker

T When you select a marker in the list, the clip opens automatically, and the playhead jumps to the marked frame.

Navigating to Markers

FCP offers a variety of ways to find and navigate to your markers both in the Event Browser and in the Timeline.

If you typically use markers to identify specific moments in the raw footage (before you've added clips to a project), you'll want to be able to find those frames in the Event Browser.

To find a marker in the Event Browser:

1. In the Event Browser, type a search term in the search field in the upper-right corner **S**.

   FCP applies your search terms and filters the Event Browser display to show only clips, markers, and keywords that contain the selected text.

2. Click the marker item in the Event Browser to select it.

   The clip containing the marker is selected and displayed in the Viewer **T**.

To find a marker in the Timeline:

1. Make the Timeline window active by clicking in it; then press Command-F.

   The Timeline Index opens (if it's not already showing) with the search field automatically activated .

2. In the Timeline Index search field, type any of the text that's labeling the marker you want to find; then click the Tags button to open the Tags pane.

   A list of markers and keywords that contain the search term appears in the Timeline Index **V**.

Search field   Click to open the Tags pane.

U You'll find the Timeline search field at the top of the Timeline Index.

Show all tag types

Show only markers

Show only keywords   Show analysis keywords

Show To Do Items

Show completed To Do Items

V Just like in the Event Browser, the view is filtered to show only the items with the search text. Here there are several markers and keywords that all have the word *stretch*.

The marker selected in the Timeline index.   *The playhead jumps to selected marker.*

W The selected object in the Timeline Index is also selected in the Timeline.

X The Timeline Index filtered to show only the markers containing the word *stretch*.

3. Click the marker you searched for in the Timeline Index.

    The Timeline playhead jumps to the selected marker **W**.

TIP Double-click the marker in the Timeline Index to move to the marker and automatically open the **Modify Marker** window.

TIP If you'd like to restrict your search results to show markers only, click the **Show Only Markers** button at the bottom of the Timeline Index **X**.

To jump from marker to marker:

1. Make the desired window active, and *then do one of the following*:

    ▸ Press Control-' (apostrophe) to move the playhead to the next marker.

    ▸ Press Control-; (semicolon) to move the playhead to the previous marker.

    The playhead moves to the next or previous marker in the selected window.

Other Clip Metadata

In addition to ratings, keywords, markers, and other information you can assign to a clip, a huge amount of additional information is associated with each clip. This information is called *metadata*.

Metadata can be hard-coded information such as the frame size, frame rate, audio format, and so on; it can be data supplied by the camera, such as the f-stop, shutter speed, GPS location, and other information; or it can be user-editable fields such as scene number, take number, camera reel, and so on.

You can even add your own custom metadata fields that will be available to all your clips.

All of this metadata is displayed in the Info Inspector, and the Info Inspector can be configured to display a variety of different views, each showing a different set of metadata.

To enter metadata for a clip:

1. Select the clip in the Event Browser.

2. Open the Inspector and click the Info button to open the Info pane.

   The Info pane opens showing the metadata for the clip **Ⓐ**.

3. If needed, choose a Metadata view from the View pop-up that contains the field you want to change **Ⓑ**.

4. Type text directly in the field **Ⓒ**.

   The metadata is added to the clip.

> **TIP** Many metadata fields are hard-coded, meaning you can't manually enter data. These fields appear uneditable in the Inspector.

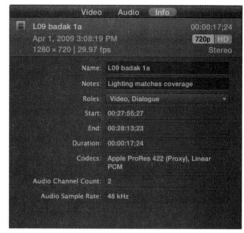

Ⓐ Open the Info Inspector to see the clip's metadata.

Ⓑ Choose a view from the View pop-up.

Ⓒ Type directly in the field to enter metadata for the clip.

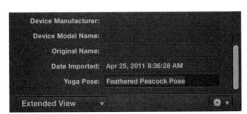

D Choose Add Custom Metadata Field from the Action menu.

E Enter a name and description for your custom field.

F Your custom field appears at the bottom of the current view.

To create a new metadata field:

1. In the Info Inspector, click the Action menu, and choose Add Custom Metadata Field **D**.

   The Add Metadata Field sheet appears **E**.

2. Enter a name and optional description for the new field, and click OK.

   The new field is added to the bottom of the current view **F**.

Metadata Views

There are seven different views in the Info Inspector, each showing a specific set of criteria. You can customize these views by adding or removing fields or reordering the fields in the view.

You can also create your own custom metadata views containing just the fields you want to see and in the order you want to see them.

To select a metadata view:

- Click the View pop-up menu, and select one of the items from the menu **G**.

  The Info Inspector updates to show the new view **H**.

To rearrange the order of fields in a metadata view:

- Drag the name of the field to a new position in the view **I**.

G Choose from one of the seven preset metadata views available in the View menu.

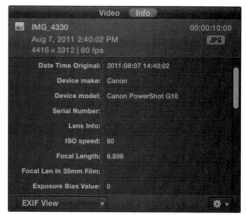

H The Inspector updates to show the current view.

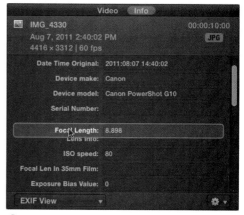

I Drag fields up or down to rearrange their order.

J Choose
Edit Metadata View
from the View
menu.

To add or delete fields from the view:

1. Click the View pop-up menu, and choose Edit Metadata View **J**.

   The Edit Metadata View window opens **K**.

   continues on next page

Categories pop-up menu

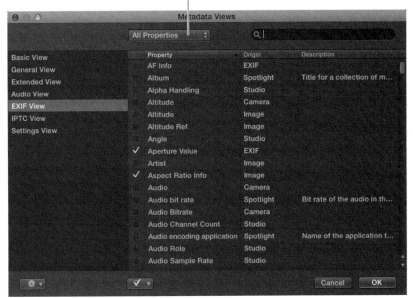

K The Edit Metadata View window opens.

2. Choose a category of fields from the Category pop-up menu .

3. Click the checkbox to select fields you want to add to the view or deselect fields you want to exclude ⓜ.

4. Repeat steps 2 and 3 for additional categories as needed.

TIP You can search for specific fields by typing a name (or part of a name) in the search field at the top of the window ⓝ.

5. Click OK.

The metadata view is updated to reflect the changes you made.

TIP Optionally you can also save the changed metadata view as a new view by clicking the Action menu in the Edit Metadata Views window and choosing Save Metadata View As.

ⓛ Choose a category of fields.

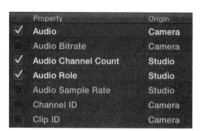

ⓜ Select the fields you want to include in the view, and deselect those that you don't.

ⓝ Search for a specific field by typing in the search field.

To create a new metadata view:

1. Click the View pop-up menu, and choose Edit Metadata View.

   The Edit Metadata View window opens **O**.

continues on next page

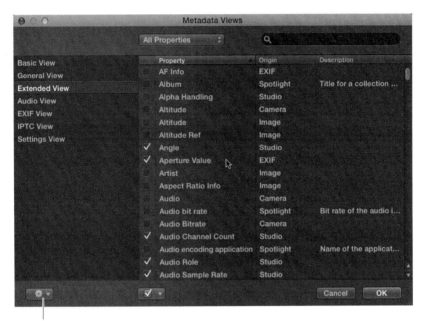

Action menu

O The Edit Metadata View window

2. Click the Action menu, and choose New Metadata View **P**.

   A new view is added to the list on the left **Q**.

3. Click the name of the new view, and type a custom name **R**.

4. Select the fields you want to include in the new view **S**.

5. When you're finished, click OK.

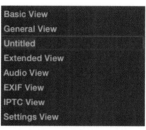

P Choose New Metadata View from the Action menu.

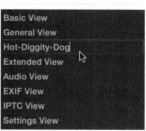

Q The new view is added to the list on the left.

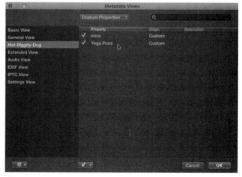

R Name the view something practical.

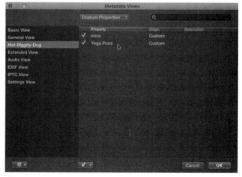

S Select the fields you want to include in your custom view.

A Type your search term in the field at the top of the Event Browser.

B The Event Browser is filtered to show only clips containing the search term.

Searching for Clips

The ultimate value of all the metadata you add to your clips using any of the forms described in this chapter is the ability to search your library of clips to find exactly the ones you're looking for.

Final Cut Pro has a robust search mechanism that allows you to filter the Event Browser based on a wide variety of different criteria, filter on multiple criteria at once, and even save searches as *Smart Collections* that act as folders in the Event Library, updating automatically whenever a new clip fits the collection criteria.

The way filtering works in FCP X is that the results of the search replace the current view in the Event Browser. In this way, you need to clear the search or switch to a new view to see all the items in the browser again.

To filter the view by text only:

- Type text into the search field at the top of the Event Browser **A**.

  The view is filtered to show only clips that contain the text in the search field **B**.

  The text can appear in the name of the clip, in the name of a marker, or in any of the metadata text fields in the Info Inspector (reel, scene, take, and so on).

To Filter the Event Browser:

1. Choose Edit > Find, or press Command-F.

TIP You can also click the magnifying glass in the Search field at the top of the Event Browser.

The Filter window opens **C**.

2. Optionally type text in the Text search field.

3. Click the Plus button, and select an additional type of criteria you want to search on **D**. Choices include the following:

   ▸ **Text:** Finds text in any field (name, markers, reel, scene, take, angle, and so on). You can include or exclude the entered text, and you can specify exact text or partial text.

   ▸ **Ratings:** Choose Favorites **E** or Rejected.

   ▸ **Media Type:** Choose video only **F**, audio only, video + audio, or stills. Then choose to include or exclude the selection **G**.

C The Filter window

D Add criteria by clicking the Plus button and choosing a type.

E The Ratings option lets you specify Favorites or Rejected.

G You can also choose to include or exclude the selected media type.

F The Media type lets you choose audio, video, both, or still images.

 Any available keywords appear as checkboxes for you to select.

 Choose whether the results have to include all selected keywords or any.

 Choose any of the people-related analysis keywords.

 Choose a specific metadata field, and type text into it.

 Choose a specific date.

 Or choose a relative date range.

 The search field shows icons indicating what types of criteria are being used to filter the current view.

▸ **Stabilization:** Choose whether to include or exclude clips containing excessive shake. This information is gathered during clip analysis (for more, see "Video Analysis" in Chapter 6, "Importing Footage").

▸ **Keywords:** Each of the keywords used in the event are listed with checkboxes . Check the keywords you want to include in (or exclude from) your search. Assuming you select more than one keyword, you can choose whether the search must include all or any of the selected terms .

▸ **People:** Choose to find clips containing analysis keywords identifying different types of shots as gathered during clip analysis  (for more, see "Video Analysis" in Chapter 6, "Importing Footage").

▸ **Format Info:** Enter text and choose a specific field to search on . This allows you to find only clips from a specific scene or reel (or other fields) based on the information in the Info Inspector.

▸ **Date:** Choose clips from a specified date  or date range .

▸ **Roles:** Choose to find clips tagged with a Role designation such as Dialogue, Music, Effects, Video, or Titles.

As you add criteria, icons are added to the search field at the top of the Event Browser . Even if you close the Filter window, the filters will remain in place until you manually clear the search.

To clear the search filter:

- Click the Clear Search icon in the search field at the top of the Event Browser **O**.

TIP You can also remove all of the criteria in the Filter window.

To remove an individual criterion from the search results:

- Click the Remove Criteria button to the right of the criteria name in the Filter window **P**.

To filter based on all criteria:

- Click the pop-up menu in the upper-left of the Filter window, and choose All **Q**.

  Only clips containing every listed criterion will appear in the Event Browser.

To filter based on any criteria:

- Click the pop-up menu in the upper-left of the Filter window, and choose Any.

  Any clip meeting at least one of the listed criteria will appear in the Event Browser.

Clear Search Field button

O Clear the search field by clicking the circled x.

Remove Criteria button

P Remove any individual search criterion by clicking the red Remove Criteria button.

Q Choose whether search results must meet all criteria or any criteria.

New Smart Collection button

R Click the New Smart Collection button to save your filter settings as a collection.

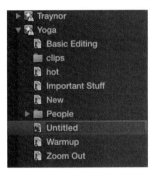

S A new Smart Collection appears in the Event Library.

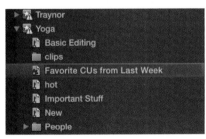

T Rename the Smart Collection so you'll remember what it represents.

U The Filter window shows the settings that define the selected Smart Collection.

To save the filter results as a Smart Collection:

1. Open the Filter window, and enter any desired search criteria.

   The selected event is filtered.

2. Click the New Smart Collection button **R**.

   A new Smart Collection appears in the Event Library **S**.

   This collection contains clips that meet the criteria selected in the Filter window. Any clip that later meets the same criteria will automatically be added to the Smart Collection.

3. Click the collection's name in the Event Library, and enter a custom name **T**.

To modify the criteria of a smart collection:

1. Double-click the Smart Collection icon in the Event Library.

   The Filter window opens, showing the criteria for that collection **U**.

2. Make necessary changes to the search criteria.

To delete a smart collection:

- Right-click the smart collection, and choose Delete Smart Collection from the pop-up menu (or press Command-Delete).

Folders

You can also add another level of organizational structure to your Event Library: *folders*. Folders are simply a way to group elements in events to simplify your view.

Strangely, you cannot stick individual clips inside folders. Folders can hold only collections.

To create a folder:

1. Select an event in the Event Library.

2. Right-click the event and choose New Folder **A**, or press Shift-Command-N.

   A new empty folder is added to the event **B**.

3. Click the name of the folder, and type a name **C**.

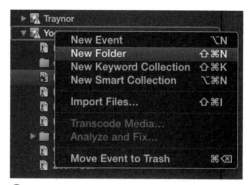

A Right-click the event, and choose New Folder.

B A new folder is added to the event.

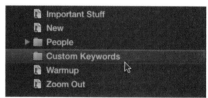

C Rename the folder something useful.

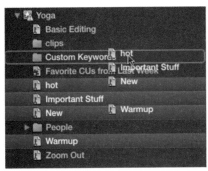

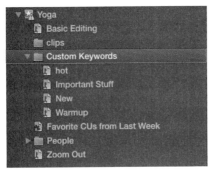

D Drag collections or other folders into the folder. Don't bother trying to drag individual clips; inexplicably, folders can hold only collections of clips.

E The items are added to the folder.

To add items to a folder:

- Drag Keyword Collections, Smart Collections, or other folders into the folder **D**.

  The items are added to the folder **E**.

To remove an item from a folder:

- Drag the item from the folder onto the event name.

  The item is moved from the folder back into the root of the event.

To delete a folder:

- Select the folder and press Command-Delete.

5

Projects

A *project* is an edited assembly of audio and video clips. In Final Cut Pro X, projects are stored in a separate file from FCP clip information, and you can have only one project open at a time.

Once you've assembled a project, you can manipulate that project as if it were a single clip by creating a compound clip. You can open a project and play it in the Viewer, mark In and Out points, and insert all or part of that project into another project. Inserting a project into another project creates what's known as a *compound clip*.

In this chapter, you'll learn about creating and managing your projects.

All of your editing genius—all of the time and inspiration you invest in assembling and refining your finished movie—is stored in this modest data file, so you should treat project files with respect.

One final note, and it's important: FCP automatically saves your work as you go. If you're interested in experimenting with your edit, you should read up on your options for duplicating and saving project versions. (See "To duplicate a project" later in this chapter.)

In This Chapter

Anatomy of the Project Library

FCP's Project Library displays all projects on any connected hard drive. When your project list gets too lengthy for easy access to your current work, it's time to create some folders to organize your library.

To display the Project Library:

- Click the Project Library button in the lower-left corner of the main window **A**.

Time Stamp for Projects

The Last Modified listing in the Project Inspector tab makes it easy to find the most recently revised version of your project—a real lifesaver when you're returning to a project after a long absence.

Share indicator appears when a project has been exported. Click to view export details in the Project Inspector.

Click the triangle to reveal the contents of a connected hard drive.

Project files can be organized into folders.

Double-click a project's icon to open it in the Timeline and Viewer.

Click to display/hide the Project Library.

Click to create a new project.

Click to create a new folder.

Project filmstrips can be previewed by skimming.

A Project management options in the Project Library

A Open the Project Library, and then click the New Project button. The Project Library buttons are visible only when the Project Library is open.

B Type a new name for the project, choose a default event folder, and don't change the default properties settings in the New Project window unless you have a solid reason to customize your settings.

Creating a New Project

A new project created in FCP automatically generates a new, untitled project in your default project format. Note that you probably won't need to change project settings unless you change your media format.

To create a new project:

1. *Do one of the following*:

   ▸ Choose File > New > Project, or press Command-N.

   ▸ Open the Project Library, and then click the New Project button **A**.

   FCP's New Project window appears, displaying a default, highlighted name.

2. In the New Project window, type a new name for the project **B**.

continues on next page

FCP X Update: New Organizing Framework

FCP X introduces a reconfigured FCP organizing framework. Media clips (which are stored in event folders) and edit information (which is stored in the Project Library) are now independent of one another.

Final Cut Pro X's organizing framework breaks down into the following key components:

▪ **Event:** An event folder stores references (file location information) to all the media files you use in your projects. Events are stored in the FCP's Event Library.

▪ **Project:** A project (called a *sequence* in earlier versions of FCP) is an edited assembly of audio and video clips, along with the sequencing information (your cuts) and all settings for special effects you apply to any clip in the project. The project file contains no media—it's strictly the "brains" of your project—but this one file is your project's most valuable asset. Projects are stored in the Project Library.

▪ **Clip:** The ground level of the FCP organizing framework, the clip represents an individual unit of media in Final Cut Pro. A clip can stand for a movie, a still image, a nested sequence, a generator, or an audio file. Clips are stored in event folders and appear in the Event Browser.

3. Choose the event folder that contains the clips you want to work with from the Default Event drop-down menu.

4. Unless you have a special need to do so, leave Starting Timecode, Video Properties and Audio and Render Properties on their default (automatic) settings, and then click OK.

The Timeline opens with your new, empty project displayed **C**.

To open a project for editing:

- *Do one of the following*:
    - ▸ Double-click the project's icon or filmstrip in the Project Library **D**.

The project opens in both the Viewer and the Timeline.

TIP If you are editing a long program in multiple segments, you might want to set the starting timecode to reflect each segment's start time in the master program. You can do that by entering the start time in the New Project window's Starting Timecode field. To modify the starting timecode of an existing project, see "Changing Project Properties" later in this chapter.

C The Timeline opens, displaying your new, empty project.

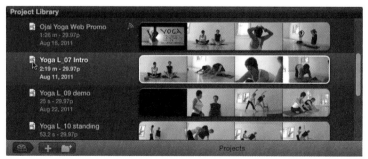

D Double-click the project's icon in the Project Library to open it for editing.

A The Final Cut Projects folder is FCP's default location for project files is inside your Home folder's Movies folder. See the Final Cut Events folder just above the Projects folder? That's the default location for your event folders—the folders holding your projects' media files. It's also located in the Movies folder.

B Right-click the project in the Project Library, and then choose Duplicate Project; or press Command-D.

Managing Projects

As they shape the final version of their movie, editors frequently cut, copy, and paste together partial sequences to assemble the full program. This section offers tips on duplicating projects, switching between projects, copying clips from one project into another, and organizing your Project Library with folders.

TIP It's a wondrous thing to be able to e-mail an FCP project file to a friend or colleague who can then open and edit it—assuming you both have the same media files on disk. To share or archive a project file, you first need to know its default location on your hard drive. FCP's default location for project files is inside your Home folder's Movies folder **A**.

To duplicate a project:

1. Right-click the project in the Project Library, and then choose Duplicate Project **B**; or press Command-D.

2. In the Duplicate Project window, choose a disk location to store your duplicate project file.

continues on next page

3. Specify which project elements you want to duplicate, and then click OK . Your duplication options are as follows:

   ▸ **Duplicate Project Only:** Duplicates only the project file **D**.

   ▸ **Duplicate Project and Referenced Events:** Duplicates the project file, any events referred to by the project file, and all of the media in the referenced events.

   ▸ **Duplicate Project + Used Clips Only:** Duplicates the project file and the media files for any clips used in the project.

   ▸ **Include Render Files:** Duplicates the project's render files.

C Specify your Duplicate Project selection in this window.

D Your duplicated project in the Project Library.

Stop Saving! Duplicate Your Project to Archive a Version

FCP automatically saves your work as you go. If you're interested in experimenting with your edit, you need to duplicate your project file to create an archival copy of your project that won't change as you continue to edit.

The copy procedure described here is a convenient way to "safety copy" a version of a project and associated media files. With a safety copy of the project, you can feel free to experiment because any changes you make to the duplicate project will not affect the original project or its render files.

E Open the first project in the Timeline, select the clips you want to copy, and then press Command-C.

F Double-click a project's icon in the Project Library to open it as a second project in the Timeline.

G In the second project, position the playhead where you want to paste the clips, and then choose Edit > Paste; or press Command-V.

To copy multiple clips from one project to another:

1. Open the source project in the Timeline.

2. In the Timeline, select the clips you want to copy, and then press Command-C **E**.

3. Click the Project Library button to return to the Project Library.

4. Double-click the project's icon to open it as a second project in the Timeline **F**.

5. Position the playhead where you want to paste the clips, and then choose Edit > Paste; or press Command-V **G**.

   The clips now appear in both projects and reference the same source media files on disk, but you'll need to rerender any previously rendered project material in the new project location **H**.

H The clip copies are pasted into the second project and reference the same source media files on disk.

To move a project to another hard drive:

1. Select the project in the Project Library, and *then do one of the following*:

   ▸ Choose File > Move Project .

   ▸ Command-drag the project to the destination hard drive's icon in the Project Library.

2. In the Move Project window, choose a destination for your project from the Location pop-up menu.

3. Specify which project elements you want to move, choosing from the following 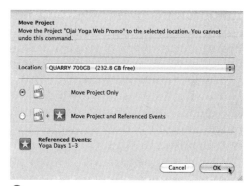:

   ▸ **Move Project Only:** Select to move just the project file and no events (media files).

   ▸ **Move Project and Referenced Events:** Select to move the project file plus all events (media files) to which the project file refers.

4. Click OK.

   FCP moves your project and any events you specify to the new location you selected .

> **TIP** You can't undo a project move operation. To return the project to its original disk location, you'll need to perform another project move operation.

I Select the project in the Project Library, and then choose File > Move Project.

J Specify which project elements you want to move in the Move Project window, and then click OK.

K The project you moved appears in its new hard drive location.

Ⓛ Right-click the project in the Project Library, and then choose Move Project to Trash from the shortcut menu.

Ⓜ Click and hold the Timeline History feature's Forward button to switch to a project you opened later than the currently displayed project.

TIP Timeline History buttons are dimmed if there are no previously opened projects.

TIP Timeline History buttons also allow you to navigate up and down compound clip levels. What is a compound clip? It's a way to nest projects within other projects. See Chapter 16, "Compound Clips," for the full rundown.

To delete a project:

- Select the project in the Project Library, and *then do one of the following*:
  - ▸ Choose File > Move Project to Trash.
  - ▸ Right-click the project, and then choose Move Project to Trash from the shortcut menu Ⓛ.

  The project is moved to the Finder's Trash and disappears from the Project Library. To permanently delete the project, empty the Finder Trash.

TIP By selecting a Project Library folder containing multiple projects, you can transfer them all to the Trash in a single operation. Gutsy move.

Switching Between Projects

You can have only one FCP project open in the Timeline at any one time. You can use FCP's Timeline History feature, however, to make switching between projects fast. Timeline History is designed to operate like your web browser's History list: Your last open project is at the top of the list.

To switch between projects using the Timeline History feature:

- *Do one of the following*:
  - ▸ Click and hold the Timeline History's Back button to switch to a project you opened earlier.
  - ▸ Click and hold the Timeline History's Forward button to switch to a project you opened later than the currently displayed project.

  A drop-down list appears below the button; select the project you want to switch to from the list Ⓜ.

Using Folders to Organize Your Project Library

If you've been using FCP long enough to generate a lengthy list of projects and project versions, Project Library folders can be an enormous help. FCP's compact Project Library interface works a whole lot better when you've hidden old and irrelevant projects away from view in a well-labeled folder.

To create a new folder in the Project Library:

1. Open the Project Library.

2. Select the hard disk, folder, or project level where you want to add a new folder, and *then do one of the following*:

   ▶ Click the New Folder button.

   ▶ Right-click its icon, and choose New Folder from the shortcut menu **N**.

   A new folder appears on the disk or in the folder you selected, at the same level as the selected disk, folder, or project **O**.

3. Select the folder, click the folder name, and type a new name.

4. Drag a project you want to group into the folder. You can select only one project at a time.

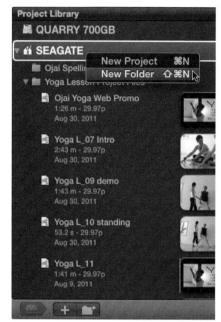

N In the Project Library, select the hard disk, folder, or project level where you want to add a new folder; then right-click its icon and choose New Folder from the shortcut menu.

O A new folder appears on the disk or folder you selected, at the same level as the selected disk, folder, or project.

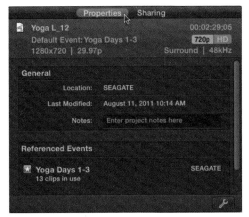

A In the project's Inspector window, click the Properties button at the top of the pane.

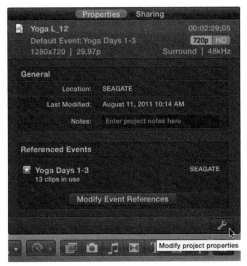

B Click the "Modify project properties" button (that's a wrench icon on the button) at the bottom of the project's Inspector window.

Changing Project Properties

Most project settings are determined by the video and audio of your project's source media; your project settings should almost always match your source media's format settings. Final Cut Pro does a fine job of automatically assigning the best settings to your project, but occasionally you need to make a change. Here's how:

1. In the Project Library, click the project's icon to select it.

2. Choose File > Project Properties, or press Command-J.

   The Inspector window displaying the project's default property settings appears in the upper-right corner of the interface.

3. In the project's Inspector window, click the Properties button at the top of the pane **A**.

4. Click the "Modify project properties" button at the bottom of the project's Inspector window.

   The project's Properties window appears **B**.

   continues on next page

5. In the project's Properties window, modify any of the settings listed next .

   ▸ **Name:** Rename the project.

   ▸ **Default Event:** Specify the default event folder and disk location for any media dragged directly to this project's Timeline from the Finder or the FCP Media Browser.

   ▸ **Starting Timecode:** Enter a value to modify the starting timecode for your project.

   ▸ **Video Properties:** Modify the project's frame size, resolution, or frame rate.

   ▸ **Timecode Display:** Specify the timecode display options. Available frame rate options depend on the project's source media format.

   ▸ **Audio Channels:** Specify surround sound or stereo for the project's audio output format.

   ▸ **Audio Sample Rate:** Specify a sample rate for the project's audio.

   ▸ **Render Format:** Specify a codec to use for the project's rendered material.

6. Click OK.

C In the project's Properties window, modify the format, timecode display, audio output, or render format settings, and then click OK. You should leave the project's default settings as they are unless you have a specific reason to modify them.

A Right-click the project's icon, and then choose Consolidate Project Media from the shortcut menu.

Consolidate Your Project's Media Files

You've been working on your project for a while—perhaps you changed cameras or computers during production—and now your project's media files are scattered across multiple external drives and your internal hard drive. Relax, it's not hard to clean up. FCP's Consolidate Project Media feature can automatically consolidate all the media used in the project on the same hard disk as the project.

To consolidate a project's media clips at a single disk location:

1. In the Project Library, right-click the project's icon, and then choose Consolidate Project Media from the shortcut menu A.

    The Consolidate Project Media window appears.

    continues on next page

2. In the Consolidate Project Media window , select a consolidation method from the following options:

▸ **Copy Referenced Events:** Select this option to copy all events (media files) referenced in the project file to a single disk location.

▸ **Move Referenced Events:** Select this to move all events (media files) referenced in the project file to a single disk location.

▸ **Copy Used Clips Only:** Select this option to copy only media files used in the project. This creates a new event folder for storing your consolidated media clips.

▸ **New Event Name field:** Select this option to create a new event folder to hold the consolidated media. This choice is available only if you choose Copy Used Clips Only.

3. Click OK.

Final Cut Pro consolidates the media using the method you selected. The consolidated event folder or folders appear on the same hard disk as the project.

TIP If you invoke the Consolidate Project Media command and an alert window appears informing you that there is "nothing to consolidate," all of your project's media files are already consolidated on one disk.

B Select a consolidation method in the Consolidate Project Media window, and then click OK.

6

Importing Footage

One of the things that differentiates Final Cut Pro from most other software is that you can't really do anything until you import some files. In most programs, you can create a document from scratch and begin working, but with a video editor, you need to start with some existing video.

This video will invariably come from one of three sources: a file-based camera, such as most modern camcorders, cell phones, DSLRs, Flips, GoPros, and so on; a tape-based camera, such as legacy DV and HDV camcorders that were popular way back in the *aughts*; or digital video files on your hard disk, such as a computer-generated animation, a downloaded video file, a screen-capture file, or something similar.

Regardless of your source media's provenance, you need to import it into FCP so you can remove the bad bits, polish the rest, add some music, and call it a movie.

Importing from File-Based Cameras

The engineers who developed FCP X made the mildly controversial choice of assuming that most users will be using modern file-based cameras. While this potentially alienates the poor, the Luddite, and the professional who is deeply invested in technology they bought three years ago, the reality is that file-based cameras are the future (at least for the next decade until some even newer technology makes them obsolete). Plus, you can still import other video sources, either by using one of FCP's other import methods (detailed in the remainder of this chapter) or by using third-party solutions.

FCP X can also optionally perform a number of useful tasks during the import process that will greatly improve your editing experience thereafter. These include organizing your files for you, transcoding your footage into editing-friendly formats, and analyzing both audio and video in search of potential problems, as well as providing details about the content such as whether there are people in the shot and how far away from the camera they are standing.

This method works for most file-based cameras, including iPhones and other Apple devices.

TIP If your camera or memory card doesn't appear in the Cameras list (in the Camera Import window), try following the instructions in "Importing Files" later in the chapter. That is the recommended procedure for popular DSLR cameras such as the Canon 5D and 7D.

Import from Camera button

Ⓐ Click the Import from Camera button in the toolbar to open the Camera Import window.

Ⓑ On a Mac with a built-in camera, the Camera Import window defaults to showing your own face. Check your hair before proceeding.

Ⓒ Select your device from the Cameras list on the left. Its contents appear under the preview area.

Ⓓ The clips on the current device are displayed as filmstrips beneath the preview area.

To import files from a file-based camera:

1. Connect the device to your Mac via USB (or FireWire for P2-based media), or insert the memory card containing the video clips into a connected card reader.

2. Choose File > Import From Camera, or click the Import from Camera button in the toolbar. **Ⓐ**

   The Camera Import window opens **Ⓑ**.

3. Select your camera or volume from the list on the left side of the window **Ⓒ**.

   Filmstrips for each of the clips appear below the preview area. The width of the thumbnails indicates the relative duration of the clips **Ⓓ**.

TIP Customize the view by zooming in and out on the thumbnails, modifying the track height, and optionally displaying the audio waveforms using the controls in the lower-right corner (just like the identical controls in the Event Browser and in the Timeline) **Ⓔ**.

continues on next page

Ⓔ Customize the filmstrip view just like you modify the view in the Event Browser. Sadly, there's no List view.

4. Preview the clips by skimming the thumbnails or using the playback controls at the bottom of the preview area.

5. Press I and O to select the beginning and end of the section of a clip you want to import **F**.

6. Click Import Selection.

The Import Settings sheet appears **G**.

7. Select the event to which you want your imported footage stored, or create a new event and assign a hard disk on which to save it **H**.

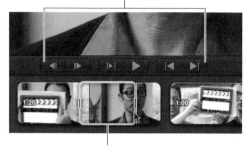

Playback controls

Marked selection

F Use the playback controls in the preview area as well as familiar keyboard shortcuts such as J-K-L, I, and O to select the range of a clip you want to import.

G The Import Settings sheet allows you to choose your desired settings and analysis options prior to beginning the import.

H Select an event or create a new one where you plan to save the imported clips.

I Choose the import settings required for the current selection.

J The imported video appears in the selected event (behind the Camera Import window).

K As you import footage, orange marker bars indicate areas that have been imported.

8. Enable the Transcoding, Video, and Audio analysis settings you want to apply, and click Import **I**.

   For more on using these settings, see the "Import Settings" section.

   If you move the Camera Import window out of the way, you'll see that the imported footage appears immediately in the chosen event **J**.

   In the Camera Import window, the imported section is indicated with an orange bar **K**.

   As you're working, you may want to hide the sections of your footage that have already been selected.

9. Enable the Hide Imported Clips checkbox.

   Any imported footage is hidden **L**.

continues on next page

Clip is split in two

L If you enable the Hide Imported Clips setting, the imported areas are hidden. In this example, the remaining footage (before and after the selected area) was made into two separate clips.

10. Repeat steps 4–8 until you've imported all the clips you want to use.

TIP You can also select multiple clips at once by Shift-clicking or Command-clicking **M**. Also, when no clips are selected, the Import Selected button becomes an Import All button **N**, allowing you to quickly import all the footage from the camera in one step.

11. To close the Camera Import window, click the Close button at the top left or the bottom right, or press Command-W or Command-I.

Note there are some devices whose media is not automatically recognized by FCP at this time. In such cases, such as when importing footage from Sony XDCAM or RED cameras, you'll need to use a separate utility to convert the video files into a format recognizable by the software. Consult your camera's documentation for more information.

M Shift-click or Command-click to select multiple clips at once.

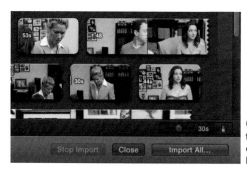

N If no clips are selected, the Import Selected button changes to an Import All button.

How Files Are Imported So Fast

One wonderful innovation FCP X brings is the way it makes clip importing truly instantaneous, even when the files must be copied, transcoded, or otherwise manipulated.

When you import files of any type, FCP instantly creates an alias to the original files in the FCP events folder in your User Movies folder. The Event Browser points to that alias, and therefore you can instantaneously play, edit, and do anything else you want with that media inside FCP.

Little progress pie indicators ![icon] appear for each clip as it being imported (both in the Camera Import window as well as in the Event Browser).

When the clip is fully imported, the indicator disappears, and you're working with the final version of the clip.

As the files are copied, transcoded, analyzed, or otherwise modified, the new versions secretly replace the aliases, so the Event Browser doesn't even know the difference.

Any edits you make, metadata and keywords you add, or other modifications you perform remain intact as the newly created clip transparently replaces the alias. To you, it doesn't matter how long the import operation really takes because you can keep working all the while!

Importing from Tape-Based Devices and Live Cameras

Of course, millions of tape-based cameras are still in use around the world, and as long as those cameras have a FireWire port, you'll still be able to get their footage into your computer.

While FCP X does not facilitate the robust logging features found in previous versions, you can control a connected video device to rewind, cue up, and play back the video stored on the tape.

You can then choose to record the footage (in its native format—usually DV or HDV) and apply the same settings and analysis options described in the "Import Settings" section.

You can also import footage directly from the built-in camera found on all MacBooks, MacBook Pros, and iMacs, as well as any other connected webcam.

To import footage from a FireWire-enabled video device:

1. Make sure the device is turned on, and connect it to your Mac using a FireWire cable.

2. Choose File > Import from Camera, press Command-I, or click the Import from Camera button in the toolbar **A**.

   The Camera Import window appears **B**.

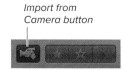

Import from Camera button

A Click the Import from Camera button in the toolbar (or press Command-I).

B The Camera Import window opens.

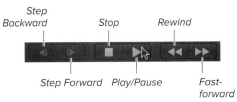

C Select the device from which you want to import footage from the Cameras list on the left.

Step Backward   *Stop*   *Rewind*

Step Forward   *Play/Pause*   *Fast-forward*

D Use the device control buttons to navigate the tape and cue up the section you want to record.

Camera Import

○ Add to existing event: New Event 8–15–11

◉ Create new event: Imperfectly Raw

Save to: Macintosh HD   (2.2 GB free)

Transcoding: ☐ Create optimized media
☐ Create proxy media

Video: ☐ Remove pulldown
☑ Analyze for stabilization and rolling shutter
☑ Analyze for balance color
☐ Find people
☑ Consolidate find people results
☑ Create Smart Collections after analysis

Audio: ☐ Analyze and fix audio problems
☑ Separate mono and group stereo audio
☑ Remove silent channels

Cancel   Import

E The Import Settings sheet allows you to choose your desired settings and analysis options prior to beginning the import.

3. If it's not already selected, choose the device from the Cameras list on the left **C**.

The main play-through window will display the contents of the tape-based device.

For a deck or a camcorder in play-back mode, you can use the playback controls, allowing you to rewind, fast-forward, step forward or backward, play, or pause the device **D**.

TIP For a camcorder in camera mode, you can still capture video, but the device control buttons will have no effect.

4. Cue up the tape, and begin playback on the device a few seconds prior to the section you want to import.

TIP There may be a momentary lag before recording begins, so be sure to give yourself a few seconds of lead-in time.

5. Click Import.

The Import Settings sheet appears **E**.

6. Select the event to which you want your imported footage stored, or create a new event and assign a hard disk on which to save it.

TIP When importing from tape, the resulting files are always stored in the event folder.

7. Enable the Transcoding, Video, and Audio Analysis settings you want to apply, and click Import.

For more on using these settings, see the "Import Settings" section later in this chapter.

Recording begins automatically.

continues on next page

8. When you are done recording, click the Stop Import button or press Escape **F**.

The imported footage appears immediately in the chosen event **G**.

TIP Clips imported from tape will automatically be split into multiple clips when a timecode break or scene break is encountered.

9. To close the Camera Import window, click the Close button at the top left or the bottom right, or press Command-W or Command-I.

Note that for tape-based cameras without a FireWire port, there are numerous third-party capture utilities you can utilize to import the footage and turn it into digital video files that can be edited in FCP. You can find more information on this topic online.

To import footage from an iSight/FaceTime camera:

1. Choose File > Import from Camera and press Command-I, or click the Import from Camera button in the toolbar.

The Camera Import window opens **H**.

2. If it's not already active, select the camera from the Cameras list on the left **I**.

The main play-through window displays the contents of the attached camera.

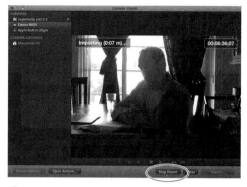

F To stop recording, click the Stop Import button (or press Escape).

G The imported video appears in the selected event.

H The Camera Import window opens.

I Select the built-in FaceTime camera (or any attached webcam) from the Cameras list on the left.

J The Import Setting sheet allows you to set your choices for how the clip is handled upon import.

K The imported footage appears in the selected event.

3. Click Import.

   The Import Settings sheet appears **J**.

4. Select the event to which you want your imported footage stored, or create a new event and assign a hard disk on which to save it.

5. Enable the Transcoding, Video, and Audio analysis settings you want to apply, and click Import.

6. When you're done recording, click the Stop Import button or press Escape.

   The imported footage appears immediately in the chosen event **K**.

7. To close the Camera Import window, click the Close button at the top left or the bottom right, or press Command-W or Command-I.

Backing Up Your Footage

It's a very wise idea to back up the footage from your camera, ideally to multiple hard drives. This is your most valuable asset, and in many cases it is irreplaceable.

FCP has a mechanism for creating a backup of your camera volume that is an identical copy of the original with all the camera metadata and file structure intact. This is called a *camera archive*.

Once the camera archive is created, you can access it in the Camera Import window and recover the files long after the camera memory has been erased.

To create a camera archive:

1. In the Camera Import window, select the device you want to archive from the Cameras list **L**.

2. Click Create Archive.

   The Create Archive sheet opens **M**.

   The archive appears in the Camera Archives list. As it's being saved, an indicator to the right of the name displays the progress **N**.

   By default, the archive is saved in a folder called Final Cut Camera Archives in your Movies folder.

TIP For a more useful backup, you should save the archive on a different volume than where your events are stored.

To open an archive:

- In the Camera Import window, select the archive from the Camera Archives list **O**.

  The volume is loaded and works exactly the same as if you were looking at the camera original.

TIP If the archive you want to mount does not appear in the list, click the Open Archive button at the bottom of the Camera Import window and navigate to the archive file on your hard disk.

You can also create archives from tape-based cameras. The entire tape will be stored as an archive, and later you can import sections just as you can when importing from file-based archives.

L Select the device from the Cameras list, and click Create Archive.

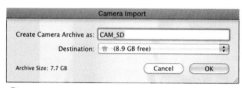

M Name your archive, and click OK.

Archive Progress indicator

N The archive appears in the Camera Archives list, and as it's being saved, an indicator shows the progress.

O Select the archive you want to restore. The volume automatically loads into the window.

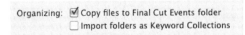

Organizing: ☑ Copy files to Final Cut Events folder
☐ Import folders as Keyword Collections

Ⓐ The Organize section controls whether files are copied to the events folder and whether folder names are imported as keywords.

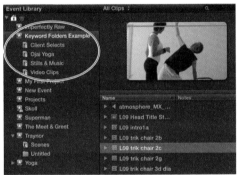

Ⓑ When enabled, the original folder names from the disk you're copying from are assigned as keywords to the clips within them. In this example, all of the clips were in the folder called Ojai Yoga, so all of the clips get that keyword, but only two clips were in the Client Selects folder, so only those two get that keyword, and so on.

Import Settings

These Import settings (or a subset of them) appear in different windows depending on the import method you choose, but no matter where they appear, they have the same effect.

Organizing Settings

There are two checkboxes in the Organizing section of the Import Settings window **Ⓐ**.

This section appears only when you're using the Import Files command.

- **Copy files to Final Cut Events folder:**
  This option will copy all the data in your original media files into the event folder on your hard disk.

  You need to enable this if you're importing files directly from a device that is only temporarily available (such as a flash drive or a client's hard drive, and so on).

  If the files are already stored on a local hard disk, you may choose to disable this; however, in that case, it's imperative that you do not delete the original media files.

  If this setting is disabled, aliases will be added to the event folder that point to the original files.

- **Import folders as Keyword Collections:**
  This setting re-creates the folder structure from the disk containing the files to be imported as sets of keyword collections in the FCP Event Browser **Ⓑ**.

  Disable this checkbox if you're importing files directly from a camera or camera memory card. Optionally, enable it if you're importing files from another location on your hard disk.

  For more on keyword collections, see Chapter 4, "Marking Clips."

Transcoding Settings

The Transcoding section allows you to instruct FCP to create duplicate copies of all your media files in alternative file formats 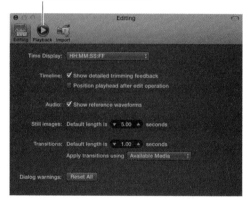.

TIP You can transcode clips at any time (not just during Import) by right-clicking a clip, folder, collection, or whole event, and choosing Transcode Media from the shortcut menu.

- **Create Optimized Media:** Enabling this checkbox will create a duplicate copy of all your files in one of the ProRes formats. The specific ProRes format is determined automatically based on the quality level of the source footage being transcoded.

This can improve performance, ensure wider compatibility, and ensure consistent image quality across varied source footage types. On the other hand, it takes a long time and uses up a lot of disk space.

When optimized media exists, FCP will automatically use that version of the media instead of the original source footage. Optimized media is always stored in the event folder.

- **Create Proxy Media:** Enabling this checkbox will create a duplicate copy of all your files in the ProRes 422 (Proxy) format.

Once proxy media exists, you can select whether to use the proxies instead of the original source footage (or the optimized footage if it exists). Proxy media is always stored in the event folder.

To enable use of proxy media across all projects:

1. Choose Final Cut Pro > Preferences.

   The Preferences window opens **D**.

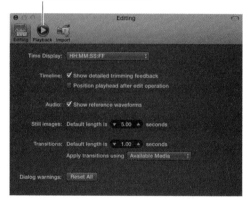

Transcoding: ☐ Create optimized media
☐ Create proxy media

C The Transcoding settings enable you to convert your imported video into ProRes format clips that are optimized for playback in FCP.

Click to open the Playback pane of the Preferences window.

D Open the Preferences window, and click the Playback icon to open the Playback pane.

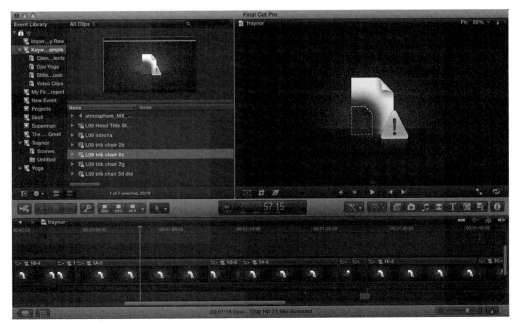

E In the Playback pane, select the "Use proxy media" setting.

2. Click the Playback icon to open the Playback pane.

The Playback pane opens.

3. Click the "Use proxy media" radio button, and close the Preferences window **E**.

FCP substitutes the proxy media (if available) for all other media.

IMPORTANT: If you enable the Use proxy media setting, it applies to all events and projects in FCP. If proxy media does not exist for a particular event or project, you will see the Offline Files warning instead of the video clips **F**.

F If you have your preferences set to use proxies but there are no proxies in one of your events or projects, you will see the Offline Media warning in the Event Browser, the Viewer, or the Timeline.

To stop using proxies and use original or (if available) optimized media:

- In the Playback pane of the Final Cut Pro Preferences window, choose the "Use original or optimized media" setting 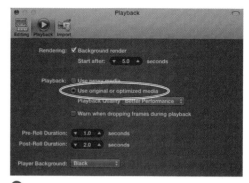 **G**.

  Your original media or (if available) your optimized media will be used instead of the proxies.

Video Analysis

This section contains settings enabling different types of data analysis of the video image **H**.

- **Remove pulldown:** This setting is available only for footage at certain frame rates.

  If prior frame-rate conversion (as occurs during telecine or when using some formats such as some frame rates in DVCPro HD or 24fps DV) has inserted duplicate frames, selecting this option will remove the extra frames and return your footage to its native frame rate (usually 24fps).

- **Analyze for stabilization and rolling shutter:** This option searches the footage for instances of extremely shaky camera work and instances of rolling shutter artifacts.

  Once analyzed, analysis keywords are automatically added to areas in your footage where such problems might exist **I**.

G Disable the "Use proxy media" setting to stop using proxies and use the original or (if available) optimized media instead.

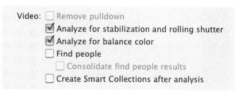

H Video settings provide options to analyze your clips for a variety of information that will speed up and ease your editing work.

Analysis keyword indicators

Analysis keywords

I Analysis keywords are added to sections of the footage where the camera was shaken excessively or had rolling shutter artifacts.

By analyzing during import, you can correct these problems instantaneously during the editing process rather than waiting for analysis to occur after adding a clip to a project and enabling one of the correction settings in the Video Inspector **J**.

TIP Image Stabilization and Rolling Shutter controls are available only for clips in a project. Raw clips in the Event Browser cannot be stabilized.

On the other hand, this analysis takes a very long time, and you wind up potentially analyzing gobs of footage you never intend to use, whereas analyzing later allows you to examine only the specific footage you choose to edit into your project.

continues on next page

J If analysis hasn't yet occurred, enabling the Image Stabilizer or Rolling Shutter controls in the Video Inspector forces analysis to begin. A warning appears in the Viewer to alert you that stabilization cannot yet be applied.

- **Analyze for balance color:** This setting instructs FCP to examine the color balance settings of your source footage. That way, if you later enable the Balance Color setting in the Color section of the Video Inspector, the color balance will happen instantaneously.

  If you skip the analysis, you can still balance a clip's color, but you will have to wait for the analysis to occur upon activation of the Balance Color control 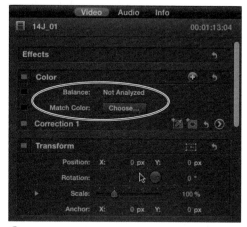.

  For more on balancing color, see the "Color Balance" section of Chapter 15, "Color Correction."

- **Find People:** This setting uses facial recognition technology to search your footage for clips containing human faces.

  It then uses the approximate size of the faces it finds in the frame to assign a shot size (Close-up, Medium Shot, Wide Shot, and so on) and the number of faces (two-shot, group shot, and so on)

  Once analyzed, analysis keywords are automatically added to your footage identifying areas spotted by the analysis 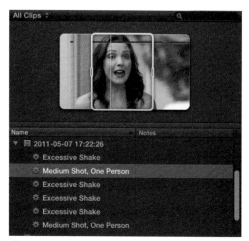.

  While this sort of analysis is a nice idea in theory, its usefulness is limited in practice. Shots frequently change over time in ways that defeat the analysis: A person turning away from the camera is not recognized; people entering or exiting the frame change the number of faces. Occasionally inanimate objects are misread as faces, and the decision the software makes about what constitutes a close-up, medium shot, or wide shot seems fairly inconsistent or at least oversimplified.

K If analysis hasn't yet occurred, the Balance Color setting indicates such.

L Analysis keywords are added to indicate clips containing faces. In this example, the analysis thinks this is a Medium Shot of One Person. Most humans would consider this a close-up, and technically, it has two people in the frame.

Consolidating the results means keywords will be grouped. This figure shows the same image analyzed without consolidation (on top) and with consolidation (on bottom). The top example is more precise; when the actor moves out of frame temporarily, the keyword (indicated by the purple bar) goes away. The bottom example might be more convenient however, since overall the shot is of this subject, even if there are a few frames here and there where he isn't visible.

Still, if you have a bunch of interviews peppered throughout a large pile of nonhuman subject footage, this analysis will do a great job of identifying those moments automatically.

- **Consolidate find people results:** If you choose to enable the Find People analysis, you can further choose whether to mark the analysis keywords for the duration of the shot versus only for the exact frames where the people are visible .

- **Create Smart Collections after analysis:** Enabling this checkbox will add smart collections based on any keywords added during the analysis.

So, if there are sections of your footage with rolling shutter issues or clips containing close-ups of people, smart collections are automatically added to the event, enabling you to easily locate those keyworded sections .

Because they are *smart*, any new clips with similar attributes that get added to the event will automatically be added to the existing collection.

Smart collections are created within the event based on the applied keywords.

Smart collections are automatically generated based on the analysis keywords.

Audio Analysis

This section contains three checkboxes to facilitate automatic correction of common audio problems:

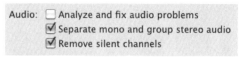

- **Analyze and fix audio problems:** This checkbox enables analysis of clip audio to identify areas that could benefit from audio compression (aka loudness), background noise reduction, and hum removal.

  You can then use the controls in the Audio Enhancements Inspector to make these common corrections .

> **TIP** Because audio analysis is very quick, it's largely irrelevant whether or not you perform the analysis during import or later, when you want to adjust specific audio settings.

  For more on audio enhancements, see Chapter 12, "Audio Effects."

O The Audio Enhancements Inspector relies on this analysis, but if you haven't already done it, the analysis can be performed manually at any time.

P Mono audio tracks displayed in the Audio Inspector

Q Stereo audio tracks displayed in the Audio Inspector

- **Separate mono and group stereo audio:** This option scans your audio files to identify tracks that were recorded in stereo (more common on consumer camcorders) or mono (more common on professional audio recording equipment). Based on the results, it assigns the relevant settings in the Audio Inspector appropriately: Mono tracks are kept discrete, and the pan settings are assigned as centered **P**. Stereo tracks are grouped into pairs with the pan settings split to the left and right **Q**.

- **Remove silent channels:** Selecting this option instructs FCP to scan your footage for audio tracks containing no data. Such tracks are hidden in the Audio Inspector and are never included when a clip is edited into a project.

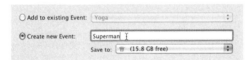

A The Import Files window

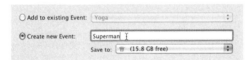

B Chose an event where you want to import the files, or create a new event and specify a disk on which to save it.

C Select the appropriate import settings, and click Import.

Importing Files

If you have any video, audio, or still-image files on a connected hard disk and you want to use them in FCP, you can import them into an event using the Import Files window.

TIP You can also use this method for some camera-original files when the volume doesn't appear in the Camera Import window (such as from the Canon 5D or 7D).

You can also drag and drop files from any folder on your hard disk into a FCP event or even directly into an open Timeline.

To import files:

1. Choose File > Import > Files.

    The Import Files window opens **A**.

2. Navigate to the folder containing the files you want to import.

TIP When importing files from a camera volume, select the top-level folder, and FCP will figure out where the usable video files are.

3. Select the event into which you want to import the files, or create a new event. If you create a new event, specify the disk where you want to save it **B**.

4. Specify the Import Settings you desire as described in the "Import Settings" section earlier in this chapter **C**.

continues on next page

5. Click Import.

If the folder you selected contains unreadable files, FCP will show a warning, identifying the files that cannot be imported 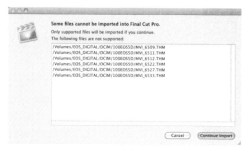.

6. Click Continue Import.

The files are imported into the selected event **E**.

D You will be warned if there are files inside the selected folder that cannot be imported.

E The files are instantly added to the selected event.

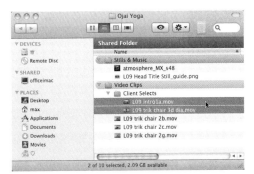

F Select the files in the Finder that you want to import.

G You can drag directly to the Timeline.

H You can also drag the files to an event in the Event Library.

To drag and drop files from the Finder into FCP:

1. Open the Finder window containing the file(s) you want to import **F**.

2. Select the file(s), and *do one of the following*:

   ▸ Drag the files to the FCP Timeline **G**.

   ▸ Drag the files to an event in the FCP Event Library **H**.

   Note that you cannot drag files to the Event Browser.

Import Preferences

When importing files using drag and drop, you can still determine whether to transcode the files or perform analysis on either video or audio.

These settings are determined by the controls in the Import preferences, which are identical to the settings described in the "Import Settings" section earlier in this chapter.

To choose import settings for clips dragged and dropped into FCP from the Finder:

1. Choose Final Cut Pro > Preferences.

   The Preferences window opens **I**.

2. Click the Import icon to open the Import pane.

   The Import pane opens **J**.

3. Enable the checkboxes for the settings you want to apply.

4. Close the Preferences window.

   For more information about the specific settings, see "Import Settings" earlier in this chapter.

Click to open the Import pane.

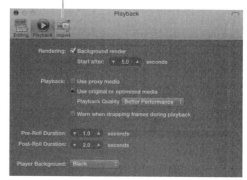

I Open the FCP Preferences window.

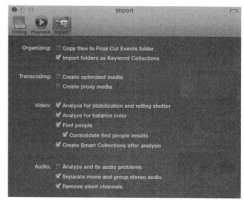

J The Import pane contains all the familiar import settings.

Show/Hide Photos Browser

K Click the Show Photos Browser button.

Categories pop-up menu

L The Photos Browser opens.

M Choose a category of photos from the pop-up menu.

Importing from iPhoto, Aperture, or Photo Booth

You can import still images from any folder on your computer using the steps described in the earlier "Importing Files" section, but if you want to import photos directly from your iPhoto, Aperture, or Photo Booth libraries, you can do that from the Photos Browser.

To import photos from other Apple applications:

1. Click the Show Photos Browser button in the toolbar **K**.

   The Photos Browser opens to the right of the Timeline **L**.

2. Click the Categories pop-up menu to choose a specific library, album, place, or other category **M**.

   The photos in that group are displayed in the stack **N**.

continues on next page

N The contents of the category are displayed in the stack area.

3. Select one or more photos from the stack area **O**.

Selected photos are highlighted in blue.

TIP You can shift-click to select a range of photos or Command-click to select a group of individual photos.

TIP You can double-click a photo to see a larger preview of it. Double-click again to return to the full list.

4. Drag the selected photo(s) to the Timeline or to an event in the Event Library **P**.

O Shift-click or Command-click to select more than one photo.

P Drag your selection into the Timeline or Event Library.

Show/Hide Music and Sound Browser

Q Click the Show/Hide Music and Sound Browser button.

R The Sound and Music Browser opens.

S Choose a category of sound effects or music from the pop-up menu.

Importing from iTunes

Similarly to working with photos, you can manually import any audio file from a folder in the Finder using the steps described in the earlier "Import Files" section, or you can directly access the library, playlists, and individual songs in your iTunes library from within FCP using the Music and Sound Browser.

The Music and Sound Browser contains all the sound effects files that come bundled with FCP, all the files bundled with iMovie, and all the files in your iTunes library.

To import sound and music files:

1. Click the Show Music and Sound Browser button in the toolbar **Q**.

   The Sound and Music Browser opens to the right of the Timeline **R**.

2. Click the Categories pop-up menu to select a specific library, category, or iTunes playlist **S**.

continues on next page

The files in the selected item appear in the stack **T**.

3. Optionally type in the search field to refine the list of results displayed **U**.

4. Click any individual item in the list, and click the Preview button to hear a preview of that audio clip **V**.

Click the Preview button again to stop the preview.

TIP You can also select a sound file in the stack and click the Preview button to the left of the search field to hear a preview.

5. When you find the file you're searching for, drag it to the Timeline or to an event in the Event Library.

T The stack shows the contents of the selected category. In this example, an iTunes playlist has been selected.

Search field   Clear Search button

U Use the search field to refine your list. Clear the search field by clicking the Clear Search button.

Preview button

V Click the Preview button, or double-click any item in the list to preview it.

A Choose Import iMovie Events from the File menu.

B Acknowledge the warning that only new events will be imported.

C Your iMovie Events are added to your FCP Event Library.

Importing from iMovie

Despite the complaints from previous FCP users that FCP X was nothing more than just "iMovie Pro," for existing iMovie users, FCP X really is like the best upgrade you could ever desire!

Best of all is that you can easily import your existing iMovie events and projects directly into FCP X and pick up right where you left off working in iMovie.

To import your iMovie Events Library:

1. Choose File > Import > Import iMovie Events Library A.

   An alert appears, indicating that if you previously imported your Events Library, only new events will be imported B.

2. Click OK.

   The iMovie events are added to your FCP Event Library C.

To import an iMovie project:

1. Choose File > Import > Import iMovie Project.

   The Import iMovie Project window opens and displays a list of existing iMovie projects **D**.

2. Select the project you want to import, and click Import.

   The project is added to your FCP Project Library **E**.

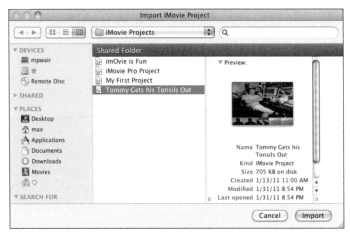

D The Import iMovie Project window opens, already pointing at the iMovie Projects directory in your Movies folder.

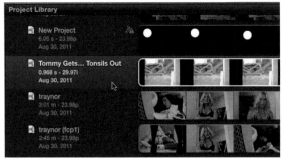

E The iMovie Projects are added to your FCP Project Library.

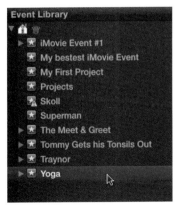

A Open the Record Audio window.

B Choose the event in the Destination menu where you want the audio files to be saved.

C To ensure that you're recording only to an event (and not a project), click an event in the Event Library to make that pane active.

Importing Live Audio

It's not uncommon that you need to record some voice-over, replacement dialogue, or even *foley* sound effects during the editing process.

For best results, you probably want to connect a high-quality, professional microphone to your computer to do such recordings, but in a pinch you can just use the built-in mic that comes on any Mac with an iSight/FaceTime camera.

You can store the newly recorded audio in an event to later be edited into a project, or if you have a project open, you can record the audio directly into the Timeline while it plays.

This second option allows you to easily replace existing audio (also known as *ADR—alternate dialogue replacement*) or to record a voice-over while watching your movie play.

To record live audio to an event:

1. Choose Window > Record Audio.

   The Record Audio window opens **A**.

2. Click the Destination pop-up to select an event where you want the new audio file to be saved **B**.

3. Click the event in the Event Library to make sure the Timeline is not selected **C**.

TIP You can also open the Project Library window to ensure your new audio doesn't accidentally wind up inside some project.

continues on next page

4. Select the microphone you want to use from the Input Device pop-up menu .

5. Perform a test example of the audio, and using the audio meters at the top of the Record Audio window, adjust the Gain slider until the audio is at a nice, solid level without hitting the red at the top of the meters' range .

6. When you're ready to record, click the red Record button .

   Recording begins immediately.

7. When you're finished recording, click the Record button again.

   Recording is stopped.

D Select a mic input from the Input Device pop-up menu.

E Test your audio levels, and adjust the gain slider as needed to ensure a good level (lots of green and no red in the audio meters).

Record button

F Click the Record button to begin recording, and click it again to stop recording.

G Set the event where you want the audio recording to be saved.

H Set the Timeline playhead to the position where you want recording to begin.

I Enable the checkbox next to the Monitor setting, and use the pop-up menu to choose which sound output you want to monitor.

To record live audio directly to the Timeline:

1. In the Record Audio window, select the destination (event) where you want the new audio file to be saved **G**.

2. Position the playhead in the Timeline at the point where you want to begin laying down the new audio **H**.

TIP For best results, set the starting point a few seconds before the moment where you want the audio to begin. You can always trim off that beginning edge later.

3. In the Record Audio window, select the microphone you want to use from the Input Device pop-up menu.

4. Perform a test example of the audio, and using the audio meters at the top of the Record Audio window, adjust the Gain slider until the audio is at a nice, solid level without hitting the red at the top of the meters' range.

5. If you have headphones connected to your Mac, you can optionally enable the Monitor section and select an audio output from the pop-up menu **I**.

   This allows you to hear the existing audio in the Timeline while you're recording.

6. Adjust the Monitor Gain slider so it is loud enough that you can comfortably hear the audio but quiet enough that the audio doesn't spill out of the headphones and get picked up by the microphone recording the new audio.

continues on next page

7. When you're ready to record, click the red Record button.

   The Timeline playhead begins moving, and recording begins immediately.

8. When you're finished recording, click the Record button again.

   Recording is stopped. The new audio clip is laid into the Timeline on a new track as an audio-only clip connected to the primary storyline ⬤.

   The file is saved in the designated event.

9. If you're not satisfied with the recording, you can repeat steps 7 and 8.

   Each time you record, a new audio track is recorded and added to the Timeline ⬤.

   TIP You may want to delete or disable previous recordings prior to recording a second (or more) time. Otherwise, you'll hear the old recording while you're trying to re-record a new version, which can be distracting.

   TIP You can also edit different sections of the different recordings to patch together the perfect overall recording.

⬤ When you're done recording, the audio clip is laid into the Timeline at the selected position.

⬤ Make as many passes at recording the audio as you like. When you're done, disable or delete all the ones you didn't use.

7

Basic Editing

Editing tasks can be divided into two main categories: creating a rough *assembly* of your story and refining and fine-tuning those edits to create a finished product. This chapter will focus primarily on the first stage, that is, getting stuff into (and out of) the Timeline.

Final Cut Pro offers at least five ways to add a clip to your project, with multiple options within each. We'll start by showing you a couple of the most commonly used methods and then elaborate on the remaining methods, identifying when and why you might choose one over another.

We'll also explore ways to limit those edits, such as making an audio-only or video-only edit.

Next, you'll learn various ways of removing clips from a project. FCP offers a variety of options here too.

Finally, we'll get into the basics of moving objects around and making simple modifications to clips once they're in the project.

Anatomy of the Timeline

The Timeline displays audio and video clips as colored bars. The horizontal position of a bar indicates the clip's position in time, and the width of a bar represents the clip's duration **A**. The bars can display video thumbnails, audio waveforms, or both. At the top of the window the ruler displays frame numbers, providing a reference for where each item exists in time.

The middle row (or *track*) contains your *primary storyline*, where you place most of the clips that make up your movie. These clips can contain both audio and video.

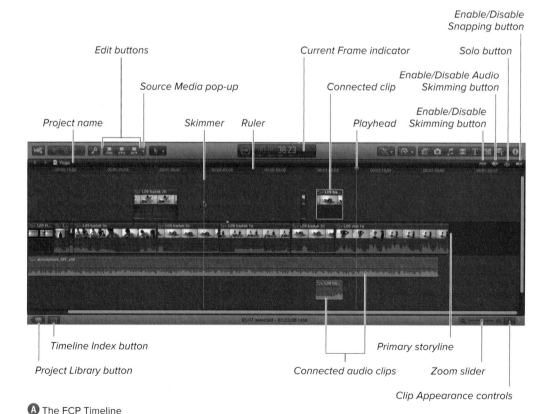

Edit buttons

Source Media pop-up

Project name

Skimmer   Ruler

Current Frame indicator

Connected clip

Playhead

Enable/Disable Snapping button

Solo button

Enable/Disable Audio Skimming button

Enable/Disable Skimming button

Timeline Index button

Project Library button

Connected audio clips

Primary storyline

Zoom slider

Clip Appearance controls

A The FCP Timeline

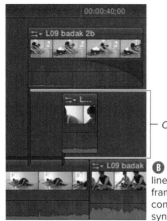

Connection lines

B Connection lines show the frame to which the connected clip is synced.

Clips that came directly from your camera will likely contain both. Video-only or clips with both video and audio appear in blue. Audio-only clips appear in green.

You can *connect* additional clips above or below the primary storyline to synchronize them with a particular frame in one of the primary clips.

In the Timeline, a connected clip is indicated by a connection line that extends from the first frame of the connected clip to the sync point in the primary storyline **B**.

Once you've connected a clip, it's *attached* to that point in the primary storyline and will move any time that primary storyline clip is moved **C**.

Video clips obscure the contents of any tracks below them. So, attaching a full-size video clip on top of your primary storyline effectively replaces the underlying image when the video is played back. If the object on the higher track is partially transparent (such as a logo or a title) or if its size is reduced, the underlying video will show through, creating a *composition*.

Audio that overlaps in time is mixed together based on the relative volume and fade settings of each object.

Connected video clips

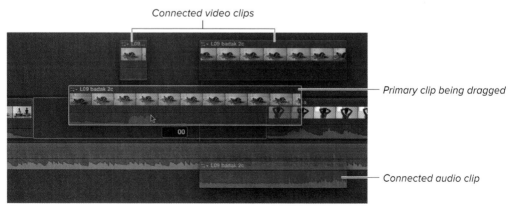

Primary clip being dragged

Connected audio clip

C Dragging a clip moves any connected clips along with it.

Timeline View Options

You can customize clip height as well as clip appearance; specifically, you can choose how much of the clip area displays the thumbnails and how much displays the audio waveforms. Changing these settings applies to all clips in the Timeline.

Click the Show Connections checkbox to show (or hide) the connection lines that indicate where each connect clip is linked to the primary storyline (see again **B**).

Connection lines are always visible when a connected clip is selected. The Show Connections checkbox controls whether the lines appear even when connected clips are unselected.

To change clip appearance and height:

1. Click the Clip Appearance button that is beneath the Timeline and to the right of the Timeline Zoom slider **D**.

   The Clip Appearance controls appear.

2. Click one of the six Clip Appearance icons (see again **D**).

   The icons on the left display larger audio waveforms, and the icons on the right display larger video thumbnails.

   The rightmost icon displays a simplified track view, with neither audio waveforms nor video thumbnails and a fixed clip height.

3. Drag the Clip Height slider to the left for shorter clips and to the right for taller clips.

4. Once you have made your selections, click anywhere outside the Clip Appearance panel to close it.

   The clips in the Timeline change to reflect the style and height you selected.

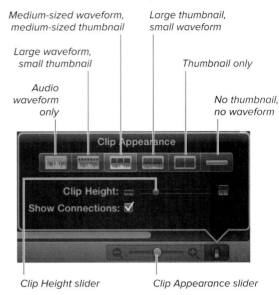

Medium-sized waveform, medium-sized thumbnail

Large thumbnail, small waveform

Large waveform, small thumbnail

Thumbnail only

Audio waveform only

No thumbnail, no waveform

Clip Height slider

Clip Appearance slider

D Choose a clip style from the row at the top, and use the slider beneath to control the track height.

A The first time you create a project, click the icon in the middle of the Timeline area.

B Name the project, and leave the rest of the settings at their defaults.

C The dotted clip outline indicates that the project is empty.

D Press I to set the In point and press O to set the Out point to mark the section of the clip you want to include.

Adding Clips to a Project

To get started editing, begin by adding your first clip to your project. Then, you can add additional clips using a variety of methods.

To add your first clip to a project:

1. If you haven't yet created a project, click the Create New Project icon in the Timeline area **A**.

   The New Project dialog appears **B**.

2. Enter a name for the project, specify a default event, and click OK.

   A new project is added, and an empty Timeline appears **C**.

3. In the Event Browser, select the clip you want to edit, and select the portion of the clip you want to edit **D**.

4. Click the Append button, or press E.

   The clip is added to the project and appears in the Timeline **E**.

Append Edit button

E Click the Append Edit button or press E to add the first clip to the project.

To add additional clips:

1. In the Event Browser, mark the section of the clip you want to edit **F**.

2. Click the Append Edit button or press E to add the clip the end of the project **G**.

   The clip is added to the project after the other clips.

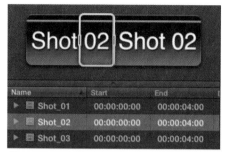

Name		Start	End	
▶ 🖿 Shot_01		00:00:00:00	00:00:04:00	
▶ 🖿 Shot_02		00:00:00:00	00:00:04:00	
▶ 🖿 Shot_03		00:00:00:00	00:00:04:00	

F For best results, play the video clip, and then press I and O on-the-fly to mark the selection.

Append Edit button

G Append is only one way to add a clip to the project. See the next section for more edit types.

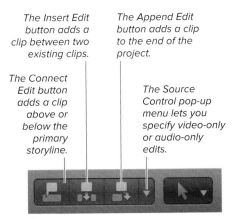

The Insert Edit button adds a clip between two existing clips.

The Append Edit button adds a clip to the end of the project.

The Connect Edit button adds a clip above or below the primary storyline.

The Source Control pop-up menu lets you specify video-only or audio-only edits.

H The toolbar contains one-click buttons for performing three of the five types of edits.

Skimmer vs. Playhead

One important aspect of performing edits in the Timeline is that if you edit using keyboard shortcuts with skimming enabled, edits will be applied at *the position of the skimmer*, not at the position of the playhead, unless the skimmer is not active because your pointer is not over the Timeline.

This can very easily create misplaced edits if your pointer drifts even a few pixels away from the playhead and the intended edit location. For more reliable and precise results, disable skimming while editing.

Which Edit Type Should You Use?

Different situations call for different edit types. Traditional editing technique often involves inserting a *master shot* and then going back and overwriting bits and pieces of it with other shots until your whole scene is assembled. In other cases, you may want to *insert* a clip between two existing ones, or you may want to *append* a new clip to the end of the movie.

FCP offers five ways to add a clip to a project: *inserting*, *appending*, *overwriting*, *connecting*, and *replacing* **H**. The Replace function (which works entirely differently from the Replace Edit function in previous versions of FCP) can be employed in four ways, bringing the total number of editing options up to eight.

Each of these edits can be performed in multiple ways including clicking on-screen buttons, pressing keyboard shortcuts, choosing menu items, and using drag and drop.

The following are the three most common edit types you'll use for assembling your clips:

- Appending adds the selected clip to the end of the active storyline.

- Inserting adds the selected clip to the active storyline, beginning at the playhead (or skimmer) position and pushing any existing clips *downstream* (to the right) to make room for the new clip.

- Overwriting adds the selected clip to the active storyline, beginning at the playhead (or skimmer) position and deleting any existing frames for the duration of the source clip.

TIP The first time you add a clip to your project, you can perform an append, insert, or overwrite edit and get identical results: The clip will be added to the beginning of the project.

Append Edits

Appending adds the selected clip to the end of the active storyline. Appending a clip always makes your project longer.

To append a clip:

1. In the Event Browser, select the clip you want to add to the project.

2. Play the clip, and press I to set the In point and press O to set the Out point to identify the specific range of the source clip you want to use .

3. Click the Append Edit button in the toolbar, or press E .

   The clip is appended to the end of the storyline .

Insert Edits

Insert edits add the selected clip to the active storyline, beginning at the playhead (or skimmer) position and pushing any existing clips *downstream* (to the right) to make room for the new clip.

You can also use three-point editing to perform an insert edit. For more on three-point editing, see "Three-Point Editing" later in this chapter.

Inserting clips always makes your project longer.

Name		Start	End	
▶ 🎞 Shot_01		00:00:00:00	00:00:04:00	
▶ 🎞 Shot_02		00:00:00:00	00:00:04:00	
▶ 🎞 Shot_03		00:00:00:00	00:00:04:00	

I Mark the area of the clip you want to select.

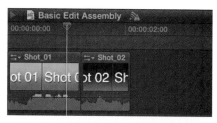 **J** Click the Append Edit button or press E to add the clip to the end of the project.

K Append edits add the new clip to the end of the project, regardless of where the Timeline playhead is.

L Mark the range of the clip you want to edit.

M The bottom image shows a new clip inserted into the project between the last two clips. Notice that the marker (the cyan diamond) is pushed to the right.

N Click the Insert button or press W to insert the clip into the Timeline at the playhead position.

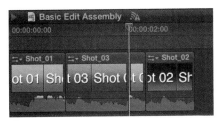

O The clip is inserted, splitting clips if necessary. In this example, Shot_01 has been split into two pieces.

To insert a clip:

1. In the Event Browser, select the clip you want to edit into the project.

2. Play the clip, and press I to set the In point and press O to set the Out point to identify the specific range of the clip you want to use **L**.

3. In the Timeline, position the playhead where you want the clip to be inserted **M**.

4. Click the Insert Edit button in the toolbar, or press W **N**.

   The clip is inserted in the storyline at the designated location **O**.

   Alternatively, you can drag the clip to the Timeline and drop it between any two clips in the storyline **P**.

   The existing clips will move out of the way to make room for the new clip.

P When you drag and drop, a blue outline appears to show you where the new clip will be added to the project.

Overwrite Edits

Overwriting adds the selected clip to the active storyline, beginning at the play-head (or skimmer) position and deleting any existing frames for the duration of the source clip.

You can also use three-point editing to perform an overwrite edit. For more on three-point editing, see "Three-Point Edit-ing" later in this chapter.

To overwrite a clip:

1. In the Event Browser, select the clip you want to edit into the project.

2. Play the clip, and press I to set the In point and press O to set the Out point to identify the specific range of the clip you want to use.

3. In the Timeline, position the playhead at the first frame you want the clip to be overwritten **Q**.

4. Choose Edit > Overwrite, or press D **R**.

   The clip is overwritten in the storyline beginning at the designated location.

TIP You can also overwrite a clip by pressing P to select the Position tool and then drag-ging the selection from the Event Browser to the Timeline and dropping it anywhere in the Timeline.

Q Note the playhead position prior to the edit.

R The new clip (Shot_03) overwrites the end of Shot_01 and all of Shot_02.

S Prior to the edit, the playhead is positioned near the end of Shot_01.

T Click the Connect Edit button or press Q to add the clip to the project as a connected clip.

U Shot_03 is added as a connected clip, linked in time to the frame in Shot_01 where the playhead was when the edit was performed.

Connect Edits

Connect edits add a selected clip to a project by attaching it to the primary storyline beginning at the playhead (or skimmer) position. Rather than deleting the underlying clips, as with an overwrite edit, a connect edit composites the clip above the storyline.

You can also use three-point editing to perform a connect edit. For more on three-point editing, see "Three-Point Editing" later in this chapter.

To connect a clip:

1. In the Event Browser, select the clip you want to edit into the project.

2. Play the clip, and press I to set the In point and press O to set the Out point to identify the specific range of the clip you want to use.

3. In the Timeline, position the playhead where you want the clip to be connected **S**.

4. Click the Connect Edit button in the toolbar, or press Q **T**.

   The clip is added to the Timeline **U**.

   The clip is connected to the storyline at the designated location.

> **TIP** Alternatively, you can drag the clip to the Timeline and drop it in the area above the storyline and to the position in time where you want the clip to be connected.

Replace Edits

Replace edits add a selected clip to a project by exchanging it with a clip that currently exists in the project (the *target clip*). The target clip is always completely removed (unlike an overwrite edit, where only the section beneath the source clip is removed).

When performing a replace edit, you must choose from one of the following options: Replace, Replace from Start, Replace from End, and Replace and Add to Audition. That last option will be covered in Chapter 10, "Auditioning Clips." The other three are described next.

Replacing a clip may or may not change the overall duration of the project depending on the situation.

Types of Replace Edits

The following are types of replace edits:

- **Replace:** The target clip is entirely replaced by the source clip selection. If the source clip is shorter than the target clip, the overall sequence will be shortened. If the source clip is longer, the overall sequence will be lengthened .

- **Replace from Start:** The target clip is replaced with the source clip. The first frame of the source clip is aligned with the first frame in the target clip, and the rest of the footage is added to fill the remaining duration of the target clip . If there are not enough frames after the source In point to fill the remaining duration, FCP will display a warning, and the resulting clip will be only as long as is possible based on the source footage.

V In this figure, movingBall2 has replaced Shot_04. Because movingBall2 is longer, the resulting clip in the project is longer.

W Replace from Start replaces Shot_04 with the beginning frames of movingBall2 (where the ball is in the upper left and the background is orange). The resulting clip in the project is limited to the original length of Shot_04.

X Replace from End replaces Shot_04 with the last frames of movingBall2 (where the ball is in the lower right and the background is yellow). The resulting clip in the project is limited to the original length of Shot_04.

Y The white highlight is the clue you are entering Replace mode. The pop-up menu allows you to choose the type of replace edit you want to perform.

Z Shot_03 replaces Shot_02. Notice that the resulting edit is longer, because the selected area of Shot_03 was longer than Shot_02.

- **Replace from End:** The target clip is replaced with the source clip. The last frame of the source clip is aligned with the last frame in the target clip, and the rest of the footage is *backtimed* to fill the remaining duration of the target clip **X**. For more about backtiming, see the "Backtiming Edits" section of this chapter.

If there are not enough frames before the source Out point to fill the remaining duration, FCP will display a warning, and the resulting clip will be only as long as is possible based on the source footage.

Note there are additional options in the Replace drop menu regarding auditions. For more information, see "Creating Auditions in the Timeline" in Chapter 10.

To replace a clip:

1. In the Event Browser, select the clip you want to edit into the project.

2. Play the clip, and press I to set the In point and press O to set the Out point to identify the specific range of the clip you want to use.

3. Drag the clip to the Timeline over an existing clip (making the clip turn white), and drop it.

   The Replace options drop menu appears **Y**.

4. Choose the type of replace edit you want to make.

   The target clip is replaced by the source clip in the manner you chose **Z**.

TIP You can also select a clip in the Timeline and press Shift-R to replace it with the currently selected clip in the Event Browser or press Option-R to invoke a Replace from Start command.

Controlling Edits

You can use additional tools and techniques to further customize and control how your edits are performed.

Backtiming Edits

In most of the edits described so far, the In point in the source footage is aligned with the playhead (or skimmer) position in the Timeline. However, sometimes it's more important to align the end of the clip with the Timeline playhead position.

In such cases, rather than performing a regular edit, you can perform a *backtimed* edit. In a backtimed edit, it is the Out point of the source clip that is aligned with the playhead (or skimmer).

To overwrite a clip (backtimed):

1. In the Event Browser, select the range of the clip you want to edit into the project **A**.

2. In the Timeline, position the playhead at the last frame where you want the clip to be overwritten **B**.

3. Press Shift-D **C**.

   The clip is overwritten in the storyline ending at the designated location with the last frame lined up with the playhead (or skimmer) position.

To connect a clip (backtimed):

1. In the Event Browser, select the range of the clip you want to edit into the project **D**.

A MovingBall3 begins with a red background and a ball in the upper left and ends with a blue background and the ball in the lower right. In this case, the end of the clip is selected.

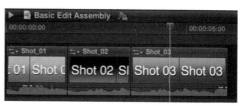

B With a regular edit, the playhead indicates where the first frame of the new clip will go.

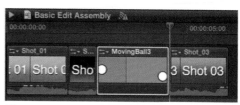

C With backtiming, the playhead indicates where the last frame of the new clip goes. The rest of the selected frames from the new clip are added *prior to* the playhead position.

D Again, a section near the end of the clip is selected.

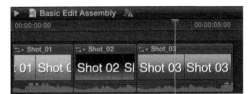

E The playhead is used to define where the new clip will end.

F The new clip is connected, ending at the playhead position. Notice that despite the backtimed edit, the connection line is still aligned with the first frame of the connected clip.

G Click the small arrow to the right of the edit buttons to access the Source Media controls. The selected option displays a check mark, and the adjacent edit buttons turn blue for video-only (as shown) or green for audio-only.

TABLE 7.1 Basic Editing Shortcuts

Edit Type	Keyboard Shortcut
Append	E
Insert	W
Overwrite	D
Overwrite-backtimed	Shift-D
Connect	Q
Connect-backtimed	Shift-Q
Replace	Shift-R
Replace from start	Option-R

2. In the Timeline, position the playhead at the last frame you want the clip to be connected **E**.

3. Press Shift-Q.

   The clip is attached to the storyline at the designated location with the last frame lined up with the playhead (or skimmer) position **F**.

   Table 7.1 lists shortcuts for append, insert, overwrite, connect, replace, and backtimed edits.

Performing Audio-Only or Video-Only Edits

By default, FCP will edit all your tracks (video and audio) into a project whenever you make an edit, but oftentimes you want to edit just the audio or just the video tracks from the source clip.

For example, you may be adding a shot where the picture was great but the audio was no good, or you may be stealing the dialogue from one angle to be used for another.

FCP allows you to limit edits to video-only or audio-only. This limit affects all types of edits.

You cannot specify individual tracks during the edit process as you could in previous editions of FCP. However, you can choose which tracks are active for any specific shot in the Info window for that shot.

To perform a video-only edit:

1. Click the Source Media button in the toolbar, and choose Video Only or press Option-2 **G**.

continues on next page

2. In the Event Browser, select the range of the clip you want to edit .

3. Perform any one of the edits described in the previous section **I**.

To perform an audio-only edit:

1. Click the Source Media button in the toolbar, and choose Audio Only or press Option-3 **J**.

2. In the Event Browser, select the range of the clip you want to edit **K**.

3. Perform any one of the edits described in the previous section **L**.

H The selected clip has both audio and video.

I A video-only append edit. Notice the waveform area (the bottom half of the clip) is empty.

J Select Audio Only from the Source Media pop-up menu, or press Option-3.

K The selected clip has both audio and video.

L An audio-only append edit. Audio-only clips appear in green, even in the primary storyline.

M Select All from the Source Media pop-up menu, or press Option-1.

N The selected clip has both audio and video.

O A video plus audio append edit. The new clip contains both video and audio.

P The Current Frame indicator can display the exact duration of your selected range. When viewing the current duration, the numbers turn blue, and the icon on the right side changes to the duration icon.

To perform a video-plus-audio edit:

1. Click the Source Media button in the toolbar, and choose All or press Option-1 **M**.

2. In the Event Browser, select the range of the clip you want to edit **N**.

3. Perform any one of the edits described in the previous section **O**.

Three-Point Editing

Often you want to use specific frames in the project to determine where an edit should occur. For example, you may want to ensure that a *cutaway* covers a section where the microphone dipped into the frame. Or you may want to replace a wide shot with a close-up and control precisely where in the sequence the new shot should begin and end.

FCP allows such edits by permitting you to identify a range in the project (using In and Out points) and limit the edit to occur only inside that range.

Note that when you press I to set an In point in the Timeline, FCP automatically adds a corresponding Out point at the end of the clip under the playhead. If you set an Out point first, it will automatically add a corresponding In point. Just ignore them and manually set your own specific Out or In points exactly where you want them! The Current Frame indicator can display the duration of your selected range **P**.

When you set a range in the Timeline, you can run into a potentially confusing situation where you have a certain duration selected in the project and a selection in the source clip of a different duration . In such cases, the Out point of the source clip is never used to determine the position or duration of the edit.

If the selected source clip is longer than the selected range in the Timeline, the extra frames will not be included in the edit.

For a normal edit, that means the frames at the end of the clip will be ignored. For a backtimed edit, it means the frames at the beginning of the clip will be ignored.

If the selected source clip is shorter than the selected range in the Timeline, additional frames from the source clip will be included in the edit (even though they were outside the marked selection).

If there is not enough footage after the In point in the source clip to fill the selected range in the Timeline, FCP will warn you that the resulting edit will be shorter than expected 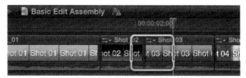.

If you proceed, all the frames from the marked In point to the last frame of the media in the source clip will be edited into the project.

To perform a three-point edit:

1. In the Timeline, identify the area you want to affect by playing the project and pressing I to mark an In point and pressing O to mark an Out point 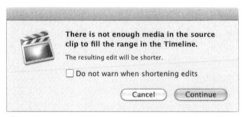.

Q The selection in the Event Browser (top) is 2:20, and the selection in the project (bottom) is 6:08. How do you fit one into the other?

R FCP will warn you if you don't have enough frames in the source clip. You can still make the edit, but it's going to come out shorter than what you requested.

S Select the range of the project you want to edit into using In and Out points.

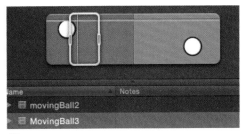

T Set an In point where you want the source clip to start. Ignore the Out point that FCP automatically creates.

U In this case, an overwrite edit was used to add the new shot to the project. The new clip is overwritten precisely within the selection you marked in step 1.

2. In the Event Browser, select the clip you want to edit, and mark an In point where you want the edit to begin **T**.

3. Perform an insert, overwrite, or connect edit to add the clip to the project **U**.

   The clip is edited into the project, beginning at the In point marked in the Event Browser and extending until the Out point marked in the Timeline.

   For more information about specific edit types, see "Which Edit Type Should You Use?" later in this chapter.

> **TIP** You can also perform a backtimed edit using three-point editing. In that case, the Out point in the Event Browser would be observed, and the In point would be ignored. For more about backtiming, see "Backtiming Edits" earlier in this chapter.

Matching Project Settings to Your Clips

FCP can work with an extremely wide range of frame sizes, frame rates, and video formats. Furthermore, you can mix and match source video types in the same project, and they will all play back smoothly and without requiring rendering. Still, it's important to understand what your project settings are and how they relate to the source footage you're working with.

For example, if you put SD-resolution footage in an HD-resolution project, it will need to be scaled up to fill the screen, lowering the image quality. Similarly, if you put 24p footage into a 60i sequence, additional frames will need to be generated on-the-fly to play back the project. This can result in your video looking different when viewed in the project than it does natively.

For best results, you want your project to match the settings of your source footage. Fortunately, FCP makes this easy: By default, the first time you edit a clip into your project, FCP automatically matches the project settings to those of your source clip. If the application doesn't recognize the format of the source footage, a sheet appears asking you to confirm or change the relevant project settings.

If all your source footage is from the same camera, this is very straightforward. However, if you're mixing and matching footage from different sources, you need to decide what the best settings for your project should be. For more about project properties, see Chapter 5, "Working with Projects."

Removing Clips from a Project

Someone once described the process of editing as the job of "removing the bad bits," and, indeed, often the choice of what to remove is just as important as what to add. In this way, editing is often compared to sculpting: The goal is to chip away at the overall mass to reveal the movie hiding within it, just as a sculptor chips away at a mass of marble to uncover the figure within it.

FCP has two primary ways to remove footage from a project: deleting clips and replacing clips with gaps.

Deleting Clips

The default function for removing footage is Delete. It was called *Ripple Delete* in previous versions of FCP (and *Extract* in Avid parlance). Delete removes the selected range and closes the gap so no black frames are left behind.

To delete footage from the Timeline:

1. Select the range you want to delete in the Timeline *by doing one of the following*:

   ▸ Click a clip to select the entire clip.

   ▸ Use the I and O keys to mark a selection.

   ▸ Choose the Range Select tool from the Tools pop-up menu in the toolbar (or press R), and drag in the Timeline to select a range 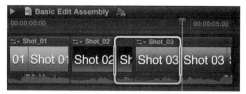.

2. Choose Edit > Delete, or press Delete.

   The footage is deleted, and the gap is closed .

A Selections can span multiple clips.

B The selected region is removed from the project, and no gap is left behind.

TIP To select more than one item with the Select tool, press Command and click additional objects; alternatively, press Shift and click additional objects to create a contiguous selection.

C Select the area you want to replace with a gap.

D The selected region is removed, and no automatic rippling occurs. This used to be called *Lift* and was the default behavior when you pressed Delete.

Replacing Clips with a Gap

Replace with Gap removes the selection and leaves a gap in its place. This function was simply called *Lift* in previous versions of FCP and was the default behavior when you pressed the Delete key.

To replace footage from the Timeline with a gap:

1. Select the range you want to delete in the Timeline *by doing one of the following*:

   ▸ Click a clip to select the entire clip.

   ▸ Use the I and O keys to mark a selection.

   ▸ Choose the Range Select tool from the Tools pop-up menu in the toolbar (or press R), and drag in the Timeline to select a range **C**.

2. Choose Edit > Replace with Gap, or press Shift-Delete (or Forward-Delete).

   The footage is removed, and a gap is left in its place **D**.

Moving Clips in the Timeline

One of the most discussed aspects of FCP X is the cleverly named *Magnetic Timeline*. This is an innovative feature that allows you to move complex clip selections around in the Timeline without overwriting any objects.

Clips that are connected to a shot on the primary storyline automatically move when you move the primary clip.

The software automatically moves neighboring objects out of the way so everything can fit together nicely, overlapping all the objects .

Gapless Editing

By default, the FCP Timeline is designed to never create gaps (which would play back as black flashes between edits) and to never allow you to accidentally overwrite any existing footage.

When you move objects, they automatically align themselves to the edges of existing objects. So, for example, if you move a clip anywhere past the last clip in the project, when you release your mouse, the clip will automatically move itself snugly up against the end of that last clip.

Similarly, if you move a clip over an existing clip (or gap), that existing object will automatically move out of the way to make room for your new clip.

To deliberately overwrite an object, you must use the Position tool (see the upcoming "Positioning Clips" section).

Ⓐ The connected clips above and below the second clip automatically get out of the way to make room for the new clip.

Mark and Carol exit the restaurant and walk down the street.

B Placeholders are highly customizable and can optionally contain descriptive notes. You can customize the framing, number of people, gender, background environment, sky type, interior or exterior, and whether to display on-screen text notes.

C Place the playhead wherever you want the gap added. If you're not positioned precisely on an edit point, inserting a gap will split the clip under the playhead.

D The default gap is three seconds long. Simply drag the right edge of the gap to make it longer or shorter.

Inserting Space into the Timeline

If you deliberately want to leave a gap between two clips, you can either insert a gap or insert a placeholder.

Insert a gap when you want actual black frames to play, such as you might after a fade-to-black effect or in a place where you want audio to be heard over a blank screen. Use a placeholder when you want to leave room for a missing shot that you intend to drop in later.

Gaps and placeholders are *generators*— that is, content automatically generated by the software. A gap is simply black video, and placeholders display customizable generic images to represent a specific type of shot, such as a close-up of a man and a woman in a city on a cloudy night **B**.

When inserted from the Edit menu, gaps and placeholders default to a duration of three seconds. After you've added either to your project, you can use any of the editing tools to change the duration as needed.

> **TIP** If you use the replace edit to substitute the actual footage for a gap or placeholder, the new shot's duration will override the place-holder's, so it may not be critical to ensure the placeholder has the "correct" duration at the time you add it.

To insert a gap in the Timeline:

1. In the Timeline, position the playhead (or skimmer) where you want the gap inserted **C**.

2. Choose Edit > Insert Gap, or press Option-W.

   A three-second gap object is added to the project **D**.

To insert a placeholder
in the Timeline:

1. In the Timeline, position the playhead (or skimmer) where you want the gap inserted .

2. Choose Edit > Insert Placeholder, or press Command-Option-W.

   A three-second placeholder is added to the project .

3. If you have enabled the placeholder's View Notes option, you can double-click the "enter notes here" text object in the Viewer, and type a note 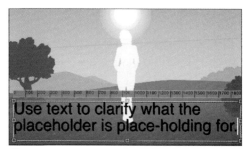.

4. Customize the placeholder by opening the Info window, clicking the Generator pane, and modifying the Published Parameters settings .

TIP A placeholder's notes field for entering text is hidden by default. To display a placeholder's notes field, select the placeholder and then check the **View Notes** checkbox on the **Generator** tab of the placeholder's Inspector window.

E Place the playhead where you want the placeholder to be inserted.

F The placeholder is added just like any other clip. Later drag a clip to the placeholder, and choose Replace.

G Customize the text in the placeholder to make the clip more useful for yourself and your clients.

H Create the placeholder image of your dreams with all the controls in the Info window's Generator pane. You can also customize the format and style of the note text by clicking the Text pane at the top of the Info window.

I Selected clips are highlighted in yellow.

J The blue insertion bar helps you see where the edit can occur.

The blue box shows where the new clip will be inserted.

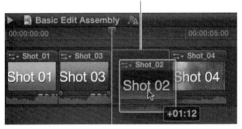

K The clips automatically move out of the way to show you what your new edit will look like.

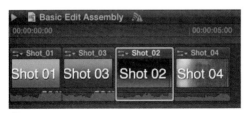

L Using the Select tool, you can never overwrite other clips.

Moving Primary Storyline Clips

You can easily change the order of existing objects in the Timeline's primary storyline, rearranging scenes without changing any of the specific clips' durations.

You can move one primary shot at a time or select multiple clips and move them all together. Any connected clips will automatically move along with their primary clips, maintaining their relative positions. As discussed earlier, should there be an overlap at the destination location, FCP will simply move the conflicting clips onto new tracks so all the objects can coexist peacefully.

To rearrange shots in the Timeline:

1. Click the clip or clips you want to move **I**.

2. Drag the object to a new position in the Timeline, and pause **J**.

   Once you pause at an insertion point, the other clips move out of the way to show what the new edit will look like once you release your mouse button **K**.

3. When the insertion bar is at the desired position, release the mouse button **L**.

   The order of the clips is rearranged.

Moving Connected Clips

Although connected clips move around automatically when you drag the primary shots they're attached to, you can also reposition the connected clips, separate from the primary shots. You can adjust the connection point (the frame where the connected clip begins) or even move the clip to connect it to a different primary clip.

To move connected clips:

1. Click the connected clip you want to move **M**.

2. Drag the selected clips to a new position **N**.

   The clips are moved to the new location. Any existing connected clips that might overlap the moved clips will automatically move out of the way.

M Click the connected clip you want to move. Command-click to select more than one connected clip.

N Connected clips can be aligned with any frame in the primary storyline.

Which Clip Goes on Top?

If you ever move a connected clip into a position where it may overlap another connected clip, FCP will automatically move one of the objects out of the way.

Because clips on higher tracks obscure the clips beneath them, it's important to know which video clip is placed on the higher "track" in the Timeline.

If you move a connected clip into an overlapping position with another connected clip, the one you're moving will go below the static clip if you deliberately drag it to the lower half of the static clip clip in the Timeline. Drag to the static clip's upper half and the new clip will be placed above the static clip **O**.

O Make sure you know which clip you want on top.

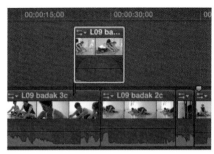

P Commit your edits by collapsing connected clips into the primary storyline.

Q The connected clip is overwritten into the primary storyline. Note that the audio in the clips underneath were automatically moved out of the way to make room for the audio in the new clip.

Moving Connected Clips into and out of the Primary Storyline

Often you will connect a clip rather than overwriting it because you're not entirely sure if it's the right shot or if it's in the right position. Once you've committed to the clip's placement, you may want to overwrite it into the primary storyline to simplify your Timeline view.

Conversely, you may find that a clip or group of clips in the primary storyline is mispositioned, or you want to remove a clip from the primary storyline because you're no longer sure you want to use it.

FCP has some specific commands to address these situations.

To overwrite a connected clip into the primary storyline:

1. Select the connected clip (or clips) in the Timeline **P**.

2. Choose Edit > Overwrite to Primary Storyline, or press Command-Option-Down Arrow.

   The connected clip is overwritten into the primary storyline **Q**.

To lift a clip out of the primary storyline:

1. Select the clip (or clips) in the primary storyline .

2. Choose Edit > Lift From Primary Storyline, or press Command-Option-Up Arrow.

    The clip is removed from the primary storyline, leaving a gap **S**.

Positioning Clips

Although there are advantages to the way FCP prevents you from ever overwriting clips, oftentimes overwriting is exactly what you want to do.

This allows you to add one clip in the middle of another while keeping everything in the primary storyline. You can also use this technique to cover up duplicate action at an edit point, or even to simply replace one clip with another that is already in the Timeline.

FCP calls this type of moving *positioning* since it allows you to chose a precise position for your new clip without the software shifting other clips around to make room for it. To position a clip, you must select the Position tool.

Positioning works only on clips in the primary storyline.

R Hedge your bets by moving clips out of the primary storyline and converting them into connected clips.

S Even though there's now a gap in the primary storyline, you won't see any black frames because the connected clip covers the empty space.

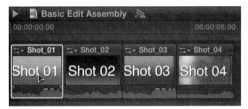

T Press P to activate the Position tool.

To overwrite clips in the Timeline using drag and drop:

1. Choose the Position tool from the Tools pop-up menu in the toolbar, or press P **T**.

2. Select the clip (or clips) in the Timeline you want to move **U**.

3. Drag the clip to a new position in time **V**.

   The clip will overwrite whatever is in the destination location.

You can also use positioning to deliberately add a clip at a point beyond the end of the current project. If you drag a clip to a point past the last clip, FCP automatically adds a gap between the last clip and the newly positioned one **W**.

U The Position tool selects only whole clips.

Snapping

When dragging objects in the Timeline, it's important to be able to position them precisely so they go exactly where you intend. Often, you want to ensure that objects align with existing edit points, with other objects in the project, with markers, and so on. When you enable *snapping*, dragging a tool or an object near one of those common targets will cause your pointer to automatically align, or *snap*, to the target.

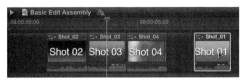

V Pick up clips and put them exactly where you want them with the Position tool (P).

In addition to dragging objects, snapping affects the playhead and the skimmer, as well as tools such as the Select tool, the Position tool, the Trim tool, the Range Selection tool, and the Blade tool.

continues on next page

W You can even deliberately leave some gap after the last clip.

When snapping is enabled, the following objects act as snap points:

- Edit points
- Existing clip boundaries
- The playhead
- Markers
- Keyframes

TIP Snapping is especially useful when using the Position tool, which allows you to move objects freely or when moving connected clips.

When snapping is enabled and you drag an object near a snap point, yellow vertical lines appear to indicate the precise snap point .

Although snapping can be of great benefit, preventing you from accidentally positioning an object near to, but not exactly on, your desired target, sometimes snapping can prevent you from placing your object where you want it to go. For example, if you are zoomed out or have a project with many small edits close together, snapping will force your drags to align with the various objects and prevent you from positioning with frame-accurate precision.

Fortunately, you can enable and disable snapping quickly, and you can even turn it on or off temporarily *during* a dragging operation (which is often when you realize you need to change it).

To enable or disable snapping:

- *Do one of the following*:
  - ▸ Choose View > Snapping **Y**.
  - ▸ Press N.
  - ▸ Click the Snapping button in the upper right of the Timeline **Z**.

X Yellow vertical lines indicate exactly to which point you're snapping.

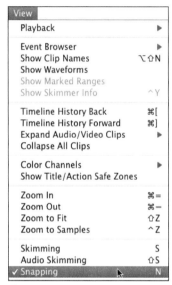

Y A check mark in the menu indicates whether snapping is currently enabled.

Enable/disable snapping

Z When snapping is enabled, the button turns blue. When disabled, it is gray.

8

Editing Tools

Chapter 7, "Basic Editing," got you started cutting in earnest. Final Cut Pro offers a wide array of additional tools and techniques that can take you beyond the basics and greatly improve your editing efficiency.

In this chapter, you'll explore secondary storylines and the Timeline Index, two tools that help you view and organize your projects.

You'll also find tips on how to navigate and work with multiple projects simultaneously and many other tools and tasks that will improve your skill level dramatically.

In This Chapter

Splitting Clips

In some cases, you may want to deliberately break one clip into multiple pieces.
This can happen automatically if you insert
a new clip in the middle of an existing one,
but you can also manually split a clip using
the Blade command or the Blade tool.

Blading a clip does not, by itself, change
what the movie looks like when you play
it back. It simply divides the bar in the
Timeline into two pieces. This allows you
to perform other tasks, such as moving or
deleting a portion of a clip, applying an
effect to part of a clip, and so on.

To split a clip into two pieces:

- Identify where you want to split the clip,
  and *then do one of the following* **A**:

  ▸ Position the playhead at the desired
    split location, and choose Edit > Blade
    or press Command-B **B**.

  ▸ From the Tools pop-up menu, choose
    the Blade tool (or press B), and then
    click the clip in the Timeline at the
    frame where you want to divide the
    clip **C**.

  The clip is split into two pieces.

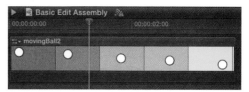

A Find the precise frame where you want the clip
to be split.

B Select the Blade
tool from the Tools
pop-up menu located
above the Timeline
on the main toolbar,
or press B.

C Add an edit point to your clip by using the
Blade tool or command.

A You can cut or copy anything you can select: a portion of a clip, a whole clip, a group of clips, or even *noncontiguous* selections like this one.

Copying and Pasting Clips

The Cut, Copy, and Paste commands are frequently used to move clips from one part of a project to another or from one project to another. You can also use the copy commands to duplicate a selection and make multiple copies.

You can opt to either *cut* or *copy* the selection you want to move.

- Choosing Cut removes the initial instance of the selection (automatically closing any created gaps) and saves it in the clipboard until you are ready to paste it in a new location.

- Choosing Copy stores the selection on the clipboard but leaves the original in place.

Once you've stored the selection on the clipboard, you can paste it to a new location. When you paste, cut, or copy clips into a project, the clips will be pasted into the same tracks you cut them from. So, copying a clip from the primary storyline will paste to the primary storyline. Copying a connected clip will paste the copy as a connected clip.

Nonadjacent (or *noncontiguous*) selections will remember the relative positions of the clips. When you paste a noncontiguous selection of clips, FCP will add gaps as necessary to maintain the clips' relative positions **A**.

To select a portion of a clip or a range across multiple clips:

1. From the Tools pop-up menu, choose the Range Selection tool; or press R .

2. In the Timeline, click at the point in the clip where you want your selection to start, and then drag the Range Selection tool to mark your selection **C**.

   The range is selected and ready to be cut or copied.

Pasting Clipboard Contents

Clips are pasted at the position of the playhead—or the skimmer if skimming is enabled. Pasted clips will be either inserted or connected to the primary storyline.

TIP You cannot paste a clip as an overwrite.

To paste as an insert:

1. Make a selection in the Timeline using any selection method **D**.

2. To copy the selection to the clipboard, *do one of the following*:

   ▸ To copy the selection to the clipboard and delete the original, choose Edit > Cut or press Command-X.

   ▸ To copy the selection the clipboard and leave the original intact, Choose Edit > Copy or press Command-C.

3. Place the Timeline playhead (or skimmer) at the frame where you want to paste the selection **E**.

B The Range Select tool can select a portion of a clip or a range across multiple clips in a single storyline.

C Drag in the Timeline with the Range Select tool to define your selection. You can select right across edit points, selecting portions of two or more adjacent clips.

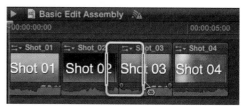

D Select the clip or range of clips that you want to copy to the clipboard.

E Because the playhead position is midway through Shot_04, that clip will be split when the paste is performed.

F The clips are inserted, pushing the last part of Shot_04 downstream. In this example, the original clips were copied, not cut, so now there are two *instances* (copies) of the selected range.

G In this example two nonadjacent clips are selected.

H The playhead position will determine where the first frame of the first selected clip will be pasted.

I FCP pastes the selection as connected clips, adding a gap to the primary storyline in order to reproduce the original spacing of your nonadjacent clip selection in the pasted copies.

4. Choose Edit > Paste, or press Command-V.

The selection is pasted as an insert into the Timeline **F**.

To paste as a connected clip:

1. Make a selection in the Timeline using any selection method **G**.

2. To copy the selection to the clipboard, *do one of the following*:

  ▸ To copy the selection to the clipboard and delete the original choose Edit > Cut or press Command-X.

  ▸ To copy the selection the clipboard and leave the original intact, Choose Edit > Copy or press Command-C.

3. Place the Timeline playhead (or skimmer) at the frame where you want to paste the selection **H**.

4. Choose Edit > Paste as Connected Clip, or press Option-V.

A copy of your selection is pasted as clips connected to the primary storyline **I**.

Table 8.1 shows all Cut, Copy, and Paste keyboard shortcuts.

TIP **FCP also allows you to copy and paste effects such as filters and color correction settings.**

TABLE 8.1 Copy and Paste Shortcuts

Command	Keyboard Shortcut
Cut	Command-X
Copy	Command-C
Paste (Insert)	Command-V
Paste as Connected Clip	Option-V

Navigating in the Timeline

The more time you spend editing, the more you'll appreciate how important it is to be able to quickly and easily move around the Timeline, zoom in and out, jump right to specific edits, and so on.

Many of the tasks described here can be accomplished with the help of keyboard shortcuts. FCP has an army of key commands; many professional editors prefer a keyboard-intensive working style. This section demonstrates some other ways to approach the Timeline interface because, frankly, keystrokes don't make good illustrations. Check out the keyboard shortcuts in Table 8.2.

Before you skip past this section, though, consider the alternatives described here. FCP has a variety of tools, commands, and controls to help you get around.

You can play your project back in a wide variety of ways. You can play forward and backward, and you can play in slow motion and in fast motion; in addition, you can play from start, play to end, play just the selection, play around the current playhead position, and so on.

> **TIP** You can use the playhead's locator line to help identify the exact timecode location of an item way down at the bottom of the Timeline window. Set the playhead's locator line on the point you want to identify, and the Current Timecode indicator will give you its exact timecode location.

TABLE 8.2 Playback Shortcuts

Play Mode	Keyboard Shortcut
Play Forward	Space or L
Play Backward	Shift-Spacebar or J
Stop Playback	Spacebar or K
Play from Beginning	Control-Shift-I
Play to End	Control-Shift-O
Play Selection	/ (backslash)
Play Around	Shift-/ (backslash)
Play Fullscreen	Shift-Command-F
Loop Playback	Command-L

TABLE 8.3 Timeline Navigation Shortcuts

Command	Keyboard Shortcut
Go to Next Edit	' (apostrophe) or Down Arrow
Go to Previous Edit	; (semicolon) or Up Arrow
Go to In point	Shift-I
Go to Out point	Shift-O
Go to Beginning	Home
Go to End	End
Go to Next Marker	Control-'
Go to Previous Marker	Control-;

To jump the playhead to a new location:

■ Click the location on the Timeline ruler to move the playhead to that location.

To scrub through a project in the Timeline:

■ Drag the playhead along the Timeline ruler.

TIP Click directly on a Timeline clip to move the playhead to that position and select the clip in a single operation.

To jump the playhead from edit to edit:

■ *Do one of the following*:

▸ Press the Up Arrow key (for the previous edit) or the Down Arrow key (for the next edit).

▸ Press ; (semicolon) for the previous edit, or press ' (apostrophe) for the next edit. (These are the most convenient alternatives if you use the J, K, and L keys for navigation.)

▸ In the Viewer, click the Previous Edit button or the Next Edit button.

▸ Choose Mark > Previous (or Next) > Edit.

▸ Press Home to jump to the beginning of the sequence, and the playhead jumps to the first frame of the clip. If you've enabled Show Overlays on the View menu, an L-shaped icon appears in the lower left or right of the Canvas, indicating that you are on the first or last frame of the project clip.

▸ Press End to jump to the end of the project.

Table 8.3 lists the Timeline navigation shortcuts.

Navigating with Timecode in the Timeline

Just as in the Event Browser, using timecode values to position the playhead in the Timeline results in frame-accurate positioning. The timecode input function in FCP is very flexible.

There are a couple of ways to use timecode to navigate the Timeline:

- You can type a specific number of frames (preceded by a plus or minus sign) to move the playhead by the number of frames you specify.

- You can type a specific timecode number into the Current Timecode indicator to jump the playhead to the frame you specify.

To jump the playhead a specified number of frames using timecode values:

1. Start in the Timeline. Make sure all clips are deselected, or you'll move the selected clip and not the playhead.

2. Type a specific number of frames, preceded by a plus (+) or minus (–) sign. You don't need to click in the Current Timecode indicator; just type the numbers.

3. Press Enter.

   The playhead moves to the new timecode value, and the new timecode position displays in the Current Timecode indicator.

TIP Deselecting everything in the Timeline is easy—especially if you know the keyboard shortcut. Press Shift-Command-A, and you're completely deselected. You can also just click on an empty space in the Timeline.

Playhead indicator appears

Numbers zero out

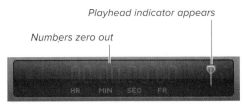

A When you click the Current Frame indicator, FCP indicates that it's waiting for you to enter new timecode information.

B Type the exact timecode number of the frame to which you want to navigate.

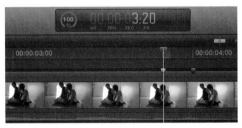

C In this example, the playhead moves to three seconds and twenty frames.

D Be sure the Timeline is active (press Command-2) before you click the Current Frame indicator.

E When you type a plus (+) sign, a plus (+) icon appears to the left of the numbers, and a right-facing arrow lights up to the right of the playhead icon.

F When you type a minus (–) sign, a minus (–) icon appears to the left of the numbers, and a left-facing arrow lights up to the left of the playhead icon.

To move the playhead to a precise frame:

1. Click the Current Frame indicator (be sure not to double-click), or press Control-P.

   The Current Frame indicator display lights up blue, the numbers turn to all zeros, and a playhead icon appears to the right of the numbers **A**.

2. Type a timecode number, following the rules laid out in the "Timecode Entry Rules" sidebar **B**.

3. Press Enter (or Return).

   The playhead moves directly to the frame you selected **C**.

Alternatively, you can enter a specific number of frames preceded by a plus (+) or a minus (–) to move the playhead forward or backward by that amount.

To move the playhead by a specific number of frames:

1. Click the Current Frame indicator (be sure not to double-click), or press Control-P **D**.

   The Current Frame indicator display lights up blue, the numbers zero out, and a playhead icon appears to the right of the numbers.

2. Type plus (+) or minus (–) and a number of frames following the rules laid out in the "Timecode Entry Rules" sidebar **E F**.

continues on next page

3. Press Enter (or Return).

The playhead moves forward or backward by the number of frames you selected 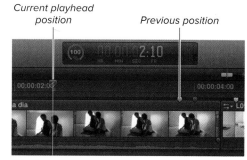.

Note you can also use the Current Frame indicator to move or trim specific clips. For more information on trimming numerically, see "Numerical Trimming" in Chapter 9.

Changing Time Display

You can also make the Current Frame indicator display in frames or in seconds. For very short projects, such as animations, this may be more useful than traditional timecode. For longer projects, traditional timecode is generally easier to comprehend.

Current playhead position   *Previous position*

G In this example, the playhead moved 34 frames (1 second, 10 frames) to the left.

Timecode Entry Rules

For many years, video frames have been counted using a standardized eight-digit code called *timecode*. It can be a little intimidating or confusing until you get used to it, but once you do, it's very handy and allows for great precision.

FCP displays the frames in your movie in four two-digit sections: Hours, Minutes, Seconds, and Frames, abbreviated as HH:MM:SS:FF **H**.

H The Current Frame indicator shows abbreviations under the numbers to help you remember what the numbers mean.

So, a timecode of 10:00:01:00 corresponds to ten hours and one second, and 00:10:00:10 corresponds to zero hours, ten minutes, and ten frames.

When entering timecode numbers, there are three shortcuts you can remember to speed your work:

- You don't actually need to type the colons to separate the frames, seconds, and so on. Instead of typing *12:34:56:12*, just type *12345612*. FCP will know what you mean.

- Don't bother entering leading zeros. Any zeros to the left can be ignored. Rather than typing *00:00:01:14*, just type *1:14* (or *114*).

- If there's a pair of zeros to the right, you can substitute those with a period. So, rather than typing *12:00*, just type *12.* (12 and a period). Rather than typing *05:00:00:10*, just type *5..10* (5, two periods, 10).

FCP is even smart enough to calculate the correct number of seconds based on the current frame rate. So, if you're working in a 24fps project and you type *50*, FCP automatically interprets that as 2:02 (two seconds and two frames).

Click the Editing icon to open the Editing preferences.

Choose the Time Display settings.

I The Editing pane of the Final Cut Pro Preferences window is where you'll find the Time Display pop-up menu.

J Choose from standard timecode, timecode plus subframes, frames, and seconds.

To change the display of the Current Frame indicator:

1. Choose Final Cut Pro > Preferences.

The Final Cut Pro Preferences window opens **I**.

2. If it's not already showing, click the Editing button to open the Editing preferences.

3. Set the Time Display pop-up menu to the frame-counting method of your choice **J**.

Changing the Time Display preference affects all instances of time display throughout the program, so the Event Browser, Timeline Index, Timeline ruler, and so on, will all switch to the different frame-counting method when you change that preference.

Zooming In and Out

Although there aren't quite as many ways to zoom in and out in FCP X as there were in FCP 7, there are still quite a few to choose from.

As you edit, you'll frequently want to zoom way in to manipulate a specific edit and then quickly jump back out to see the big picture of the whole project.

There are three ways to zoom the Timeline view: the Zoom tool, the zoom commands, and the Zoom slider.

To zoom using the Zoom tool:

1. Choose the Zoom tool from the Tools pop-up menu in the toolbar, or press Z .

2. Click anywhere in the Timeline to zoom in.

3. Option-click to zoom out.

> **TIP** You can also drag a box in the Timeline with the Zoom tool to zoom into a specific range **L**.

Once you're zoomed in, you can use the Hand tool to move earlier or later in time.

K Press Z to select the Zoom tool.

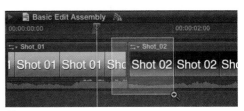

L Drag with the Zoom tool to zoom in on a specific selection.

 Press H to select the Hand tool.

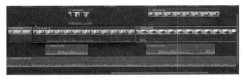

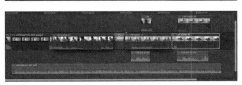

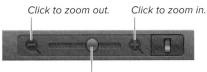

Whether you're zoomed in as pictured in the top image or zoomed out as in the middle image, the Zoom To Fit command automatically fills the Timeline window with all the clips in your project (as shown in the bottom image).

Click to zoom out.   *Click to zoom in.*

Drag left to zoom out and right to zoom in.

O The zoom slider zooms in and out centered around the playhead—even if a clip is selected.

To navigate using the Hand tool:

1. Choose the Hand tool from the Tools pop-up menu in the toolbar, or press H **M**.

2. In the Timeline, drag right to view a later portion of the project, and drag left to view an earlier portion of the project **N**.

TIP If you're using a multi-touch device such as a trackpad or a Magic Mouse, you can use a two-finger swipe to move earlier or later in time.

To zoom using the Zoom commands:

- Choose View > Zoom In or press Command-+ to zoom in.

- Choose View > Zoom Out or press Command-− (minus) to zoom out.

- Choose View > Zoom to Fit or press Shift-Z to activate the Zoom to Fit command.

- Choose View > Zoom to Samples or press Control-Z to zoom all the way in to the audio samples level.

To zoom using the Zoom slider:

- Drag left to zoom out, and drag right to zoom in **O**.

- Click the Zoom In button to zoom in.

- Click the Zoom Out button to zoom out.

The Timeline Index

The Timeline's primary linear view is extremely helpful in terms of visualizing your project over time; it allows you to quickly see how long relative clips are, where they overlap, and where in time each item begins and ends. However, it's also a fairly inefficient way to view the contents of your project, requiring you to scroll along or zoom way out to see a large number of items at once.

Fortunately, Final Cut Pro X also provides the Timeline Index—a list of all the items in your project, arranged in chronological order. This view allows you to see a large number of items at once, but it also offers some very powerful tools that would be nearly impossible to display in the primary Timeline view **Ⓐ**.

To show the Timeline Index:

- *Do one of the following*:
  - ▸ Click the Show/Hide Timeline Index button.
  - ▸ Press Shift-Command-2.
  - ▸ Choose Window > Show Timeline Index.

    The Timeline Index appears at the left side of the Timeline.

  - ▸ Press Command-F.

    This opens the Timeline Index and also highlights the search field.

Playhead position   *Selected clip*

Click to show or hide the Timeline Index.

Ⓐ The Timeline Index can show a list of clips, a list of tags such as markers and keywords, and the controls for clip roles.

Controlling the Timeline Index View

The Timeline Index can display clips, tags, or roles. For either clips or tags, you can filter the list with great precision to quickly find exactly the elements you may be looking for **B**. The Roles view is covered in "Controlling Clips with Roles" later in this chapter.

To choose the Timeline Index view:

- Click the Clips button to display the Clips pane.

- Click the Tags button to display the Tags pane.

- Click the Roles button to display the Roles pane.

B Both the Clips (top) and Tags (bottom) views contain control tools to filter the view.

Filtering the Timeline Index

In Clips view, you can filter the list to see just video, audio, or titles. In Tags view, you can filter based on markers, keywords, analysis keywords, incomplete To Do Items, and completed To Do Items **C**. Roles can't be filtered.

To filter the Timeline Index:

- Click one of the buttons at the bottom of the Timeline Index in either the Clips or Tags pane.

  The Timeline Index is filtered to show only objects of the selected object type.

In either filterable view, you can further refine your search by typing specific text in the search field. The view will dynamically update to show only objects that contain the selected text.

To filter the Timeline Index with specific text:

- Enter text in the search field **D**.

  The Timeline Index is filtered to show only objects containing the search terms and of the selected object type.

To clear the search field:

- Click the gray X button at the right of the search field **D**.

  The Timeline Index will display all objects of the selected type.

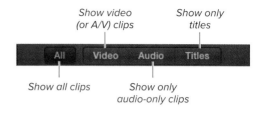

Show video (or A/V) clips   *Show only titles*
Show all clips   *Show only audio-only clips*

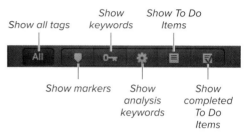

Show all tags   *Show keywords*   *Show To Do Items*
Show markers   *Show analysis keywords*   *Show completed To Do Items*

C Click one of the filtering buttons to limit the types of objects displayed. The top image shows the filtering options for clips, and the bottom shows the filtering options for tags.

Search field   *Click to clear search field.*

D Only items containing the search terms are displayed.

Navigating Within the Timeline Index

The more comfortable you are using the Timeline Index, the more you'll start to appreciate all the other things you can do in that view. You can move the Timeline playhead to specific objects and select objects based on keywords, markers, or clip names. You can even copy and paste objects to control the order of clips and arrangement of your project.

To jump to a specific object:

- Click any object in the Clips or Tags pane of the Timeline Index **E**.

  The object becomes highlighted in the Timeline Index, and the Timeline playhead moves to the first frame of the selected object.

  Selecting a keyword moves the playhead to the first frame of the keyworded range.

  Selecting a marker moves the playhead directly to the marker location.

TIP Double-click a marker in the Timeline Index to move the playhead to the marker position and open the Modify Marker window.

E Click any object to jump to the frame where that object begins in time

To copy and paste clips in the Timeline Index:

1. In the Timeline Index, click the Clips button to open the Clips pane.

2. Select the items you want to cut or copy **F**.

TIP Command-click to select multiple clips.

3. Press Command-X to cut or Command-C to copy the selected clips.

   The clips are copied to the clipboard.

4. Position the playhead at the location where you want to paste the copied objects.

5. Press Command-V to paste as an insert edit or Option-V to paste as a connected clip **G**.

   The selection is added to the Timeline at the chosen location. For more about Copy and Paste options, see "Copying and Pasting Clips" later in the chapter.

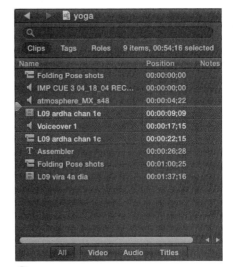

F You can copy and paste clips in the Timeline Index.

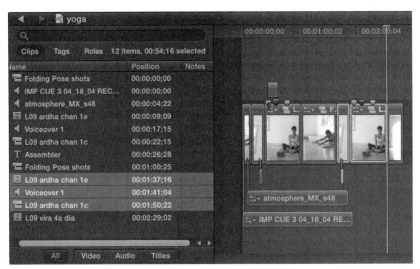

G In this example, the clips have been pasted as an insert before the last clip.

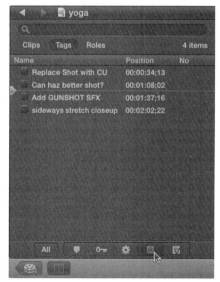

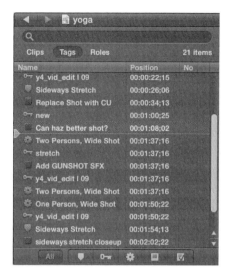 To Do Items can be shown as red checkboxes in the Tags pane of the Timeline Index.

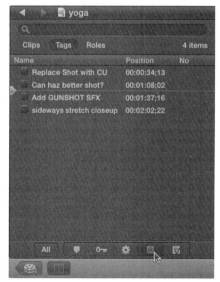 By filtering the view to show only To Do Items, you get a clean list of everything you need to do.

To Do Items and the Timeline Index

One of the great benefits of the Timeline Index is being able to see all of your To Do Items in a clean list. You can jump from item to item just by clicking them, and once the task is complete, you can mark that in the Index too.

To view a To Do Item list:

1. In the Timeline Index, click the Tags button to display the Tags pane Ⓗ.

   The Timeline tags are displayed in the Timeline Index.

2. Click the To Do Items filter button at the bottom of the Timeline Index Ⓘ.

   The list is filtered to show just To Do Items. Each To Do item has a red checkbox to the left of the name.

To check off a To Do Item list:

1. Click one of the To Do Items in the list .

   The Timeline playhead jumps to the frame where the To Do Item has been attached.

2. Perform the task assigned in the To Do Item.

   TIP There is no reason you have to go in order. It's just as easy to navigate to the last item as it is to get to the first!

3. Once the task is complete, click the red checkbox **K**.

   The To Do Item disappears from the list.

4. Repeat steps 1–3 until your list is empty.

5. To view the completed To Do Items, click the Completed To Do Items filter button at the bottom of the Timeline Index **L**.

   All the completed items appear in the list. The checkboxes now appear checked and in green.

6. Click any item to jump to the corresponding frame in the project in order to check your work.

J Selecting an item in the To Do list jumps your playhead directly to the relevant frame in the project.

K Once the task is done, click the red checkbox.

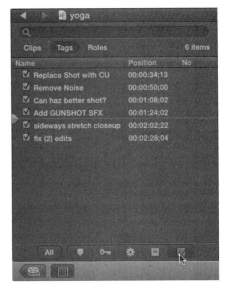

L You can view a list of completed To Do Items.

Audio Roles

You can assign every clip an identity, or *role*, such as video, dialogue, music, titles, and so on. This identity can be used to collectively hide and show, enable or disable, and otherwise group collections of otherwise disparate clips.

In fact, every clip must have some role assigned to it at all times, but you can ignore the roles if you like. Roles are primarily used for outputting different versions of your project or for outputting selected sections of your project based on user-assignable categories.

For example, you might have a set of subtitles in Spanish and a set of subtitles in Amharic. Using roles, you can turn on only the Spanish subtitles, output a version of your movie for Spanish speakers, and then turn on only the Amharic subtitles and output a second version for Ethiopians.

Similarly, you can assign specific audio to be dialogue, music, or effects, and then when outputting your audio for use in a traditional track-based audio editor like Pro Tools or Soundtrack Pro, your audio will automatically be grouped according to its role. This is how you can overcome any potential confusion that might come from exporting FCP X's trackless timeline to a track-based system.

Assigning Roles

There are two types of roles: audio roles and video roles. Audio roles can be assigned only to audio clips, and video roles can be assigned only to video clips. You cannot assign more than one role to a single clip; however, clips containing both audio and video will have one of each.

TIP If you assign an audio role to a clip in the Event Browser, every time you edit a piece of that clip into a project, the role will be maintained. If you don't assign a role until after a clip is in the project, you will need to manually assign the desired role to each individual instance of the clip.

By default all video clips have the Video role assigned, and all audio clips have the Dialogue role assigned.

To change a clip's assigned role:

- Select a clip in the Event Browser or Timeline, and *do one of the following*:
  - ▸ Choose Modify > Assign Role, and select one of the roles from the submenu 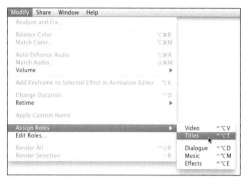.

    The submenu displays a check mark next to the currently assigned role or uses dashes for multiple selections with different roles assigned.

TIP Using this method, you can assign the same role to multiple selected clips.

  - ▸ Click the Roles pop-up menu in the Info pane of the Inspector, and select the role of your choice .

    Audio-only clips will allow only audio roles, video clips will allow only video roles and clips with both audio and video can have one role of each type.
  - ▸ Press one of the keyboard shortcuts listed in Table 8.4.

A Assign roles to the current selection in the Modify menu.

B You can assign the role for any individual clip in the Info pane of the Inspector.

TABLE 8.4 Common Role Keyboard Shortcuts

Edit Type	Keyboard Shortcut
Video	Control-Option-V
Titles	Control-Option-T
Dialogue	Control-Option-D
Music	Control-Option-M
Effects	Control-Option-E

C The Role Editor window allows you to create, name, and delete roles.

D Choose either a new audio role or a new video role.

E The role is added to the list, identified as either a video role or an audio role.

F Enter a name for the role.

Managing Roles

You can create custom roles to further customize the organization of your media. This is how you could create the multiple subtitle roles described in the previous example. You can assign as many video or audio roles as you like.

Roles can also have subroles. So, for example, rather than assigning all shots of people talking to the Dialogue role, you could create individual roles for each character's clips. That way, when you import your audio into Pro Tools or another audio editor, you can easily keep all the clips containing each character's voice on their own discrete tracks, making it easier to filter and modify them uniformly.

To create a new role:

1. Choose Modify > Edit Roles.

   The Role Editor window opens and displays all the existing roles available **C**.

   TIP You can also open the Role Editor window from the menu in the role parameter in the Info Inspector.

2. In the bottom-left corner of the Role Editor window, click the Plus button, and choose New Audio Role or New Video Role **D**.

   The new role is added to the list **E**.

3. Enter a name for the newly created role **F**.

4. Click OK.

   The Role Editor window closes, and the new role is now available for use.

To create a new subrole:

1. In the Role Editor window, select the role you want to make subroles for.

2. Click the Add Subrole button in the center of the bottom of the window ⓖ.

   A new subrole is added for the currently selected role.

3. Type a new name to customize the subrole ⓗ.

4. Click OK.

   Once subroles have been created, they appear indented in the Roles pop-up menu in the Inspector ⓘ or in the Assign Role submenu of the Modify menu.

   Roles and subroles are not project specific. They stick around until you delete them manually, no matter what project or event is active. This can result in a large number of custom roles you may have to wade through, after working on many projects.

To delete a role or subrole:

- Select the role or subrole in the Role Editor window, and press Delete.

TIP You cannot delete a role once it's been assigned to a clip.

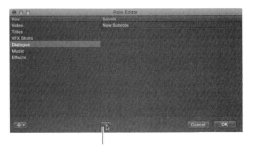

Add Subrole button

ⓖ Select a role, and click the Add Subrole button.

ⓗ Customize the subrole names to make them useful for your project.

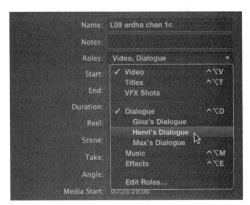

ⓘ Subroles are assigned exactly like ordinary roles; simply select them from the Roles pop-up in the Inspector, or choose them from the Modify menu.

Roles button

(J) You can manage roles in the Roles pane of the Timeline Index.

(K) Selecting the role name highlights the clips in the Timeline. In this example, the middle video clip and the bottom audio clip (IMP CUE 3 04) are highlighted.

Controlling Clips with Roles

Once you have your clips all organized with specific roles assigned to each clip's audio and video components, you can use the controls in the Roles pane of the Timeline Index to highlight, enable or disable, and expand or collapse all the clips of a particular role.

- *Highlighting* clips allows you to quickly see which clips in the sequence have a particular role applied, but playback is not affected.

- *Disabling* a clip prevents that clip from playing back.

- *Collapsing* a clip simply shrinks its display in the Timeline. Playback is not affected.

To highlight all clips of a certain role:

1. Click the Show Timeline Index window to display the Timeline Index if it's not already showing.

2. Click the Roles button **(J)** to open the Roles pane.

> **TIP** Any roles currently used by one of the clips in the Timeline are displayed in the Roles pane of the Timeline Index. If you delete the last clip containing a particular role, the role disappears from the Timeline Index.

3. Click the name of the role you want to highlight.

   The role name turns blue, and any clips in the Timeline with that role assigned light up a brighter color **(K)**.

> **TIP** You can select multiple roles by Shift-clicking or Command-clicking.

4. To deselect the role, just click its name again.

To disable all clips of a certain role:

- In the Roles pane of the Timeline Index, click the check mark to the left of the role name .

  The role name becomes dimmed, and any clips in the Timeline with that role assigned become desaturated.

  Disabled clips will not play back when the sequence is played.

  TIP To see the effect of this setting, it helps to set the Timeline Track view to display both audio waveforms and video filmstrips at a moderate size.

- To reenable the clips, just click the role checkbox again.

To minimize all clips of a certain role:

- In the Roles pane of the Timeline Index, click the Minimize icon to the right of the role name **M**.

  The Minimize icon turns blue and affected clips in the Timeline shrink vertically to a minimum size.

  TIP Titles are collapsed by default.

- To expand minimized clips back to their normal height, just click the Minimize button again.

L The checkbox to the left of the role name controls which roles are active. Disabled clips appear in black-and-white in the Timeline. Notice that some of the A/V clips have active video and disabled audio.

Minimize button

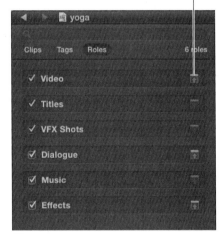

M The Minimize button to the right of the role name collapses the clips associated with that role. In this example, the middle video clip (but not its audio) and the bottom audio clip are minimized.

Secondary Storylines

In Chapter 7, "Basic Editing," you learned how to create and work with connected clips. As you get more used to working with such clips and the benefits they provide (such as always moving in tandem with the primary clip they're connected to), you may come to a point where you want to group multiple connected clips into their own storyline.

This allows you to move multiple connected clips as a single unit and apply transitions between connected clips. One common example of when you would employ this would be if you were editing a group of B-roll shots in a documentary film. Such shots might illustrate what an interview subject is describing.

Creating Secondary Storylines

By converting the clips into a *secondary storyline*, you could treat the group as a single connected clip and move it around to find the best place in the interview where it could be attached **A**.

The gray bar indicates that this is a secondary storyline.

Ordinary connected clip

A Secondary storylines are like mini-movies floating above your main movie. They can contain transition effects, gaps, and more.

To create a secondary storyline:

1. Select one or more connected clips **B**.

2. Choose Clip > Create Storyline, or press Command-G.

   The connected clips are converted into a storyline **C**.

Editing in Secondary Storylines

Once you create a secondary storyline, you can work with it just like you do with your primary storyline: insert, append, replace, move, trim, apply transitions, and so forth. The only thing you can't do is connect clips to it. Connected clips always connect to the primary storyline.

B Select one or more connected clips. Secondary storylines can be created based only on connected clips.

C The gray bar above the clips indicates that the connected clips are now part of a secondary storyline.

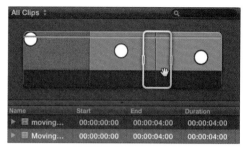

Select the clip you want to edit into the secondary storyline.

E Select the storyline by clicking the gray bar. When selected, it turns yellow.

F In this example, the clip was appended to the end of the secondary storyline.

To edit clips into a secondary storyline:

1. In the Event Browser, mark the range of the clip you want to add to the secondary storyline using In and Out points **D**.

2. In the Timeline, select the gray bar above the secondary storyline clips.

   The entire storyline is highlighted in yellow **E**.

3. Depending on the type of edit you want to perform, *do one of the following*:

   ▸ Choose Edit > Insert, or press W.

   ▸ Choose Edit > Append, or press E.

   ▸ Choose Edit > Overwrite, or press D.

   ▸ Drag the selection directly onto a clip in the secondary storyline, and choose one of the Replace edit types from the drop menu.

   The clip is edited into the secondary storyline **F**.

TIP You can also drag clips already in the Timeline directly into a secondary storyline. Such clips will be inserted or replaced depending on where you drop them. Your added clips will overwrite if you're using the Position tool.

Deconstructing Secondary Storylines

Like most parts of editing, getting stuff out is just as important as getting stuff in. With secondary storylines, you can take them apart in a variety of ways. You can remove individual items from the storyline, break apart the entire storyline, or delete the storyline.

To remove a clip from a secondary storyline:

1. Select the clip (or clips) you want to remove **G**.

2. *Do one of the following*:

   ▸ To delete the clips entirely, press Delete (or Shift-Delete to replace the clip with a gap) **H**.

   ▸ To convert a clip back into a free-standing connected clip, drag the clip out of the storyline and into the adjacent area of the Timeline above the primary storyline **I**.

   TIP If there is only one clip remaining in the secondary storyline, select the clip inside the storyline (not on the the bar) and drag it out of the storyline boundary either up, down, left, or right.

G Select a whole clip or a range.

H Deleting a clip from a secondary storyline does not affect the overall duration of the project.

I Connected clips can be added or removed from a secondary storyline by just dragging them into or out of the secondary storyline.

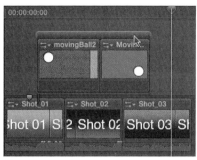

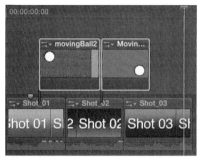

J Select the gray bar to select the storyline rather than the clips within it.

K When you break apart a storyline, the clips retain their position, but they are no longer part of a storyline.

L Transitions cannot exist on connected clips if they are not part of a secondary storyline.

To break apart a secondary storyline:

1. Click the gray bar above the secondary storyline clips to select the whole storyline **J**.

2. Choose Clip > Break Apart Clip Items, or press Shift-Command-G **K**.

    The storyline is converted into free-standing clips.

    Note that if the secondary storyline contains transitions, FCP warns you that the transitions will be deleted if you proceed with the Break Apart command **L**.

To delete a secondary storyline:

1. Click the gray bar above the second-ary storyline clips to select the whole storyline **M**.

2. Press Delete.

The storyline and its contents are removed from the project **N**.

M Select the gray bar to select the storyline rather than the clips within it.

N The storyline and its contents are removed from the project. You can also *cut* a secondary storyline to remove it and store it temporarily on the clipboard. Later, you can paste it to a new location.

A When you click and hold the Timeline history Back button, a window appears to show you the name of the project that will open. Click the button to open the previously open project.

B The back button dims if there are no further projects to view.

Timeline History

As you work in FCP, you'll find many occasions where you will want to move between multiple projects. You may be working on more than one movie at the same time, viewing multiple versions of a single show (for example, you may want to see the same edit with two different music tracks or with a different theme applied), or viewing individual clips in their own Timeline as described in the previous section.

In any of these cases, you can quickly navigate between those projects using the Timeline history commands.

Each time you open a project, the project gets added to the history much like visited web pages get added to your web browser's history. Although you can't access a list of those previously viewed projects, the upper-left corner of the Timeline contains a left arrow and a right arrow to navigate among the projects in your history.

To go back one level in the Timeline history:

- Click the Timeline history Back button, or press Command-[**A**.

  You can keep clicking the history Back button until you're looking at the first project you opened.

  When there are no more projects to see, the Timeline history Back button is dimmed **B**.

To go forward one level in the Timeline History:

- Click the Timeline history Forward button, or press Command-] .

  The Timeline history Forward button is available only after you've clicked the Timeline history Back button to open a different project.

  If there are no projects left to view, the Timeline history Forward button will be dimmed **D**.

C When you click and hold the Timeline History Forward button, a drop-down menu appears displaying a list of all projects opened in your history after your current open project. In this case, it is the Timeline for a clip within the Basic Edit Assembly project. Notice that its icon is different from a regular project icon.

D If there are no further projects to view, the Forward button dims.

9

Fine-Tuning

Chapter 7, "Basic Editing," got you started cutting in earnest, getting your footage into the Timeline and creating a *rough cut* of your movie. However, that's only the beginning of your editing work. In fact, it might be said that the rough cut, which was 80 percent of the work, likely took only 20 percent of the overall editing time. Put another way, the last 20 percent—the finessing, perfecting, and finalizing of your edits—is likely to take 80 percent of your time.

But what exactly does fine-tuning consist of? Much of the process is about tightening edits and finding the absolute best place for each cut. Often that requires offsetting audio and video edits and finding other ways to "hide" the edits so the audience doesn't notice them. Sometimes it means removing or rearranging shots or even whole scenes to find alternative ways to tell your story.

In This Chapter

Adjusting Edits

In terms of the practical nuts and bolts, a large part of fine-tuning takes the form of *trimming*. Trimming is an editing term for two main techniques: *rippling* and *rolling*. Both of these techniques, as well as other fine-tuning tricks and techniques based on those two primary concepts, will be discussed in detail in this chapter. Fundamentally, trimming is the act of adjusting the individual edits in your project.

An edit is a deceptively simple thing: a juxtaposition of two shots. But in its way, an edit is a violent act. Every time you cut, you sever the viewer's train of thought, forcing her brain to change gears and absorb new information from a different perspective. Because of this, each edit is an opportunity for your audience to disengage from the story you are telling.

If an edit is too disruptive to the flow of information, your viewer's brain might switch to an entirely new train of thought. Suddenly, she's aware that the room is chilly or that she's hungry or has to pee. (It happens to all of us.) She might wonder if something more interesting is playing on a different channel. In that instant, on that one cut that lingered a few frames too long, you lost her. And all the work you put into the rest of the program will have gone to waste.

It could be said that the editor's primary job is to overcome these obstacles and keep viewers engrossed in the story. And in order to succeed at that job, you must make every edit perfect (or at least as perfect as the footage allows).

You can adjust edits in three basic ways:

- You can shorten or lengthen the *outgoing* clip (the clip to the left of the edit point).

Trimming and Source Footage

When you trim a clip, you're adding or removing frames from a clip's original source footage in the Event Browser.

You can't add more frames to an edit if no extra frames exist in the source footage .

A To trim an edit, there must be additional, unused frames in the source footage, illustrated here as the dimmed frames to the left of the edit.

If, when you first edited your footage into the project, you used all of the frames in the source clip (that is, you didn't specify a selected range using In and Out points), you will only be able to shorten the clip during the trimming process.

- You can shorten or lengthen the *incoming* clip (the clip on the right side of the edit).

- You can change both sides of the edit at the same time, shortening one while simultaneously lengthening the other by the same number of frames.

The first two ways are called *rippling*, because changing the duration of either clip has a ripple effect on all the other edits in the movie. When you ripple an edit, by definition you make the overall movie longer or shorter.

Rippling is commonly used to fix the timing of a bad edit. For example, if you have a cut that shows a door closing in the outgoing shot and then it closes again in the incoming shot, one of the two shots must be shortened.

The third trimming method is called *rolling*. In this case, the change you make is limited to the two clips on either side of the edit at hand, and the rest of the project remains unaffected.

Rolling will never fix bad timing. In the previous example, you could roll the edit in either direction, but the door is still going to close twice.

However, once you've fixed the timing of the edit by rippling, you can then roll the edit to select precisely where the cut should occur: Do you want the cut to happen before the door closes or after it's already closed? Or do you want the edit to land on the exact frame where the door hits the jamb? By rolling the edit, you can experiment and find the timing that feels just right.

Because of this, you typically ripple before you roll, fixing timing by rippling, and then roll the edit to its optimal location in time.

Rippling Edits

In Final Cut Pro, rippling edits is simple and intuitive. Whenever you drag the edge of a clip that abuts another, the edit (and subsequently the entire sequence) is automatically rippled .

Whenever you position the Selection (Arrow) tool over an edit point, the Ripple pointer appears.

If you position the mouse over the left side of the edit, the pointer turns into the Ripple Outgoing tool (pointing left) .

If you position the mouse over the right side of the edit, the pointer turns into the Ripple incoming tool (pointing right) .

This pointer change helps indicate what will happen if you click and drag. You click the left side to shorten or lengthen the outgoing clip. You click the right side to shorten or lengthen the incoming clip.

In either case, as you change the duration of one clip, the rest of the clips in the project automatically move along in sync.

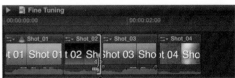

B The bottom image shows that Shot_02 has been rippled to make it (and the whole movie) shorter.

C The Ripple Outgoing tool

D The Ripple Incoming tool

E Position your pointer over the left side of the edit.

F Drag the left side of the edit to ripple the outgoing clip. In this case, the clip was rippled to the left, shortening Shot_02.

G An Info window shows how many frames are being trimmed.

H Position your pointer over the right side of the edit.

I Drag the right side of the edit to ripple the incoming clip. In this example, the clip was trimmed to the left, lengthening Shot_03.

J If you ripple to the last frame of the source media, the edge of the clip turns red.

To ripple the outgoing clip:

1. In the Timeline, position the pointer over the left side of an edit point.

   The pointer changes into the Ripple Outgoing tool **E**.

2. Drag the edge of the edit to the left to shorten the clip **F**, or drag to the right to lengthen the clip.

   As you drag, an Info window appears to show you how many frames you are rippling **G**.

   When you release the mouse, the clip's duration has changed, with no gap left in the Timeline.

To ripple the incoming clip:

1. In the Timeline, position the pointer over the right side of an edit point.

   The pointer changes into the Ripple Incoming tool **H**.

2. Drag the edge of the edit to the right to shorten the clip, and drag to the left to lengthen the clip.

   As you drag, an Info window appears to show you how many frames you are rippling **I**.

   Note that if you ripple a clip all the way to the last frame available in the source footage, the clip edge turns red **J**. This indicates that the clip cannot be trimmed any further in that direction.

Viewing Detailed Trimming Feedback

As you drag to ripple an edit, it can be difficult to know exactly which frame you should choose for the new edit point. As you drag, Final Cut Pro displays the frame you're dragging in the Viewer .

This is helpful, but often you're trying to match the action on both sides of the edit, so it's essential to see the frame from the adjacent clip that you're trying to match.

Fortunately, you can instruct Final Cut Pro to display a two-up preview of the frames on either side of the edit .

If you're dragging the edge of the outgoing clip, the frame on the left changes to show the new frame you're choosing, and the frame on the right displays the first frame of the incoming clip.

K The Viewer shows the changing frame as you trim.

Note the right side doesn't change, because when rippling, you modify only one clip.

If you're dragging the edge of the incoming clip, the frame on the right side updates, and the one on the left shows the last frame of the outgoing clip.

L Detailed trimming feedback allows you to compare the incoming and outgoing frames.

To enable two-up trimming preview:

1. Choose Final Cut Pro > Preferences, or press Command-, (comma).

   The Preferences window opens.

2. Click the Editing icon to open the Editing pane.

3. In the Timeline section, select the "Show detailed trimming feedback" checkbox **M**.

   The two-up display is now enabled.

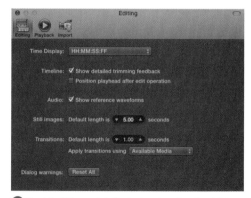

M Enable "Show detailed trimming feedback" in the Editing pane of Final Cut Pro Preferences.

Rolling Edits

Once the timing of your edit is just right, you can finesse exactly where it should occur in time by *rolling* the edit.

One of the tricks editors use to keep audiences engaged across edit points is to cut in the middle of an action. That way, the viewer's brain is too busy following the movement of the action to notice the cut. If you cut from one static shot to another static shot, the cut is the only change, and thus it draws the viewer's attention. But if there is movement within the frame, the attention is pulled there, and the cut can sneak by unnoticed.

For example, if two on-screen people are about to shake hands and you want to cut from a *wide shot* to a *close-up*, the best place to hide the edit would be just as their arms are reaching toward each other but before the hands are grasped.

The viewers' eyes will track the movement of the moving arms, and as long as that movement is smooth and consistent in both sides of the edit, the cut will go unseen.

Every edit is unique, so you will likely need to experiment a bit to find exactly the right moment to make the cut.

The beautiful thing about rolling edits is that once you get the timing of the edit correct, you can roll the edit to any frame at all, and the timing will always look right.

Think about it: If the action of the handshake takes 50 frames to complete and the hands grasp on frame 30, as long as they grasp on frame 30 in both the outgoing wide shot and the incoming close-up, you can move the actual cut point to frame 10, frame 20, or frame 43, and the action will still appear smooth and the edit will be disguised.

In Final Cut Pro, you use the Trim tool to select an edit as a roll. However, as you'll see in the next few pages, once that edit is selected, you have a variety of ways to actually perform the edit.

To roll an edit:

1. Click the Tool pop-up menu in the toolbar, and choose the Trim tool or press T .

   Your pointer turns into the Trim tool.

   TIP While the Trim tool is required to perform a roll edit, you can also make ripple edits with that tool.

2. Position the pointer over the center of the edit point until it changes to the Roll pointer .

3. Drag the edit to the left to shorten the outgoing clip and lengthen the incoming clip, or drag to the right to shorten the incoming clip and lengthen the outgoing clip .

   The edit point is rolled to the new frame.

Previewing Edits

As you trim your edits, it's very important to watch the results of your work in real time. While it may seem like you can judge the best edit point by looking at the individual frames that represent the actual edit, remember that your audience is only going to see it breezing by at full speed. To be an effective editor, you need to think like one of those viewers.

For that reason, it's critical to make your editing decisions while the video is playing whenever possible. At the very least, get used to reviewing your edit every time you make a trimming adjustment.

Ⓝ Select the Trim tool from the Tool pop-up in the toolbar.

Ⓞ Position the pointer over the middle of an edit to access the Roll pointer.

Ⓟ Rolling an edit moves the edit without disturbing the rest of the project. The bottom image shows the edit after it's been rolled to the right by 15 frames.

Q Position the playhead at the edit.

R Choose Play Around from the Playback section of the View menu.

Fortunately, Final Cut Pro has nearly ten different ways to play your movie, each one tailored for a specific situation. At least three of them are particularly helpful when trimming:

- Play Around backs up a few seconds before the current playhead position and plays for a few seconds after. You can customize the *pre-roll* and *post-roll* settings.

- Play Selection plays from the beginning to the end of a selected object. Use this method to watch a specific clip or a selected range of time.

- Play to End plays from the current playhead position to the end of a selected clip or range. This allows you to see how a clip or section ends without having to sit through the entire clip or range.

Also, turning on the Loop Playback setting can be helpful in conjunction with these commands, enabling you to repeat playback of a limited range of your project while you continue trimming.

To play around an edit:

1. Position the playhead on or around the edit you want to preview **Q**.

2. Choose View > Playback > Play Around, or press Shift-/ (forward slash) **R**.

   The playhead backs up by the pre-roll amount, plays across the edit, and stops after the post-roll amount.

Note that by default pre-roll and post-roll are both set to two seconds.

To customize the pre-roll and post-roll durations:

1. Choose Final Cut Pro > Preferences, or press Command-, (comma).

2. Click the Playback button to switch to the Playback pane **S**.

   The Playback pane opens **T**.

3. Adjust the Pre-Roll Duration and Post-Roll Duration settings to the duration of your choice, and close the Preferences window.

TIP In general, projects with more frequent cuts will benefit from shorter pre- and post-roll values. Projects with longer scenes and fewer cuts benefit from a longer pre-roll duration.

To play a selection:

1. Select a clip, a group of clips, or a range selection **U**.

2. Choose View > Playback > Play Selection, or press / (forward slash).

   The playhead backs up to the beginning of the selected area and plays until it reaches the end of the selection.

Playback button

S Open the Preferences window, and click the Playback button.

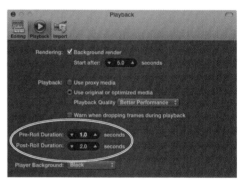

T Customize the Pre-Roll Duration and Post-Roll Duration settings as needed.

U Select the clips or range you want to preview.

V Select the range you want to preview.

W Position the playhead where you want to begin playing back.

Loop Playback button

X Click the Loop Playback button in the Viewer.

To play from the current frame to the end of the selection:

1. Select a clip, a group of clips, or a range selection (using the Range Select tool) V.

2. Position your playhead at the frame where you want to begin playback W.

3. Choose View > Playback > Play to End, or press Control-Shift-O.

   The project plays from the current position to the last frame of the selection.

To enable loop playback:

- Click the loop playback in the Viewer, or press Command-L X.

Trimming from the Keyboard

Although dragging edits to trim them allows you to "feel" how far you should move them, it's woefully imprecise and slow. When you get in the habit of trimming every one of the many edits in your program, you're likely to seek out quicker and more precise trimming methods.

In Final Cut Pro, this means you need to learn at least some of the many trim-related commands you can employ by pressing a single key or simple key combination on the keyboard.

Precise Trimming

Perhaps the most essential and useful of these keyboard shortcuts are the ones that allow you to trim an edit (in any of the three modes) one frame at a time. This way, you can trim with extreme precision and effectiveness.

To trim one frame at a time:

1. Click the left side of an edit point to ripple the outgoing clip, click the right side of an edit to ripple the incoming clip, or use the Trim tool to select the middle of the edit point as a roll .

    The edit is highlighted in yellow to indicate which edit type is selected.

2. Press , (comma) to ripple to the left by one frame and . (period) to ripple to the right by one frame.

3. Press Shift-? to play around with the edit and see the results of your work.

4. Repeat steps 2 and 3 until you are satisfied with the resulting edit.

A Select the edit as a ripple outgoing (left), roll (middle), or ripple incoming (right).

TIP Press Shift-, (comma) to ripple left by five frames at a time, or press Shift-. (period) to ripple right by five frames at a time.

B Select the edit. In this example, it's selected as a roll.

C Enter they number of frames preceded by a + (plus) or – (minus).

D The edit is moved by the specified number of frames.

Numerical Trimming

As you become more experienced as an editor, more and more you'll find yourself predicting exactly how many frames you want to trim just by looking at your movie. You'll watch a particular edit and guess that it should be rippled by precisely three frames.

When you get to that stage, you'll appreciate that Final Cut Pro will allow you to perform an edit by simply typing the number of frames you want to trim.

To perform a trim by a specific number of frames:

1. Select the edit as a ripple outgoing, ripple incoming, or roll **B**.

2. Press + or – (minus), and type the number of frames you want to trim **C**.

   The Current Frame indicator changes to show the trim amount.

3. Press Enter (or Return) to perform the edit **D**.

4. Press Shift-? to play around the edit and check your work.

5. Repeat steps 2–4 until you are satisfied with the edit.

Selecting Edits

Once you get in the habit of making your trims from the keyboard, you'll likely find that you want to be able to select the edit from the keyboard as well.

This way, you can trim the outgoing clip and the incoming clip and trim as a roll, all without ever needing your mouse.

continues on next page

To select an edit from the keyboard:

1. Position the playhead directly over the edit you want to select **E**.

> **TIP** Pressing the Up Arrow key will automatically move the playhead directly to the previous edit, and pressing the Down Arrow key will move it to the next edit.

2. *Do one of the following:*
   - To select the left edge of the edit (ripple outgoing), press [(Left Bracket) **F**.
   - To select the right edge of the edit (ripple incoming), press] (Right Bracket) **G**.
   - To select both edges (roll), press \ (Backslash) **H**.

One-Click Edits

Performing a one-click edit means you can play the project back and, when you find the frame where you'd like the edit to occur, perform the edit in a single step.

This has the benefit of being quick and easy, plus it allows you to make editing decisions while the video is playing back. Final Cut Pro has four one-step trimming commands, and each of them works slightly differently:

- Extend Edit moves the selected edit to the playhead position. It works on both ripple and roll edits. The playhead point can be located to the left or the right of the current edit.

- Trim Start moves the In point of the current clip (the clip under the playhead) to the playhead position. Trim Start always ripples (rather than rolls) the edit. The new edit must always move to the right of the existing edit position (making the resulting clip shorter).

E Position the playhead over the edit you want to select.

F Press [(Left Bracket) to select the edit as a ripple outgoing.

G Press [(Left Bracket) to select the edit as a ripple outgoing.

H Press \ (Backslash) to select the edit as a roll.

I Select the edit. In this example it's selected as a ripple incoming.

J Extend the edit to move the edit to the playhead position.

K When your playhead is over the frame to which you want to move the In point, press Option-[.

L The In point is moved to the current playhead position, trimming the clip.

- Trim End moves the Out point of the current clip (the clip under the playhead) to the playhead position. Trim End always ripples (rather than rolls) the edit. The new edit must always move to the left of the existing edit (making the resulting clip shorter).

- Trim to Selection moves both the In and Out points of a clip to a manually selected subrange within that clip. Trim to Selection always makes the resulting clip shorter.

To move an edit to the playhead position:

1. Select the edit you want to modify as a ripple outgoing, ripple incoming, or roll **I**.

2. Play the project.

3. When you find the frame where you want the edit to move, press Shift-X or choose Edit > Extend Edit **J**.

   The edit is rippled or rolled to the current playhead position.

TIP You do not need to stop playback in order to perform this command. Also, you can extend an edit in either direction (left or right) from the current edit.

To trim the start of a clip to the playhead position:

1. Play the portion of the project that includes the clip you want to shorten.

2. When you find the frame where you want to move the In point, press Option-[(Left Bracket) or choose Edit > Trim Start **K**.

   The clip under the playhead's In point moves to the current playhead position, and the clip is shortened **L**.

To trim the end of a clip to the playhead position:

1. Play the portion of the project that includes the clip you want to shorten.

2. When you find the frame where you want to move the Out point, press Option-[(Right Bracket) or choose Edit > Trim End .

   The clip under the playhead's Out point jumps to the current playhead position, and the clip is shortened .

> **TIP** Often this command is best used when playing the project in reverse (backward). To play backward, press J.

To trim both the start and the end of a clip to a selected range:

1. Play the portion of the project that includes the clip you want to shorten.

2. Press I to set the In point and press O to set the Out point to mark the range of the clip you want to keep .

   Note the range must be shorter than the existing clip's duration.

3. Press Option-\ (Backslash), or choose Edit > Trim to Selection.

   The clip is trimmed to align with the selected range .

M When your playhead is over the frame to which you want to move the Out point, press Option-].

N When your playhead is over the frame to which you want to move the In point, press Option-[.

O Set the In and Out points to mark the range you want to keep.

P Press Option-\ to trim the clip to the selection. The areas before and after the marked selection are deleted.

Trimming and Connected Clips

Any clips connected to the clips being trimmed will remain connected. If two connected clips overlap because of the trimming action, they will move out of the way accordingly **Q**.

If an edit is rolled over the connection point, the connection line will be moved from one clip to the other **R**.

If you ripple an incoming clip's edge beyond a connection point, the connection line moves along with the edit point **S**.

R Rolling under a connected clip can move the connection line from one clip to another. Here, the connection originally on Shot_02 gets moved to Shot_01.

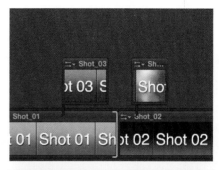

Q Connected clips automatically move out of the way when trimming makes them overlap.

S In some cases, the connection point will be moved as a clip is trimmed.

Using the Precision Editor

Final Cut Pro allows you to see how the two clips at an edit point overlap. Using the *Precision Editor*, the Timeline converts to a special view where you can quickly see the frames beyond the Out point of the outgoing clip (in the upper bar) and the frames before the In point of the incoming clip (in the lower bar).

TIP You can also see any markers in those unused frames that would not have been visible in the regular Timeline view.

This can be very helpful when you're trying to decide which side of an edit to adjust. For example, imagine that you're cutting between a medium shot of a woman reaching into a drawer and a close-up of her hand grasping a knife.

In the Precision Editor, you would be able to quickly see that a few frames after the current edit point (in the medium shot) her body obscures the action. This can guide you to move the edit so it occurs earlier and uses more frames of the close-up.

In the Precision Editor, you can perform any of the three trimming actions: ripple outgoing, ripple incoming, and roll.

Outgoing clip *Unused frames*

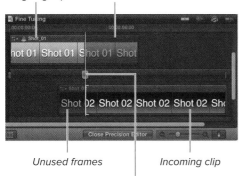

Unused frames *Incoming clip*

Current edit point

A Double-click any edit to open the Precision Editor.

Close Precision Editor button

B Click the Close Precision Editor button to close the Precision Editor.

C The Precision Editor closes, and the regular Timeline view returns.

To open the Precision Editor:

■ *Do one of the following*:

   ▶ Double-click an edit point.

   ▶ Select either edge of an edit point, and Choose Clip > Show Precision Editor (or press Control-E).

   The Precision Editor opens **A**.

To close the Precision Editor:

■ *Do one of the following*:

   ▶ Click the Close Precision Editor button **B**.

   ▶ Choose Clip > Hide Precision Editor (or press Control-E).

   ▶ Double click the grey trim handle located on the center strip between the two shots.

   ▶ Press Escape or Enter.

   The Precision Editor collapses, and the Timeline returns to its regular view **C**.

Trimming in the Precision Editor

There are two ways to ripple a clip in the Precision Editor. You can drag the edge of the clip on either side, just like you would in the regular Timeline view, or you can drag the clip itself, aligning a different frame to the edit point.

Whether you are rippling or rolling, you can also select the edit and use keyboard shortcuts to trim the edit, as described in the "Trimming from the Keyboard" section.

To ripple the outgoing clip in the Precision Editor:

- *Do one of the following:*
  - ▶ Drag the right edge of the clip to the left to shorten the clip or to the right to lengthen the clip **D**.
  - ▶ Drag the body of the clip to the right to shorten the clip or to the left to lengthen the clip **E**.
  - ▶ Click to select the right edge of the clip, and press , (comma) to shorten the clip or . (period) to lengthen the clip.

D Ripple the outgoing clip by dragging the right edge (Out point) of the clip left or right. In this example, the outgoing clip has been rippled four frames to the right.

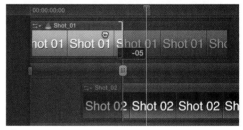

E Alternatively, drag the body of the outgoing clip to ripple it. In this example, the outgoing clip has been rippled five frames to the left.

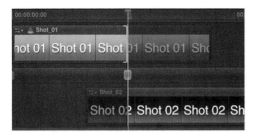

F Drag the In point of the Incoming clip to ripple it. In this example, the incoming clip has been rippled four frames to the left.

G Alternatively, drag the body of the incoming clip to ripple it. In this example, the incoming clip has been rippled five frames to the left.

To ripple the incoming clip in the Precision Editor:

- *Do one of the following*:

    ▸ Drag the left edge of the clip to the right to shorten the clip or to the left to lengthen the clip **E**.

    ▸ Drag the body of the clip to the left to shorten the clip or to the right to lengthen the clip **G**.

    ▸ Click to select the left edge of the clip, and press , (comma) to lengthen the clip or . (period) to shorten the clip.

To roll an edit in the Precision Editor:

- *Do one of the following*:

  ▸ Drag the gray trim handle to the left to shorten the outgoing clip and lengthen the incoming clip .

  ▸ Drag the gray trim handle between the two clips to the right to lengthen the outgoing clip and shorten the incoming clip.

  ▸ Click the gray trim handle, and press , (comma) to roll the edit to the left or . (period) to roll the edit to the right.

TIP Don't forget to play around with the edit as you trim to check your work and decide on the best final edit position.

Jumping Between Edits

Many editors choose to do a "trimming pass" where they walk through each of the edits in the project and fine-tune them using the various trim tools.

If you want to work this way and finesse one edit after another without having to close and reopen the Precision Editor each time, you can navigate from one edit point to another within the Precision Editor.

To navigate between edits in the Precision Editor:

- *Do one of the following*:

  ▸ Press the Up Arrow key to open the previous edit, or press the Down Arrow key to open the next edit.

  ▸ Click an edit point indicator in the middle bar .

  The window rearranges so the newly chosen edit is active .

  The outgoing clip appears on the upper bar, and the incoming clip appears on the lower bar.

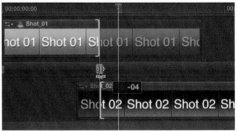

H To roll the edit, grab the gray trim handle to the left or right. In this example, the edit has been rolled four frames to the left.

Edit point indicators

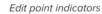

I To switch to a new edit in the Precision Editor, click one of the edit point indicators.

J The Precision Editor switches to show the new edit.

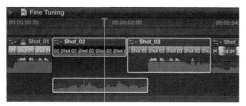

A Split edits allow you to adjust your audio edits separately from your video edits.

B Select the clips you want to expand.

C Double-click the audio waveforms to expand the audio.

Expanding Clips

Final Cut Pro does everything it can to keep your Timeline organized for you and to prevent audio and video from ever moving out of alignment with each other. But there are frequent occasions when you want to deliberately manipulate the audio and video components of an edit separately.

For example, if you want the audio from one clip to overlap the audio from an adjacent clip or if you want the video from one shot to play over the audio from an adjacent shot, you need to be able to trim the audio edit points separately from the video edit points **A**.

Edits where the audio and video cut at different points in time are called *split* edits. One way to create such split edits is to *expand* the clips. Expanding divides the audio and video elements into separate bars in the Timeline. That way, you can establish different edit points for each.

Note you cannot *move* expanded audio and video components separately. To move audio separately from video, see "Detaching Audio" later in the chapter.

To expand a clip:

1. Select one or more clips **B**.

   The clips are highlighted in yellow.

2. *Do one of the following*:

   ▸ Double-click the audio waveforms **C**.

   ▸ Choose Clip Expand Audio/Video, or press Control-S.

   The clips are divided into two bars: one for the video and one for the audio.

   Note that Clip Appearance must be set to a view option that displays both audio and video.

continues on next page

You can also instruct Final Cut Pro to expand all clips at once or to expand only clips that currently have overlapping audio and video.

To expand all clips:

- Choose View > Expand Audio/Video Clips > For All.

  All eligible clips expand.

Selecting Split Edits

Just as you learned to select edits from the keyboard in the "Selecting Edits" section when your clips are expanded, you can select just the video or just the audio edits directly from the keyboard as well.

To select a video-only edit from the keyboard:

1. Position the playhead directly over the edit you want to select **D**.

TIP Pressing the Up Arrow key automatically moves the playhead directly to the previous edit. Pressing the Down Arrow key moves it to the next edit.

2. *Do one of the following*:

   - To select the left edge of the video edit (ripple outgoing), press [(Left Bracket) **E**.

   - To select the right edge of the video edit (ripple incoming), press] (Right Bracket) **F**.

   - To select both edges of the video clips (roll), press \ (Backslash) **G**.

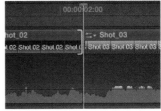

D Position the playhead precisely over the edit.

E Press [(Left Bracket) to select a video-only ripple outgoing edit.

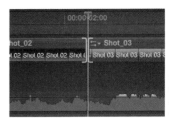

F Press] (Right Bracket) to select a video-only ripple incoming edit.

G Press \ (Backslash) to select a video-only roll edit.

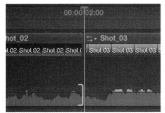

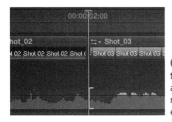

H Press Shift-[to select an audio-only ripple outgoing edit.

I Press Shift-] to select an audio-only ripple incoming edit.

J Press Shift-\ to select an audio-only roll edit.

To select an audio-only edit from the keyboard:

1. Position the playhead directly over the edit you want to select.

TIP Pressing the Up Arrow key automatically moves the playhead directly to the previous edit. Pressing the Down Arrow key moves it to the next edit.

2. *Do one of the following*:

   ▸ To select the left edge of the audio edit (ripple outgoing), press Shift-[**H**.

   ▸ To select the right edge of the audio edit (ripple incoming), press Shift-] **I**.

   ▸ To select both edges of the audio clips (roll), press Shift-\ (Backslash) **J**.

Once the edit is selected in your preferred manner, you can trim it using keyboard shortcuts or by dragging the selected clip edge.

Editing Expanded Clips

Once you've expanded your clips, you can begin trimming the audio and video elements independently.

All the same trimming tools and rules discussed earlier in this chapter apply, only now you can perform those trims to just the audio or just the video.

To edit expanded clips:

1. *Select one of the following types of edit:*

    ► Video ripple outgoing

    ► Audio ripple outgoing

    ► Video ripple incoming

    ► Audio ripple incoming

    ► Video roll

    ► Audio roll

2. Drag the clip edge or use keyboard shortcuts to add or remove frames from the selected edit 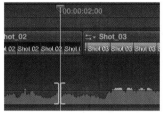 **K**.

    Any time you ripple an edit that causes the audio clips to overlap, the clips are automatically moved onto additional tracks to make room **L**.

Collapsing Expanded Clips

Expanding is temporary. Once you change the audio and video edits to your liking, you can collapse the clips again to keep the Timeline tidy and uncluttered.

Collapsing an expanded clip does not change the overlapping edits you may have created; rather, it simplifies the *appearance* of those overlaps in the Timeline. Clips can be expanded or collapsed repeatedly as needed.

K Drag or use keyboard shortcuts to trim the split edit.

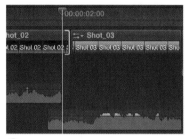

L Any trim that creates an overlap automatically adds tracks to accommodate the overlapping tracks.

M Select the expanded clips you want to collapse.

N Double-click the audio to collapse the clips.

O It can be hard to tell which collapsed clips have overlapping audio. In this example, the end of the first clip indicates a split (the dimmed audio), but there are other splits that are not so obvious.

P Expanding clips using For Splits expands only those clips with offset audio edits. Here, the first, second, and fourth clips all contained splits.

To collapse an expanded clip:

1. Select the expanded clip (or clips) you want to collapse **M**.

2. *Do one of the following*:

   ▸ Double-click the audio area of the clip.

   ▸ Choose Clip Collapse Audio/Video, or press Control-S **N**.

   The selected clips are collapsed, and any overlapping audio is displayed in the audio section of the Timeline clips.

You can also collapse all expanded clips in the project. This saves you the trouble of selecting specific clips individually.

To collapse all expanded clips:

▪ Choose View > Collapse All Clips.

   All expanded clips in the project are collapsed.

Once clips have been collapsed, it can be difficult to detect which edits are split and which are *straight* (that is, edits in which the audio and video cut at the same time) **O**.

To address this, Final Cut Pro contains an additional command that expands only those edits that are split.

To expand clips with overlapping audio and video:

▪ Choose View > Expand Audio/Video Clips > For Splits.

   Any clips containing overlapping audio and video are expanded **P**.

   Note this command will have no effect unless you have previously expanded and overlapped some clips manually.

Clearing Split Edits

There may come a time when you want to remove a split edit and reset the audio and video to cut at the same exact time (called a *straight cut*).

Although you can do this manually by trimming the individual audio clips and realigning them with the video edit point, Final Cut Pro also has a command specifically for this purpose.

To clear an audio/video split:

1. Select one or both of the clips that contain a split edit .

   Note it doesn't matter whether the selected clips are expanded or collapsed.

2. Choose Clip > Clear Audio Video Split .

   The audio edit is realigned with the corresponding video edit, removing any overlapping audio.

Ⓠ Select a clip with an offset or overlapping audio edit.

Ⓡ Choose Clear Audio Video Split to reset the audio edit to match the video edit.

A Detached audio is no different from any other connected clip.

B Select the clip you want to detach.

C Press Control-Shift-S to detach the audio.

Detaching Audio

While expanding clips allows you to trim the audio and video elements of a clip separately, sometimes you may want to treat the audio and video portions of a clip as completely separate objects.

For example, you might want to use the audio from one of them in place of the audio from a different shot. This is done frequently in dialogue scenes, where you might need to "steal" the audio from a close-up of an actor to use during another shot where you can't see the actor's lips. Or sometimes you might even use the audio from one *take* of a scene to use with a different take of the same scene. Just be sure the lips match when you play it back!

Detaching audio takes the audio component of your A/V clip and turns it into a connected clip **A**.

From that point on, you can move it or edit it in any way that you might modify any other connected clip.

Note there is no way to reattach the audio component once it has been detached, though the pieces can be combined into a compound clip. See Chapter 16, "Compound Clips."

To detach audio:

1. Select a clip (or clips) in the Timeline **B**.

2. Choose Clip > Detach Audio, or press Control-Shift-S **C**.

   The audio is extracted from the clip and added to the project as a connected clip aligned to the first frame of the corresponding video clip.

Separating Audio Channels

If you have a clip with multiple audio channels and you want to manipulate those channels independently, you must first *break apart* the clip. (To learn more about audio channels, see Audio Pan Settings in Chapter 11, "Audio Editing.")

Breaking apart an A/V clip works just like detaching audio, except that each of the individual audio channels is turned into a separate connected clip.

Once a clip has been broken apart into its individual channels, you can set the audio levels of each channel differently. (For more on adjusting audio levels, see Audio Levels in Chapter 11, "Audio Editing.")

You can also move or trim the individual channels independently, but be careful that you don't accidentally knock them out of sync. Final Cut Pro has no out-of-sync indicators to warn you that this is happening.

TIP You can also break apart an audio-only clip if it has multiple audio channels.

Note the Break Apart command is also used to separate the individual components of secondary storylines and compound clips. For more, see the "Secondary Storylines" section in Chapter 8, "Editing Tools" or Chapter 16, "Compound Clips."

To break apart a clip:

1. Select a clip (or clips) in the Timeline **D**.

2. Choose Clip > Break Apart Clip Items.

    The individual channels are each broken out into their own clips in the Timeline **E**.

Note once a clip has been broken apart, it cannot be collapsed back into a single clip, although it can be made into a compound clip. See Chapter 16, "Compound Clips."

D Select the clip you want to break apart.

E Once broken apart, each of the individual channels are separated into their own clips in the Timeline.

Select the Trim tool from the Tools pop-up menu in the toolbar.

Use the Trim tool to slip a clip by dragging the clip in the Timeline.

If you reach the end of the available media, the edge of the clip turns red.

Where Do the Extra Frames Come From?

Slipping works only when there are additional frames outside the ones you're using in the project. If, when you first edited the clip into the project, you used all of the source media, you will have no frames to slip.

Slipping Clips

If you want to adjust the timing of a single clip without disturbing the timing of any of the adjacent clips, you can *slip* the clip.

Slipping a clip ripples both its In point and its Out point simultaneously by the same number of frames. The result is that the clip's duration doesn't change, and its position doesn't change, but the frames included in the shot do change.

For example, if you had a five-second shot of a bird flying across the screen, you could slip the clip so the shot begins before the bird enters the frame, slip it so the shot begins with the bird midway through the frame, or even slip it so the bird has already left the frame before the shot began (though I'm not sure why you'd want to do that). In all three cases, the duration of the shot remains unchanged, but you're able to show a different portion of the action.

TIP Slipping is most commonly done near the end of the editing process when the overall timing of the movie is set and you want your edit to be minimally disruptive to the surrounding clips.

To slip a clip:

1. Select the Trim tool from the Tools pop-up in the toolbar, or press T .

2. Drag the clip's filmstrip in the Timeline with the Trim tool. Drag right to select earlier frames, and drag left to select later frames .

   As you drag with the Trim tool, both edges of the clip light up yellow, and the thumbnails move to display the new frames.

   When you reach the end of the source media, the edge of the clip turns red .

Slipping from the Keyboard

Just as with rippling and rolling, you can slip a clip from the keyboard, slipping one frame at a time or typing a specific number of frames to slip all at once. This allows for more precise edits than dragging usually does.

To slip one frame at a time:

1. Select the Trim tool from the Tools pop-up menu in the toolbar.

2. Click a clip to select it for slipping **D**.

   The In point and Out point of the clip are highlighted in yellow.

3. Press , (comma) to slip to the left or . (period) to slip to the right.

TIP Press shift-, (comma) or Shift-. (period) to slip by five frames.

   The clip is slipped one frame at a time.

To slip by a specific number of frames:

1. Select the Trim tool from the Tools pop-up menu in the toolbar.

2. Click a clip to select it for slipping **E**.

   The In point and Out point of the clip are highlighted in yellow.

3. Press + (plus) or − (minus), and type the number of frames you want to trim **F**.

   The Current Frame indicator changes to a slip indicator.

4. Press Enter (or Return) to perform the edit.

   The clip is slipped by the specified number of frames.

TIP Don't forget to play around with the edit after you trim to check the results of your work.

D Click a clip with the Trim tool to select it for slipping.

E Select a clip for numerical slipping by clicking it with the Trim tool.

F Type the number of frames by which you want to slip the clip.

A Select the Trim tool from the Tools pop-up menu in the toolbar.

B Option-drag the clip to Slide it.

C If you run out of available media, the edge of the clip turns red.

> **TIP** If the "Show detailed trimming feedback" setting in the Editing pane of the Preferences window is enabled, the Viewer shows the new last frame of the previous clip and the new first frame of the following clip—these are the two frames that change when you slide a clip. To learn how to enable that setting, see "Viewing Detailed Trimming Feedback."

Sliding Clips

Another way to move a clip that's similar to slipping a clip is called *sliding*. Sliding moves a clip to a new position in the Timeline by shortening or lengthening the clips on either side of it.

Whereas slipping ripples the In point and Out point of a single clip, sliding ripples the Out point of the clip *prior to* the selected clip and ripples the In point of the clip *after it*. The clip itself remains unchanged.

The result is that the clip is repositioned in the Timeline.

Like slipping, sliding is most frequently done near the end of the editing process when you want to prevent the changes you make from impacting the rest of the project.

Note that sliding will never completely delete either of the adjacent clips. If you slide a clip all the way to the end of one of the adjacent clip edges, a (useless) single frame will be left. You must then zoom in and manually delete that one frame.

To slide a clip:

1. Select the Trim tool from the Tools pop-up in the toolbar, or press T **A**.

2. Option-drag the thumbnails on a clip in the Timeline with the Trim tool **B**. Drag left to slide the clip left or right to slide the clip right.

   As you drag with the Trim tool, the adjacent clip edges light up yellow.

   When you reach the end of the clip's source media, the edge of that clip turns red **C**.

Sliding from the Keyboard

Just as with slipping clips, you can also slide a clip from the keyboard, either by sliding one frame at a time or by typing a specific number of frames to slide all at once. This allows for more precise edits than dragging usually does.

To slide one frame at a time:

1. Select the Trim tool from the Tools pop-up menu in the toolbar.

2. Option-click a clip to select it for sliding .

   The edits on either side of the selected clip are highlighted in yellow.

3. Press , (comma) to slide to the left or . (period) to slide to the right.

TIP Press shift-, (comma) or Shift-. (period) to slide by five frames.

   The clip slides one frame at a time.

To slide by a specific number of frames:

1. Select the Trim tool from the Tools pop-up menu in the toolbar.

2. Option-click the clip to select it for sliding ❻.

   The edits on either side of the selected clip are highlighted in yellow.

3. Press + (plus) or − (minus), and type the number of frames you want to trim ❻.

   The Current Frame indicator changes to a slide indicator.

4. Press Enter or Return to perform the edit.

TIP Don't forget to play around the edit after you trim to check the results of your work!

❶ Option-click a clip with the Trim tool to select it for sliding.

❶ Option-click the clip with the Trim tool to select it for sliding.

❶ Type the number of frames by which you want to slide the clip.

10

Auditioning Clips

When you find yourself needing to quickly compare how a variety of related clips fit into a particular edit, you can group the clips into an *audition*.

An audition is a single clip object that contains a collection of shots. Only one shot can be active at a time, but you can quickly switch between the choices to see how the different clips feel in the project.

You can treat an audition just as you would treat a regular clip: editing, trimming, and moving it as needed. However, at any point you can swap out the active *pick* for one of the other *alternates* stored in the audition list.

Using Auditions

The clips in an audition can vary in length, format, and number. When a new shot is selected as the pick, the Timeline automatically adjusts to make room for the new clip.

You might create an audition out of a group of related shots, such as different close-ups of birds. Later you can swap out one bird shot for another.

Similarly, if you had multiple *takes* of an over-the-shoulder (OTS) shot of an actor, each one would contain the same action but with slightly different performances. Using an audition, you can easily swap out one take for another, quickly choosing the best performance and using that one in your project.

You can also make an audition out of duplicate instances of the same shot. You might do this to see how different effects play in the context of your project. So, for example, your audition might contain three instances of an identical shot, but one is tinted pink, one is tinted green, and one is tinted orange .

Once you settle on the audition pick, you can finalize the audition, which discards the other shots in the audition list and converts the audition into a regular, flat clip.

A In this audition, one clip is tinted three different colors.

A Select the clips you want to turn into an audition.

Audition icon

B A new audition is created. The original clips
remain in the event, unaffected.

C Rename the audition clip to differentiate it from
the similarly named clips from which it was created.

Creating an Audition

You can create auditions in the Event
Browser or in the Timeline. In the Event
Browser, the audition becomes just another
source file that you can edit into a project
using any of the methods described in
Chapter 7, "Basic Editing." Later, you can
swap out the pick for one of the alternates.

To create an audition in the Event Browser:

1. Select two or more clips in the Event
   Browser **A**.

2. Choose Clip > Audition > Create, or
   press Command-Y.

   A new audition clip is created. Any keywords in the original clips are automatically copied into the audition.

   The original clips are left unaffected in
   the Event Browser **B**.

   TIP Instead of selecting whole clips, you can
   select Marked Favorites to limit the audition to
   the selected area of each clip.

3. Rename the audition clip **C**.

   Now your audition is ready to be used
   in a project.

Creating Auditions in the Timeline

In the Timeline, you can create an audition in a number of ways:

- You can add a clip to an existing clip, automatically converting the existing clip into an audition and setting the new clip as an alternate.

- You can add a clip to an existing clip, setting the new clip as the pick and saving the old clip as an alternate.

- You can duplicate an existing clip, creating an audition out of the duplicate.

- You can duplicate an existing clip with effects applied, creating an audition out of a duplicate with no effects.

The first two methods involve adding a new shot to an existing shot. The difference is that you can choose whether you want the old shot or the new shot to be set as the pick. (You can always change which one is the pick later.)

The last two methods involve duplicating an existing clip. These methods are primarily used for auditioning different effect settings.

To add a new clip as an alternate:

1. Select the clip (or range) in the Event Browser that you want to add as an alternate .

2. Drag the selection onto a clip in the Timeline, and when the clip turns white, drop the clip.

   The Replace drop menu appears .

D Select the shot you want to add as an audition alternate to the Timeline clip.

E Once the Timeline clip turns white, release the mouse. Choose Add to Audition from the drop menu.

Audition icon

F Although nothing appears to change when you play the project in the Viewer, the clip has been converted to an audition. The only clue is the Audition icon that appears next to the clip in the Timeline.

G Select the clip you want to add to the Timeline.

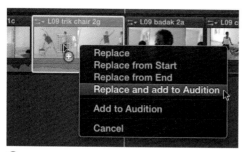

H When the drop menu appears, choose Replace and Add to Audition.

I The new clip becomes the pick, and the Timeline adjusts to make room for the longer clip.

3. From the drop menu, choose Add to Audition.

The Timeline clip is converted into an audition, and the dragged clip is saved as an alternate **F**.

Because the existing clip remains set as the pick, the content of the project does not change.

The only indication of what you've done is the Audition icon that appears to the left of the clip name.

TIP Using this technique, you can add multiple clips to an audition at once. Just select multiple items in the Event Browser in step 1.

To add a new clip as the pick:

1. Select the clip or range in the Event Browser that you want to add as an alternate **G**.

2. Drag the selection onto a clip in the Timeline, and when the clip turns white, drop the clip.

The Replace drop menu appears.

3. From the drop menu, choose Replace and Add to Audition **H**.

The Timeline clip is converted into an audition, and the dragged clip is set as the pick. The existing Timeline clip is saved as an alternate **I**.

To duplicate a clip as an alternate:

- Select a clip in the Timeline, right-click, and, from the shortcut menu, choose Duplicate as Audition (or press Option-Y) 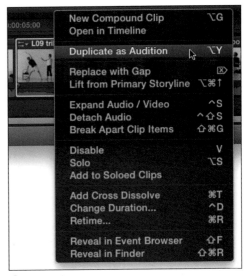.

  The clip is converted into an audition, and a duplicate of the clip is saved as an alternate **Ⓚ**.

  Now you can make whatever changes you want to the clip, and you'll always be able to return to the unaffected version of the clip.

To create an unaffected duplicate as an alternate:

- Select a clip in the Timeline, and choose Clip > Audition > Duplicate from Original **Ⓛ**.

  The clip is converted into an audition, and a duplicate of the clip is saved as an alternate. The duplicate will be a "clean" version of the shot.

  This works exactly like the previous method, except it's intended to be used after you've already made changes to the clip—for example, if you apply a filter to a clip but then want to be able to quickly switch back to an unaffected version of the clip.

Ⓙ Right-click a clip and choose Duplicate as Audition.

Ⓚ The only noticeable change is the appearance of the Audition icon to the left of the clip name.

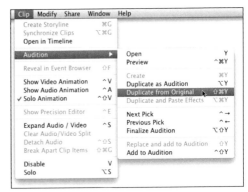

Ⓛ The Audition submenu in the Clip menu contains all the commands related to auditions.

*Number of alternates indicated
by the number of dots*

Audition icon

*Previously chosen clip
indicated with a star*

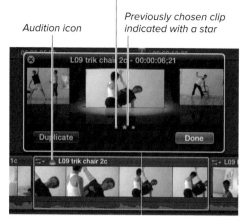

A Click the Audition icon to open the Audition window.

B Choose a new audition pick by pressing the Left Arrow key or the Right Arrow key to move to the next clip in the audition list. Note that the Timeline automatically updates to show the new pick.

Auditioning Clips

Once you've collected a group of shots into an audition, you can experiment and see which clip best fits in your project, *auditioning* each one until you find your favorite.

Simply pick one of the clips in your audition and play the project to see how well it works. Then, if you like, audition the next option, and so on. When you've settled on a pick, there's nothing more to do!

You can change your audition pick at any time. If a new pick is longer or shorter than the previous pick, the Timeline ripples automatically to accommodate the new clip length.

Note that although you can change the audition pick in the Event Browser, there's not much benefit to doing so. Primarily, auditioning should be done once the audition has been placed into a project.

To try audition clips:

1. Select an audition in the Timeline, and click the Audition icon or press Y **A**.

   The Audition window opens.

2. Press the Spacebar.

   The Timeline plays the audition area including the pre-roll and post-roll frames.

3. Press the Left Arrow key to move to the previous audition clip, or press the Right Arrow key to move to the next audition clip **B**.

   The Timeline continues to play in a loop, displaying the new audition pick. Each time you select a new pick, the loop starts over.

   continues on next page

4. When you've settled on a pick, press Enter or Escape, or click the Close button in the Audition window .

The audition window closes, and the pick remains active in the Timeline.

> **TIP** To open the Audition window and automatically start playback of the clips (combining the earlier steps 2 and 3), press Command-Control-Y.

To customize the pre-roll and post-roll durations:

1. Choose Final Cut Pro > Preferences.

2. Click the Playback icon to open the Playback pane 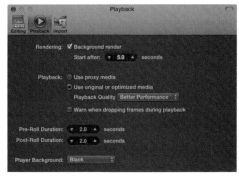.

3. In the Pre-Roll Duration and Post Roll Duration fields **E**, *do one of the following*:

- ▶ Click the increment or decrement arrows.

- ▶ Click the number and type a new value.

- ▶ Click and drag the number up to increase the value or drag it down to decrease the value.

4. Close the Preferences window.

The new pre-roll and post-roll durations are applied.

To change audition picks without opening the Audition window:

1. Select the audition clip.

2. Press Control-Right Arrow to change to the next audition clip, or press Control-Right Arrow to change to the previous audition clip.

The audition changes to reflect the new pick.

C The Audition window closes, and your last pick remains active in the Timeline.

D The Playback pane of the Final Cut Pro Preferences window contains the Pre-Roll Duration and Post-Roll Duration settings.

Click and type a new number.

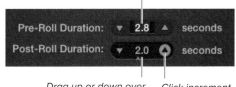

Drag up or down over one of the digits.   *Click increment or decrement arrows.*

E You can modify the duration fields in a variety of ways.

> **TIP** You can click and drag the individual digits of the number separately to change either by whole seconds or by fractions of a second.

Auditions and Effects

One of the common uses for auditions is to compare how different effects look on the same clip. For example, you might know you want a distressed look for a clip but can't decide between 50's TV, Aged Film, and Aged Paper. You can create an audition where the same clip is duplicated three times, each with a different filter applied.

Or similarly, you might have added a title graphic, but you're unsure about which font would look best and in what color. Using an audition, you can create multiple versions of the title, each with different settings.

Because this is such a common workflow, Final Cut Pro has some specific techniques for making the process of auditioning effects easy.

As described in the "Creating Auditions in the Timeline" section earlier, you can duplicate a clip, automatically saving it as an alternate. This allows you to make changes to the current pick (such as adding effects or changing text attributes), while the previous version of the shot remains unaffected in the audition list. If you ever want to return to the old version, it's just a click away.

Similarly, you can automatically generate a duplicate *as* you apply an effect. Using this technique, as you drag an effect onto a clip, a clean, unfiltered version of the clip is saved as an alternate in the audition list. You see the effect instantly, but if you change your mind, the original remains handy. And you can do this again and again, saving many versions of the clip. That way, you can very quickly audition a variety of effects (such as the various distressed looks described earlier) and then quickly switch between them, all while seeing how well they integrate with the rest of the shots in your project.

To add a new effect and save an unaffected duplicate as an alternate:

- Drag an effect from the Effects Browser onto a clip in the Timeline, and press Control before you release the mouse **Ⓐ**.

  The filter is applied, and a duplicate of the clip is saved as an audition alternate.

Ⓐ To automatically save a clean version of the shot as an audition alternate, drag an effect to a Timeline clip and then press Control before you release the mouse.

Applying Effects to All Clips in an Audition

You can also drag an effect to an audition and have it applied simultaneously to all the shots in the audition list, including the current pick.

For example, you may have a group of different shots of trees in a particular audition. You haven't yet decided whether you're going to opt for a spruce, a larch, or a horse chestnut. But you have decided that whichever tree shot you'll use, it's going to need a Simple Border effect applied to it. You can apply the effect to the entire audition list instead of just the current pick. That way, every time you switch to a different alternate, the border effect will remain.

B While dragging an effect to a Timeline audition clip, press Control-Option before you drop the clip.

L09 trik chair 2c - Simple Border - 00:00:06;21

Duplicate   Done

C Open the Audition window to see the audition list. The effect is applied to all the clips.

To apply an effect to all clips in an audition list:

1. Drag an effect from the Effects Browser to the audition clip in the Timeline, and before you drop the clip, press Control-Option **B**.

   The effect is applied to the current pick as well as any alternates in the audition list.

2. Select the audition clip, and press Y.

   The Audition window opens. You can see that the effect is applied to each of the items **C**.

TIP Once the effect is applied, each clip's effect settings remain independent from one another. To turn the border red, as in the previous example, you'd have to modify the Simple Border Color setting in the Video Effects pane of the Info window for each clip.

Adding and Removing Clips from Existing Auditions

At any point you can add clips to or remove clips from an existing audition. In this way, auditions can remain "living" objects where you can continue to modify their contents throughout the editing process.

Adding Clips to an Existing Audition

There appears to be no limit to the number of clips an audition can contain. (We successfully added more than 100, though more than 15 or so makes it pretty unwieldy.)

In the Event Browser, you can't technically add a clip to an existing audition, but you can easily create a new audition that combines the contents of an existing audition with any new items you select.

To combine an audition with new clips in the Event Browser:

1. Select the audition and the clips you want to add to the audition **A**.

TIP Command-click to add items to the current selection.

2. Choose Clip > Audition > Create, or press Command-Y.

   A new audition is created that includes all of the clips from the selected audition as well as the new clips **B**.

3. Rename the new audition **C**.

4. Select the old audition, and press Command-Delete.

   The old audition is deleted from the project.

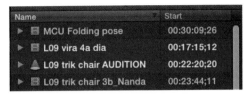

A Select both the audition and the new clips you want to add.

B A new audition is created, combining the selected audition with the additional selected clips.

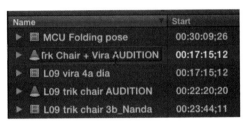

C To avoid confusion, it's best to rename the new audition and delete the old one.

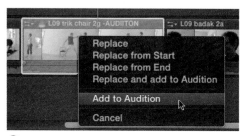

D Select the clip in the Event Browser that you want to add to the audition.

E When the Replace Edit drop menu appears, choose Add to Audition.

F Nothing appears to change in the Timeline or the Viewer, but the new clip has been added to the audition list as an alternate take.

G Select the clip in the Event Browser that you want to be the new pick.

In the Timeline, adding clips to an existing audition can be done using many of the same techniques you use to create a new audition: You can drag a new clip to an existing audition, duplicate a clip within an audition, and add an effect to an audition to create a duplicate with that new effect.

To add a new clip as an alternate:

1. Select the clip (or range) in the Event Browser that you want to add as an alternate **D**.

2. Drag the selection onto an existing audition in the Timeline, and when the clip turns white, drop the clip.

   The Replace drop menu appears.

3. From the drop menu, choose Add to Audition **E**.

   The dragged clip is added to the audition as an alternate **F**.

To add a new clip as the pick:

1. Select the clip or range in the Event Browser that you want to add as an alternate **G**.

continues on next page

2. Drag the selection onto a clip in the Timeline, and when the clip turns white, drop the clip.

The Replace drop menu appears.

3. From the Replace drop menu, choose Replace and add to Audition 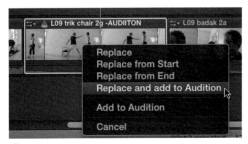.

The dragged clip is set as the pick. The existing Timeline clip is saved as an alternate .

To duplicate a clip as an alternate:

- Select a clip in the Timeline, and choose Clip > Audition > Duplicate as Audition (or press Option-Y) .

A copy of the pick is added to the alternate list. Now you can modify the current pick but quickly return to the previous state by switching to the alternate.

TIP You can press Option-Y several times consecutively to add multiple duplicates at once . That way, you can modify each of them in different ways and quickly switch between them.

H When the Replace drop menu appears, choose Replace and add to Audition.

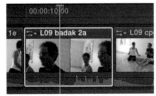

I The new clip replaces the old one in the Timeline, and the old one is stored in the audition list.

J Select the clip in the Timeline.

K Each time you press Option-Y, you're adding a new duplicate clip as an alternate. This figure shows an audition with seven copies of the clip.

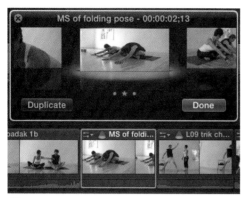

 Select the audition clip, and click the Audition icon to open the Audition window.

 Navigate to the clip you want to delete from the audition list. In this example, the leftmost clip has been selected.

 Press Delete to remove the clip from the audition list. In this example, only two audition clips remain.

Removing Clips from an Audition

As you home in on your final choice, you may want to remove some of the alternates from the audition group.

(NOTE: Deleting a clip from an audition does not delete other instances of that clip in your Event Browser.)

To remove a clip from an audition:

1. Select the audition in either the Event Browser or the Timeline, and click the Open Audition icon (or press Y) .

    The Audition window opens.

3   Press the Left Arrow key or the Right Arrow key to navigate to the alternate you want to remove .

4. Press Delete .

    The selected clip is removed from the audition.

    Note you cannot delete the last clip in an audition.

Finalizing an Audition

Once you've settled on which clip will serve as the final pick, you can lock that choice in by *finalizing* the audition.

Finalizing replaces the audition with a regular copy of the current pick. Any effects or adjustments applied to the pick will remain applied to the finalized clip.

Finalizing is not required. There's no harm in leaving auditions in your project forever (other than the continued opportunity it provides to second-guess your decisions).

To finalize an audition:

1. Select the audition in the Timeline **A**.

2. Choose Clip > Audition > Finalize, or press Shift-Option-Y.

   The audition is converted into a regular clip **B**.

A When you're ready to finalize your audition, select it in the Timeline.

A Press Shift-Option-Y, and the audition is flattened, leaving only the current pick behind as a regular clip in the project. The only obvious evidence of the change is the removal of the Audition icon from beside the clip's name.

11

Audio Editing

Editing your picture is only half the story. Your sound is just as important. In fact, a famous movie editor once quipped that sound is two-thirds of the picture. You'll likely spend much more time finessing and working on your audio edits than you will on your video.

While your picture carries the information about what's happening on-screen, the sound carries the emotion. The inflection of someone's voice often tells more than the words she is saying, and similarly, music and sound effects can often completely redefine how your viewers understand a scene. To put it simply, if seeing is believing, hearing is feeling.

Final Cut Pro contains a wide range of audio-editing tools and can facilitate myriad workflows and techniques to accommodate different types of projects.

In This Chapter

Audio Levels

The most fundamental aspect of your audio clips is the volume, or *level*, of each clip. Managing audio levels can be tricky, because your computer has a volume setting, and if you're using external speakers or headphones, those may have their own volume setting too. This can make it difficult to assess how quiet or loud your clips really are. You can turn those volume settings up or down while you're editing, but there's no way to know whether your viewers are going to have their volume settings the same as yours.

Because of this, we typically use audio *meters* to objectively measure a clip's level. Audio is measured in decibels (dB). This is a logarithmic scale, so, for example, –6 is twice as loud as –12, and –3 is twice as loud as –6. You don't need to worry about the specific numbers all that much as long as you can follow one simple rule: *Never, ever, let the level reach 0 dB.* Hitting 0 is known as *peaking*, and peaking is bad.

Less Than Zero

At 0 dB, sound will start to distort, and even if it may sound OK on your computer while you're editing, that moment of distortion can be amplified and aggravated when the file is converted into a different format for playing back on the Web or on a DVD.

Keep your audio levels safely below 0 dB, and you can be sure that your program will always sound clean and clear no matter what happens to it or where it is played back.

Audio meters

A Click the audio meters in the toolbar to open the full-size meters.

B The full-size audio meters appear to the right of the Timeline.

The problem is, keeping your overall level below zero can be trickier than you think. Audio volume is *additive*; if you play two audio clips at the same point in time, their levels are added together, and the overall sound at that point is going to be louder than either clip would be on its own.

A typical video will have dialogue, as well as some background *ambiance* to set the tone and the mood of the location, plus occasional sound effects and music. All of these will get added together to make the overall output louder than any of the individual elements on their own. It's plenty easy to accidentally hit zero, even when all of your component sounds are at perfectly reasonable levels.

Audio Meters

To help you set your audio levels properly, FCP has audio meters in two places. There are meters at the right side of the Current Frame indicator in the center of the toolbar, and, optionally, you can display a larger set of meters to the right of the Timeline **A**.

To show the large audio meters:

- *Do one of the following:*
  - ▶ Click the audio meters in the Current Frame indicator in the toolbar.
  - ▶ Choose Window > Show Audio Meters.
  - ▶ Press Shift-Command-8.

  The audio meters appear in the lower-right corner of the window **B**.

TIP A stereo project will show two audio meters. A surround project will show six audio meters. For more on the difference between stereo and surround projects, see the "Stereo vs. Surround" section of this chapter.

To enlarge the audio meters:

- Drag the divider bar between the Time-line (or the Media Browser if it's show-ing) and the audio meters **C**.

  The audio meters are expanded horizontally.

To read the audio meters:

- Play the project in the Timeline, and observe the meters. The *average level* is the approximate position of the top of the solid bar **D**.

TIP You can read the average level only while the project is playing back. The top of the bar at any one frame (as displayed when playback is stopped) is not a valid measure of average volume.

- The *peak level* is indicated by a flat line that sticks to the loudest level reached and then falls down after a moment **E**.

  If the audio reaches 0 dB, the exces-sive volume warning (a red box) lights up above the meter that peaked. This red light will stay on until playback is stopped and restarted. Be smart and don't ignore this **F**

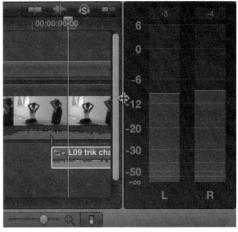

C Enlarge the audio meters by dragging the separator bar between the audio meters and the Timeline.

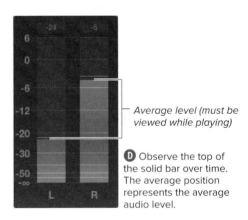

Average level (must be viewed while playing)

D Observe the top of the solid bar over time. The average position represents the average audio level.

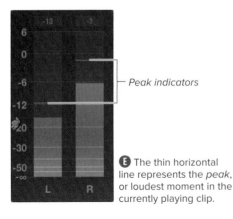

Peak indicators

E The thin horizontal line represents the *peak*, or loudest moment in the currently playing clip.

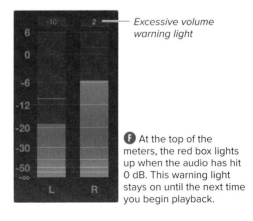

Excessive volume warning light

F At the top of the meters, the red box lights up when the audio has hit 0 dB. This warning light stays on until the next time you begin playback.

G When you position your pointer over an audio clip, the black audio level line turns white, and the pointer changes into the Adjust Levels pointer.

H Drag the line up or down to change the audio level. In this example, the audio has been attenuated to –15 dB. The little popup that appears next to the level line shows the change in decibels.

I In the Audio pane, the Volume and Pan section contains a Volume slider.

TIP The number in the warning light shows how many decibels over zero your level was at when it peaked. Use this to determine how much to lower your level to reach a safe volume. Make sure your meters are fully expanded or the warning light and numbers will be hidden.

Adjusting Audio Levels

Now that you know how to read your audio levels, it's time to learn how to change them. You can change audio levels in the Timeline or in the Audio Inspector. The controls are tied together; making a change in one place automatically updates the other.

To change audio levels in the Timeline:

1. Position your pointer over the audio portion of an A/V clip or over any audio-only clip **G**.

   The horizontal line indicating the audio level turns from black to white, and the pointer changes to the Adjust Levels pointer.

2. Drag the line up to *boost* (increase) the audio level, or drag it down to *attenuate* (decrease) the audio level **H**.

   The Info popup that appears next to the level line shows the change in decibels.

To change audio levels in the Inspector:

1. Select a clip in the Timeline, and in the Inspector, click the Audio button to open the Audio pane **I**.

2. In the Volume and Pan section, adjust the slider to boost or attenuate the audio level.

To change audio levels from the keyboard:

1. Select a clip in the Timeline.

2. Press Control-+ (plus) to boost the audio level 1 dB, or press Control-– (minus) to attenuate the audio level by 1 dB.

TIP Using the keyboard shortcut allows you to make changes while the project is playing back.

What's the Right Level?

As a general rule of thumb, set your basic dialogue and production sound to average around –12 dB.

This is not a hard-and-fast rule, but this gives you room to accommodate adding other sounds and music into your track with little danger of peaking.

It also affords you a bit of room in case you want certain sound effects or music to feel "very loud" without having to turn them all the way up to zero. If your dialogue is at –12 dB, you can have an explosion come in at –3 dB, which will be shockingly loud (as it should be), but it will still be safe from peaking.

Editors who mix films to be played in movie theaters often set their dialogue audio even quieter, such as to –20 dB or even –31 dB. This helps create that "cinematic" experience where the music swells (to four times the average volume) and breaks your heart or when the action scene reaches its climax and the motorcycle emits a deafening screech.

If you set your dialogue at –3 dB, that music or motorcycle can't be any louder than the volume of a basic conversation without distorting and sounding like a mistake. So, turn it down so you can turn it up!

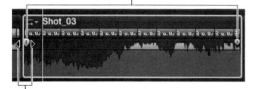

Audio Fade handles

Shot_03

Audio Fade pointer

Ⓐ When you position the pointer over an audio clip, Audio Fade handles appear, and the pointer turns into the Audio Fade pointer.

Audio Fades

If audio clips start and stop abruptly, the sudden shift in background noise can create distracting interruptions in the flow of your soundtrack. At best, they create disruptive shifts that disengage the viewer from the program; at worst, these shifts may create clicks or pops that appear as audio mistakes.

Because of this, it's common practice to make sure every single audio clip's level fades in and fades out gradually.

Fades also allow you to create smooth transitions between adjacent audio clips (commonly called a *crossfade*).

Adding such fades is typically done at the end of the editing process, because you don't want to apply a fade and then later trim the edge of the clip—which undoes the effect of the fade.

FCP makes it very easy to apply fades to your audio clips, and it provides four different fade *shapes* to accommodate different fade styles and requirements.

To add an audio fade-in and fade-out:

1. Position your pointer over the first or last frame of the audio portion of an A/V clip or any audio-only clip Ⓐ.

   The pointer changes to the Audio Fade pointer, and Audio Fade handles appear on the clip.

   TIP Zooming in on the Timeline and increasing the vertical height of the audio tracks will make it much easier to create fades effectively. For more about adjusting track height, see the "Timeline View Options" section of Chapter 7.

continues on next page

2. To create a fade-in effect, drag from the left edge of the clip toward the right  B.

3. To create a fade-out effect, drag from the right edge of the clip toward the left.

A fade-in or fade-out is applied to your clip. The longer the fades, the more gradual the fade effect will appear.

B Drag the Audio Fade handle to add an audio fade-in or fade-out.

To change the fade shape:

1. Add an audio fade as described in the previous task.

2. Right-click the Audio Fade handle.

The Fade Shape pop-up menu appears.

3. Choose from one of the four audio fade shapes 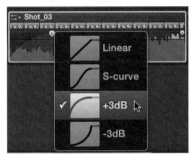 C:

- ▸ *Linear* creates a fade where the volume changes at a uniform rate.

- ▸ *S-Curve* creates a fade where the volume change begins and ends gradually.

- ▸ +3 creates a fade that accelerates the change over the course of the fade. This is the default setting and generally creates an even fade.

- ▸ –3 creates a fade that decelerates the change over the course of the fade. This creates a slower fade effect.

C The Fade Shape pop-up menu lets you choose one of four different fade shapes.

Audio level line

D The audio level line is where you add audio keyframes. Pressing the Option key turns the pointer into the Add Keyframe pointer, as shown here.

E Option-click the white line to add a keyframe.

F Drag the keyframe to set the audio level or to move it to a new point in time.

G Add multiple keyframes to create an animated effect.

Keyframing Audio Levels

Audio fades at the beginning and end of a clip are easily applied using the built-in fade controls, but there are plenty of occasions when you will want to make audio level changes midway through a clip.

You can easily do this using *audio keyframes*. Audio keyframes allow you to identify a specific audio level at a specific frame in time. By setting two or more audio keyframes, you can create dynamic audio adjustments over the course of a clip.

To add and adjust audio keyframes in the Timeline:

1. Position your pointer over the audio portion of an A/V clip or over an audio-only clip.

   The audio level line appears **D**.

2. Option-click the audio level line to add a keyframe **E**.

   TIP You must add two or more keyframes to create a change over time.

3. Drag the keyframe up or down to change the audio level at that point in time.

4. Drag the keyframe left or right to change the keyframe's position in time **F**.

   TIP You can adjust *either* the level or the timing. Once you begin dragging (either left to right or up to down), you establish the type of adjustment you're making. To switch to the other type, release the mouse and click again.

5. Repeat steps 2 through 4 to create an animated effect **G**.

To change a range of a clip audio:

1. Select the Range Select tool from the toolbar, or press R .

2. Drag a range in the clip over the area you want to change **I**.

3. Drag the Audio Level line within that range **J**.

   Keyframes are automatically added at the beginning and end of the range to create the desired effect **K**.

H Press R to select the Range Select tool.

I With the Range Select tool, drag a range over the area you want to modify.

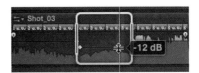

J Drag the white audio level line within the selected range.

K Multiple keyframes are added automatically to facilitate the desired adjustment.

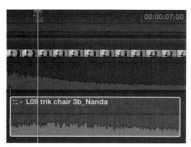

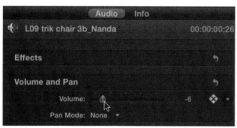

L First, position the playhead on the frame where you want the audio to begin changing.

Add Keyframe button

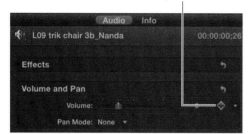

M When you position your pointer over the Volume slider, the Add Keyframe button appears. Click it to add a keyframe at the current frame.

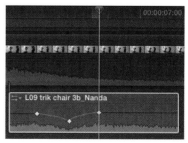

N Set the level for that keyframe.

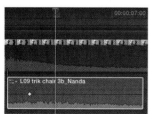

O Next, move the playhead to the next frame where you want the audio to change.

To add audio keyframes in the Inspector:

1. Select a clip in the Timeline, open the Inspector, and click Audio to open the Audio pane.

2. Position your playhead in the Timeline to the frame where you want the first keyframe added **L**.

3. In the Volume and Pan section of the Inspector, click the Add Keyframe button to the right of the Volume slider **M**.

4. Set the Volume slider to the desired level **N**.

5. Move the playhead in the Timeline to the position where you want the next keyframe added **O**.

6. Repeat steps 3 through 5 until all the desired keyframes have been set **P**.

TIP You *must* follow the exact procedure described: 1. Move the playhead. 2. Click the Add Keyframe button. 3. Adjust the Volume slider. Otherwise, you can accidentally change the level for the wrong keyframe.

P The Timeline shows the keyframes as you add them in the Inspector.

Subframe Audio Editing

FCP allows you to make audio level adjustments down to the sample level. That means you can make incredibly precise changes to your audio tracks.

You don't need to use any special tool to make such precise edits; you simply need to zoom in on the Timeline past the normal frame or 1/100th frame boundaries.

To make audio edits at the sample level:

1. Click in the Timeline to make it active, and then press Command-+ (plus) until you are zoomed in as far as possible .

   The light gray bar in the Timeline ruler indicates the duration of one video frame. By moving the playhead or adding audio keyframes, you can make adjustments at 1/100th of a frame.

   But you can zoom in even further.

2. Choose View > Zoom to Samples, or press Control-Z .

   Zoom to Samples becomes enabled. This state is saved on a project-by-project basis.

3. Press Command-+ (plus) repeatedly

   The Timeline will zoom in much further, until each pixel on the screen represents one sample in the audio track.

4. Add audio keyframes as desired.

5. When you're done, press Shift-Z to zoom the window to fit the entire project.

Note that you can change your Time Display setting in the preferences to show HH:MM:SS:FF + Subframes. This lets you see the changes you are making to the audio at the subframe sample level.

One video frame

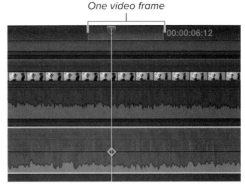

Q Zoom in as far as you can. The light gray bar in the Timeline indicates the duration of one video frame.

R Enable the Zoom to Samples setting so you can zoom in to the sample level.

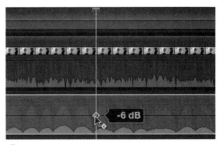

S When Zoom to Samples is enabled, you can zoom further in on the Timeline.

Audio Pan Settings

Any time you're playing audio through more than one speaker, you need to take into account the idea of *panning*—that is, how much of the sound is coming out of each speaker.

FCP allows you to control the pan settings of every clip in your project individually, and it offers some very handy preset pan settings to speed your work.

Stereo vs. Surround

With stereo output, there are two speakers, so panning is limited to left and right. You can specify whether any particular audio clip will play out of only the left speaker, only the right speaker, equally out of both speakers, or anything in between. You can even keyframe the sound so it starts in one speaker and then moves to the other.

With surround sound, there are five speakers to pan among. (Technically, there are six, but the sixth is just a subwoofer, so typically that one just plays back low-frequency sounds, regardless of which speaker the rest of the clip plays through.)

No matter how many tracks (or how few) any particular source clip might contain, you must establish the pan mode for each *project*. By default, all projects are set to surround mode, which can be a little confusing, since most projects are still distributed in stereo. Fortunately, it's very easy to switch from one to the other.

To change a project from surround mode to stereo (or vice versa):

1. If the Project Library is showing, select the project you want to modify; or, if the project is already open in the Timeline, click anywhere in the Timeline to make that window active.

2. Choose File > Project Properties, or press Command-J.

   The Project Library opens (if it wasn't open already), and the Inspector opens to display the project's properties **A**.

3. In the Properties Inspector, click the Customize Settings button (the wrench icon in the lower-right corner of the Inspector) **B**.

   The Project Properties dialog opens.

4. In the Audio and Render Properties section, click the pop-up menu for Audio Channels, select Stereo (or Surround), and then click OK **C**.

   You can verify the current status in the header area of the Project Properties Inspector **D**.

   The audio meters will display two meters for stereo projects and six meters for surround projects.

TIP If you're planning to work in surround, it's important that you connect surround-capable speakers to your Mac. This requires using a dedicated 5.1 sound card or, alternatively, a special mini-Toslink cable that will fit in the Mac's audio output port. There are also some USB-enabled 5.1 speaker sets. You'll also likely need to use Apple's MIDI setup application to configure the audio. For more information, see the documentation that came with your Mac.

Customize Settings button

A Press Command-J to open the project's properties, which appear in the Inspector.

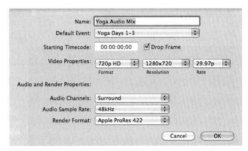

B Open the Project Properties dialog to access the Audio Channels setting.

C Set the Audio Channels setting to Stereo.

D You can see the current Audio Channels setting displayed at the top of the Project Properties Inspector.

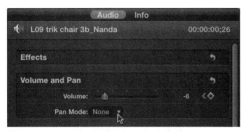

E In the Audio Inspector, set the Pan Mode option to Stereo Left/Right.

F The Pan Amount slider is where you adjust the pan values.

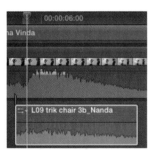

G Position the playhead on the frame where you want the pan effect to begin.

H Click the Add Keyframe button prior to adjusting the Pan slider.

Panning for Stereo

If you're working in a stereo project, panning your audio is very straightforward: You simply need to decide how much sound should come out of the left speaker and how much out of the right speaker for each individual clip in your project.

To set the audio panning setting for a clip in a stereo project:

1. Select a clip in the project, and open the Audio Inspector **E**.

2. In the Volume and Pan section, set the Pan Mode pop-up menu to Stereo Left/Right.

   The Pan Amount slider appears **F**.

3. Adjust the Pan Amount slider to the desired pan setting.

To keyframe audio panning for a clip in a stereo project:

1. Select a clip in the Timeline, open the Inspector, and click Audio to open the Audio pane.

2. Position your playhead in the Timeline to the frame where you want to add the first keyframe **G**.

3. In the Volume and Pan section of the Inspector, set the Pan Mode pop-up menu to Stereo Left/Right.

   The Pan Amount slider appears.

4. Click the Add Keyframe button to the right of the Pan Amount slider **H**.

5. Set the Pan slider to the desired position.

6. Move the playhead in the Timeline to the position where you want to add the next keyframe.

continues on next page

7. To see Pan keyframes in the Timeline, choose Clip > Show Audio Animation, or press Control-A 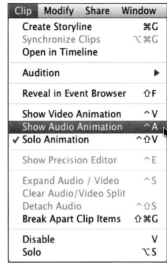.

The Audio Animation window appears in the Timeline, showing your pan keyframes ●.

8. Repeat steps 3–6 until all the desired keyframes have been set.

To modify pan keyframes in the Timeline:

1. Select the clip in the Timeline you want to modify, and make sure the Audio Animation window is showing (as described in step 7 in the previous exercise) ●.

2. In the Audio Animation window, click the Expand Graph button ●.

3. Drag the keyframes horizontally to change their location in time, or drag them vertically to change the pan value ●.

TIP You can adjust the keyframes location in time without expanding the graph. Just drag them horizontally.

TIP You can also navigate to the frame where the keyframe is located and use the slider in the Audio Inspector to change the Pan setting.

4. Once you're finished, choose Clip > Hide Audio Animation or press Control-A (or click the Close button in the Timeline) to hide the Audio Animation window.

① Turn on audio animation to see pan keyframes in the Timeline.

① Audio keyframes can be seen (and manipulated) in the Audio Animation window.

Expand Graph button

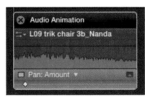

① Turn on audio animation for the clip you want to affect.

Close button

① It's not until you add a second keyframe that you create a change over time.

① Adjust the keyframes either horizontally or vertically. The Info window shows the new value or frame number (as shown here).

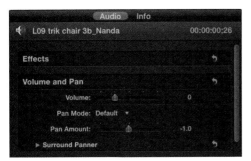

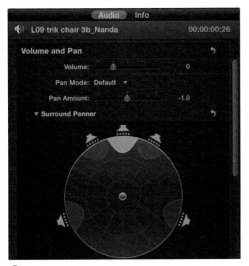

N Set the Pan Mode pop-up menu to Default to enable the Surround slider.

O Click the disclosure triangle to expose the Surround Panner.

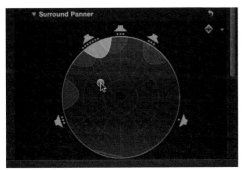

P Drag the center point toward one of the speaker icons to make the sound come out more from that speaker.

Panning for Surround

When working in surround, things get a little bit more complicated; you need to decide which of the five different speakers you want the sound to come out of.

Fortunately, FCP has an intuitive Surround Panner that lets you visualize the speakers and pan accordingly.

To set the audio panning setting for a clip in a surround project:

1. Select a clip in the project, and open the Audio Inspector.

2. In the Volume and Pan section, set the Pan Mode pop-up menu to Default **N**.

   The Pan Amount slider and a disclosure triangle that reads "Surround Panner" appear.

3. Click the disclosure triangle to reveal the Surround Panner **O**.

4. Click or drag the center point in the Surround Panner to the location where you want the sound to come out.

   ▶ The closer you drag the center point toward a specific speaker, the more the sound will come out of that speaker **P**.

   ▶ The closer to the center of the Surround Panner, the more the sound will come out of all speakers equally.

TIP You can disable a speaker entirely by clicking it directly. This will make the sound ignore that channel.

To keyframe audio panning for a clip in a stereo project:

1. Select a clip in the Timeline, open the Inspector, and click Audio to open the Audio pane.

2. Position your playhead in the Timeline to the frame where you want the first keyframe added.

3. In the Volume and Pan section of the Inspector, set the Pan Mode pop-up menu to Default.

   The Pan Amount slider and a collapsed Surround Panner appear.

4. Click the disclosure triangle to reveal the Surround Panner **Q**.

5. In the upper-right corner of the Surround Panner, click the Add Keyframe button.

6. Click or drag in the Surround Panner to move the handle to the location where you want the sound to come out, as described in the previous task.

7. Move the playhead in the Timeline to the position where you want the next keyframe added.

8. Repeat steps 5–7 until all the desired keyframes have been set.

TIP To view or modify panning keyframes in the Timeline, see "Panning for Stereo" earlier in the chapter.

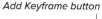

Add Keyframe button

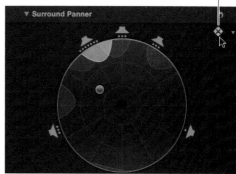

Q When you position the pointer over the Surround Panner, an Add Keyframe button appears in the upper-right corner.

Volume and Pan

Volume: 0

Pan Mode: Default (edited) ▾

Pan Amount: -1.0

▾ **Surround Panner**

<◇> ▾

Ⓡ Click the Reset button next to a specific parameter to remove all panning keyframes and adjustments, or click the Reset button for the entire Volume and Pan category to reset all parameters to their default settings.

To reset pan settings:

1. In the Audio Inspector, make sure the pan parameters you want to reset are visible.

2. Click the Reset button for the slider or for the Surround Panner as needed Ⓡ.

   Resetting removes all keyframes and resets the parameter to its default value.

Panning Presets

While dragging around in the Surround Panner is fun, it's often not the most effective or precise way to get good panning results.

FCP includes a variety of panning presets that allow you to make common but complex surround panning effects using a simple, single slider.

For example, if you want a sound effect to move from the surround speakers to the front speakers, you can choose the Back to Front preset. With that preset selected, the Pan Amount slider will allow you to pan the sound between the rear speakers and the front speakers using a regular one-dimensional slider.

Or if you want to have a sound move from the Left Surround speaker to the Right Front speaker, you can choose the preset of that name, and the Pan Amount slider will pan the sound along that specific axis.

These presets allow you to turn potentially complex panning operations into simple, reproducible tasks.

To apply a panning preset:

1. In the Volume and Pan section of the Audio Inspector, choose a selection from the Pan Mode pop-up menu 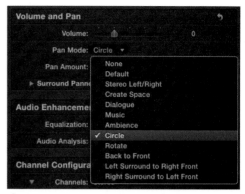.

2. To see what the preset does, click the disclosure triangle to reveal the Surround Panner, and drag the Pan Amount slider from left to right, observing what happens in the Surround Panner **T**.

3. Keyframe the Pan Amount slider using the technique described in the earlier "Panning for Surround" section.

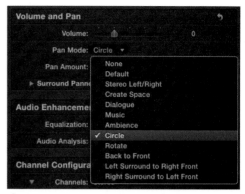

S Choose from any of the presets in the Pan Mode pop-up menu.

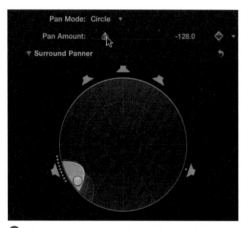

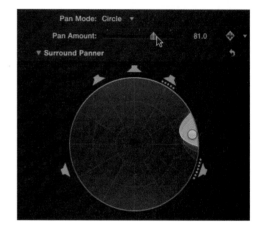

T Observe the movement in the Surround Panner while dragging the Pan Amount slider to see what the different pan modes do. In this example, the Circle mode rotates the sound around the room in a circular motion.

Audio Channel Configuration

You can configure clips with multiple audio channels so FCP can determine which channels are included when a clip is edited into a project. Additionally, you can assign whether those channels should be considered mono, stereo, surround, and so on. This setting can be autodetected during import (for more, see Chapter 6, "Importing Footage").

When you break apart audio clips, the way they're broken apart is determined based on the configuration assigned in the Audio Inspector.

Changing audio configuration can be done at any point during the editing process, so you can modify which channels are included (and how they're mixed) after a clip has been edited into a project.

To configure audio channels:

1. Select a clip containing audio in the Event Browser or Timeline.

2. Open the Audio Inspector Ⓐ.

3. In the Channel Configuration section, click the Channels pop-up, and choose from one of the options in the menu Ⓑ.

   The number of channels in the audio clip determines the options available in this menu. If you are unsure of how the channels should be configured, you can monitor the individual channels discretely.

Ⓐ Open the Audio Inspector, and scroll to the Channel Configuration section.

Ⓑ The options in the Channels pop-up changes based on the number of channels and their potential configurations.

To preview individual audio channels:

1. In the Channel Configuration section of the Audio Inspector, position the pointer over an individual audio channel .

   A skimmer appears for the channel.

2. Skim the clip or press the Spacebar to play the individual channel.

3. Move the pointer to another channel, and repeat step 2.

To enable or disable specific audio channels:

- Click the checkbox to the left of the individual channels to enable the tracks you want to include and to disable the tracks you want to exclude **D**.

TIP Disabling certain channels can be especially helpful on compound clips that contain multiple (potentially duplicate) audio channels.

C You can skim individual channels, or you can position the pointer over one and press the Spacebar to hear just that channel.

D Choose which individual channels should be included when you hear the clip play in a project. In this example, the first track is enabled, and the second track is disabled.

12

Audio Effects

The previous chapter covered the most important and fundamental aspects of working with audio: adjusting volume and working with the pan settings. But you can do much more to improve and enhance your sound or, in some cases, to fix mistakes that were made during production.

Final Cut Pro has a collection of audio-related features designed for these purposes. Some of these tools are automatic—based on the analysis you can optionally perform during ingest. Using that data, Final Cut Pro can automatically find and remove hums and other background noise, adjust your volume, and enable you to match the tone and timbre of one clip to that of another.

Additionally, there are a large number of highly customizable audio filters that you can add manually to perform a range of effects such as equalization, compression, frequency modulation, and a host of other audio-specific tasks.

This chapter will cover both of these types of audio effects.

Automatic Audio Enhancements

One of the more significant new features in Final Cut Pro is the ability to perform an optional analysis on your source footage, either at ingest or at any later point during the editing process.

You can analyze both video and audio clips for a variety of elements. The video side of things is covered in Chapter 6, "Ingesting Footage." The audio analysis evaluates your clips—looking for background noise and electrical hum—as well as determines each clip's optimal volume and equalization settings.

Analysis can be performed during ingest or at any point after your clips have been imported.

To analyze audio files during import:

- In the Audio section of the Import Files dialog, select the "Analyze and fix audio problems" checkbox **A**.

TIP You can also analyze and fix audio problems when you import directly from a camera using the Camera Import window.

To analyze audio files after import:

1. Select the clip or clips you want to analyze, and *do one of the following*:
   - ▶ Choose Modify > Analyze and Fix.
   - ▶ Right-click the selected clips, and, from the shortcut menu, choose Analyze and Fix.

   The Analyze and Fix sheet opens **B**.

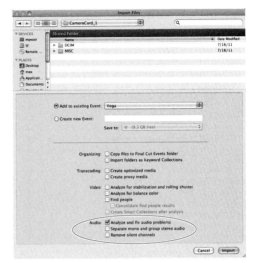

A When Importing, choose the "Analyze and fix audio problems" checkbox.

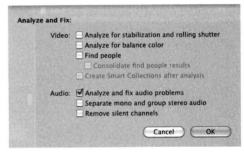

B Analyze imported clips by opening the Analyze and Fix sheet.

C Choose Auto Enhance Audio from the Auto Enhancement menu.

Applies automatic enhancements

D In the Audio Enhancements Inspector, click Auto Enhance.

2. In the Audio section, select the "Analyze and fix audio problems" checkbox, and click OK.

The analysis begins in the background.

Applying Enhancements

Once your files have been analyzed, you have several options for implementing that data in order to improve your clips' audio.

You can enable Auto Audio Enhancement, which applies enhancement settings for whatever elements Final Cut Pro thinks need improving, and you can manually control each of the enhancement options in the Audio Enhancements pane of the Inspector.

To enable Auto Audio Enhancement:

■ Select a clip, and *do one of the following*:

▶ Click the Auto Enhancement menu in the toolbar and choose Auto Enhance Audio, or press Option-Command-A **C**.

▶ If the Audio Enhancements Inspector is already showing, click the Auto Enhance button at the bottom of the Inspector **D**.

All audio enhancements are automatically applied as needed. See "Specific Audio Enhancements" for more details.

To open the Audio Enhancements Inspector:

- *Do one of the following:*

  - ▶ Click the Auto Enhancement menu in the toolbar, and choose Show Audio Enhancements .

  - ▶ In the Audio Inspector, click the Show Audio Enhancements button **F**.

  TIP If audio enhancements have been applied, the Show Audio Enhancements button turns blue **G**.

  - ▶ In the Clip Actions menu, choose Audio Enhancements **H**.

  - ▶ Press Command-8.

  The Audio Enhancements Inspector opens.

E To open the Audio Enhancements Inspector, select Show Audio Enhancements from the Auto Enhancement menu.

Opens the Audio Enhancements Inspector

F In the Audio Inspector, click the Show Audio Enhancements button.

Click here to open the Clip Actions menu.

H The Clip Actions menu also provides access to the Audio Enhancements Inspector.

G The button turns blue once you've enabled one of the enhancements.

Return to Audio Inspector

I To return from the Audio Enhancements Inspector to the Audio Inspector, click the button in the upper-left corner.

J A green check mark icon indicates the clip has been analyzed and needs no correction.

K A yellow hazard icon indicates that corrections are necessary.

L Once a correction has been applied, the status updates to descriptive text.

M If a clip hasn't yet been analyzed, you'll see a rendering-in-progress indicator.

To close the Audio Enhancements Inspector:

- *Do one of the following*:
  - ▸ Click the Return to Audio Inspector button in the upper-left corner of the Audio Enhancements Inspector **I**.
  - ▸ Click the Auto Enhancements menu in the toolbar, and choose Hide Audio Enhancements.
  - ▸ Press Command-8.

  The Audio Enhancements Inspector closes.

Specific Audio Enhancements

Once the Audio Enhancements Inspector is open, you can observe which settings Final Cut Pro thinks should be applied and which have already been applied, and you can modify the specific settings of the different enhancements.

- A green icon with a check mark indicates that no correction is necessary **J**.
- A yellow hazard icon indicates that Final Cut Pro recommends enabling the correction **K**.
- When a correction is applied, the Activation checkbox turns blue, and the icon changes to text describing the status of the effect **L**.

If you open the Audio Enhancements Inspector before a clip has been analyzed, it is analyzed immediately. While the analysis is underway, you will see a rotating progress indicator **M**.

Loudness

Loudness is a way to make your clips sound "louder" without having to actually adjust the clip's volume.

The Loudness setting applies a compressor effect to the audio clip. A compressor reduces the *dynamic range* of the clip by attenuating the peaks in the audio signal. This makes the loudest and quietest parts of the clip more uniform, which means you can turn the overall clip volume up without those peaks touching 0 dB.

TIP **Dynamic range is the distance in decibels between the loudest and quietest moments within a clip.**

To apply the automatic compressor:

1. Click the blue Activation checkbox for the Loudness section in the Audio Enhancements Inspector .

2. Adjust the Amount slider to increase the amount of compression.

3. Adjust the Uniformity slider to control how much dynamic range is affected.

Background Noise Removal

If Final Cut Pro detects a constant noise signal in the background of your audio, a frequency-specific noise gate is applied to remove the offending noise.

The Amount slider allows you to customize how much noise to remove. If you select too high of a setting, the remaining sound will begin to sound hollow and flanged.

Activation checkbox

N Enable the correction by clicking the Activation checkbox.

O Adjust the slider to create the optimal noise reduction setting.

P Choose 50 Hz in Europe and 60 Hz in North America.

To reduce background noise:

1. Click the blue Activation checkbox for the Background Noise Removal section in the Audio Enhancements Inspector.

2. Adjust the Amount slider until the noise is reduced but the rest of the signal still sounds natural **O**.

    The background noise is removed.

TIP It's often better to allow a little background noise rather than create an unnatural-sounding or over-processed clip.

Hum Removal

If electrical interference is observed in the audio clip, Final Cut Pro will determine whether the noise is of the 50 Hz (European) or 60 Hz (North American) variety, and the offending frequency (and its related harmonic frequencies) are attenuated to remove the hum.

To reduce electrical hum:

1. Click the blue Activation checkbox for the Hum Removal section in the Audio Enhancements Inspector **P**.

2. Choose the 50 Hz or 60 Hz frequency.

    The hum is removed.

Audio Equalization

Equalization (EQ) is a fancy word to describe the process of assigning different volume settings for the various audio frequencies in your audio clip.

For example, equalization allows you to turn down only the low frequencies of a clip to remove an unwanted rumble. Or you might boost a certain range of midtone frequencies that contain the bulk of an interview subject's voice to help make it pop out from the background noise.

Equalization is incredibly powerful and extremely common. There are hundreds of common EQ presets that can be implemented in a variety of circumstances. For example, a *low-pass* filter is an EQ filter that lets the low frequencies pass through the filter, thereby attenuating the high frequencies. A *high-pass* filter does the opposite. A *notch* filter lets you select a specific frequency range and control its volume separately from the rest of the clip. The Hum Remover is an example of a notch filter.

Final Cut Pro contains a built-in equalizer in the Audio Inspector for every audio clip. You can choose to apply a preset, make manual frequency volume adjustments, or match the frequency map from one clip to another.

To apply an equalization preset:

1. Select a clip in the Timeline, and open the Audio Inspector **A**.

2. In the Audio Enhancements section, click the Equalization pop-up menu, and select a preset from the list **B**.

   The EQ preset is applied to the clip.

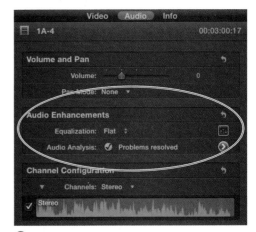

A Select a clip, and open the Audio Inspector.

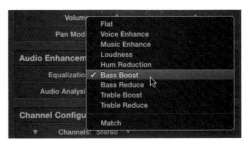

B Choose one of the EQ presets from the pop-up menu.

Graphic Equalizer

C In the Audio Inspector there is an icon to access the Graphic Equalizer.

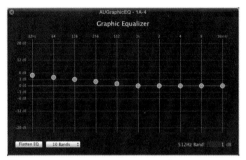

D The Graphical Equalizer window

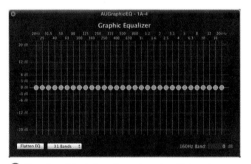

E The Graphical Equalizer showing 31 bands

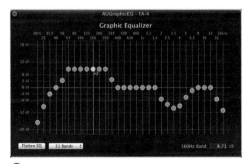

F To adjust multiple bands together, drag a box around them and adjust any of the selected sliders.

To apply a manual EQ setting:

1. Select a clip in the Timeline, and open the Audio Inspector.

2. In the Audio Enhancements section, click the Graphic Equalizer button **C**.

   The Graphic Equalizer window opens **D**.

3. Click the Frequency Bands pop-up menu to choose between 10 and 31 frequency bands **E**.

   TIP Thirty-one bands provides much more precise frequency control.

4. Adjust the individual volume sliders to change the volume for different frequencies within your clip.

   The sliders to the left control the lower frequencies, and the sliders to the right control the higher frequencies.

5. Drag a box around multiple volume sliders, and then move any of the selected sliders to move the group of sliders together **F**.

6. To reset all sliders to their default (neutral) settings, click Flatten EQ.

   The equalizer is reset.

7. To close the Graphic Equalizer, click the close box in the upper-left corner.

   The Equalization pop-up menu displays Custom **G**.

G Once you have manually changed the Graphical Equalizer, the pop-up menu displays Custom.

Matching Audio

Final Cut Pro allows you to match the sound of one clip to that of another clip. When clips are analyzed, a *frequency map* is saved that identifies the relative volumes of the various frequencies. That map is then translated into the arrangement of sliders in the equalizer, and those settings can be copied from one clip to another.

To match an audio clip's EQ to that of another clip:

1. Select a clip in the Timeline, and open the Audio Inspector.

2. *Do one of the following*:

 - In the Audio Enhancements section, click the Equalization pop-up, and choose Match ⓗ.

     ▸ Choose Modify > Match Audio, or press Shift-Command-M.

     The Match Audio window appears ⓘ.

3. Click another clip in the Timeline or in an event.

     The frequency map of the clicked clip is applied to the selected clip.

4. Click Apply Match in the Match Audio window ⓙ.

     A custom equalization setting is applied to the selected clip to approximate the sound of the clip to which you chose to match it.

To remove equalization:

 - In the Audio Enhancements section of the Audio Inspector, click the Equalization pop-up menu, and choose Flat ⓚ.

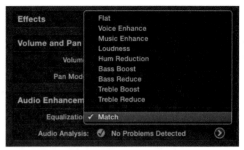

ⓗ Choose Match from the EQ presets pop-up, or press Shift-Command-M.

ⓘ The Match Audio window contains instructions to help you select the new audio clip.

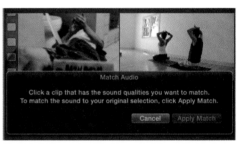

ⓙ The Match setting applies a custom EQ setting based on the frequency map of the matched clip.

ⓚ To remove all EQ settings, choose Flat from the EQ Presets pop-up menu.

Effects Browser icon

Ⓐ Click the Effects Browser icon to open the Effects Browser.

Adding Audio Filters

In addition to the automatic audio enhancements, Final Cut Pro contains a large number of audio filters you can apply to your audio clips to produce a wide range of effects, including echo and reverberation, pitch adjustments, specialized types of equalization, modulation, and many others. Some of these filters are plug-ins from Apple Logic. Third-party Logic plug-ins will also appear in Final Cut Pro.

The Effects Browser

Audio filters are found in the Effects Browser, in eight categories: Distortion, Echo, EQ, Levels, Modulation, Spaces, Specialized, and Voices. Within each category, the effects are inexplicably divided into subgroups called Final Cut, Logic, and Mac OS X.

Some of the items labeled as "Final Cut" are not specific filters; rather, they are presets that utilize other filters to create easy-to-use effects. These allow you to add a single effect, such as Vintage Radios, Cathedral, or Cartoon Animals.

To open the Effects Browser:

- Click the Effects Browser icon, or press Command-5.

  The Effects Browser opens **Ⓐ**.

The Effects Browser displays all the effects available to you, including third-party Logic plug-ins if you have any installed. Each effect is displayed with a thumbnail icon and a descriptive name. The Effects Browser contains both audio and video effects.

The Effects Browser has two parts: the stack, where the list of effects is displayed; and a sidebar, which contains category names. Scroll the sidebar down to access the Audio effects.

You can find specific effects either by searching for a particular name or by browsing through the various categories.

To find specific audio effects:

- *Do one of the following*:
  - ▶ Type the name of the effect you're looking for in the search field at the bottom of the Effects Browser 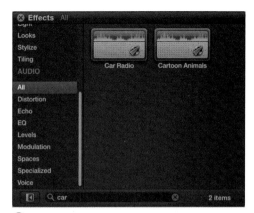.

    The stack is filtered to show only effects containing the letters in the search field.

  TIP Clear the search field by clicking the circled X at the right edge of the field or by pressing Escape.

  - ▶ Click one of the category names in the sidebar on the left side of the Effects Browser, and scroll through the main stack area on the right **C**.

    The stack is filtered by category.

  TIP Hide or show the sidebar by clicking the Show/Hide Sidebar button in the lower-left corner of the Effects Browser.

B Search for a specific effect by typing in the search field.

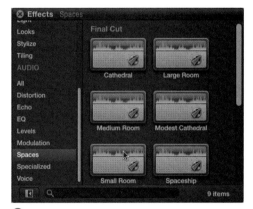

C Click a category in the sidebar to filter the list.

D Be sure to select a clip in the Timeline first, then select one of the audio effects, and finally press the Spacebar to preview the effect.

Previewing Audio Effects

You can preview what each effect sounds like prior to adding it to your project. This enables you to experiment with a variety of effects quickly.

To preview an audio effect:

- Select a clip in the Timeline; then click an effect in the Effects Browser, and press the Spacebar to hear a preview of the effect **D**.

  A preview of the effect is played.

To apply an audio effect:

- Select a clip in the Timeline to which you want to apply the audio effect, and then *do one of the following*:

  ▶ In the Effects Browser, double-click an audio effect.

  ▶ Drag the audio effect from the Effects Browser to a clip in the Timeline.

  The effect is applied to the clip.

Modifying Audio Effects

Once you have applied audio effects to a clip, many audio effects have parameters you can modify to customize the effect and tailor it to work with your particular shot.

Some effects have parameters that you can modify directly in the Inspector, others have custom interface elements that must be controlled in their own window, and some effects have a combination of such parameters.

To modify parameters in the Inspector:

1. Select the clip in the Timeline.

2. Open the Audio Inspector .

3. In the Effects category, identify the effect you want to modify, and choose menu items from pop-up menus, drag sliders, and click checkboxes as desired.

To open custom interface windows:

1. In the Audio Inspector, click the custom interface icon **F**.

   A new window opens containing the custom filter interface **G**.

2. Modify the controls within the Custom Interface window.

   TIP You can continue to preview a clip while the Custom Interface window is open, allowing you to hear the results of your changes before you close the window.

3. Close the Custom Interface window.

   The effect settings are applied.

To disable an audio effect:

- In the Effects section of the Audio Inspector, click the blue activation checkbox to the left of the effect name **H**.

  The blue light goes out and the audio effect is disabled.

To delete an audio effect:

- In the Effects section of the Audio Inspector, click the name of the effect, and press Delete.

E When audio effects are applied to a clip, their controls appear in the Effects category of the Audio Inspector.

Custom Interface buttons

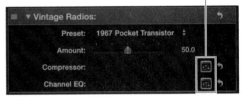

F Any effect that has a custom interface window will have the Custom Interface button to the right of the parameter name in the Audio Inspector.

G Click the Custom Interface button to open the Custom Interface.

Activation checkbox

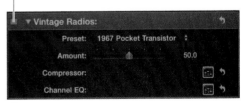

H To disable an audio effect without deleting it, simply click the blue activation checkbox.

A Position your playhead where you want the recording to begin.

B Open the Record Audio window.

C Choose the event in which you want to save the new media files that recording audio creates.

Recording Live Audio

Final Cut Pro allows you to record audio directly to the Timeline using any microphone built into, or connected to, your Mac. This allows you to add voice-overs, record *foley* (custom sound effects), or create any other sound you want to add directly to your project.

TIP For best results, use headphones. This allows you to hear the existing audio in the Timeline without the microphone hearing that sound and creating a duplicate or unwanted echo.

To record live audio into your project:

1. Position the playhead at the beginning of the section where you want to record **A**.

TIP It's a good idea to give yourself a little lead-in time, so you might want to set the playhead a few seconds before the frame where you want to begin recording.

2. Choose Window > Record Audio **B**.

   The Record Audio window opens.

3. In the Record Audio window, set the event where you want your new audio saved in the Destination pop-up menu **C**.

continues on next page

4. Select the microphone you will be recording from.

5. Practice the recording while watching the audio levels in the Record Audio window.

6. Adjust the Microphone Gain slider so your practice recording generates solid green bars, making sure you don't hit the red **D**.

7. Adjust the Monitor settings and level so you can hear the existing audio in your headphones but so that the sound will not bleed into the new recording.

8. Click the red record button at the top of the window **E**.

Recording starts immediately, causing the project to begin playing.

9. When you are done recording, click the red record button again to stop.

Recording is stopped.

A new audio-only clip is added to your project **F**.

10. If you're unsatisfied with the recording, repeat steps 8 and 9.

Each new recording will add a clip to the Timeline, attached at the frame where the recording started **G**. The clip's file is stored in the Event folder you selected.

D Be sure to practice your recording and get a good audio level (don't touch the red).

E When you're ready, click the record button to begin recording.

F When you're finished recording, a new connected audio-only clip is added to your project.

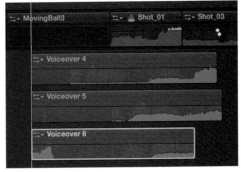

G Make as many audio recordings as you want. Each one will be added to the Timeline.

Basic Compositing

Final Cut Pro is far more than just a video editor. It enables you to perform a wide range of special effects, including a variety of *compositing* techniques. Compositing simply means having more than one image on-screen at the same time. This could be a split screen, a title superimposed over video, or an animated dinosaur chasing a live-action alpaca farmer in outer space. Your only limitation is your own imagination (and your production budget).

To see two (or more) images on-screen simultaneously, you need to scale or move the objects so they don't entirely overlap, make them partially transparent, or employ *alpha channels* (defined areas of transparency, such as the outline of a logo).

Final Cut Pro makes all of this extremely easy, utilizing intuitive controls in the Viewer and the Inspector and allowing connected clips in the Timeline to facilitate simultaneous playback of multiple shots.

In This Chapter

Transformations

The most fundamental adjustments you can perform are to change the position, scale, and rotation of an object. These manipulations are commonly called *transformations*.

Every object in Final Cut Pro can be modified in these three basic ways, and you can perform such actions either graphically in the Viewer or numerically in the Inspector.

To change the scale of a clip in the Viewer:

1. Select the clip in the Timeline.

2. In the Viewer, click the Apply Transformation button **A**.

   The transformation controls appear in the Viewer.

3. Drag any of the blue handles of the clip inward to shrink the clip and drag them outward to enlarge the clip.

   ▸ Dragging a corner point scales the clip uniformly (maintaining its aspect ratio) **B**.

   ▸ Dragging one of the side handles squeezes or stretches the clip horizontally **C**.

   ▸ Dragging one of the top or bottom handles squeezes or stretches the clip vertically **D**.

   TIP Hold the Shift key while dragging to unconstrain corner-point adjustments or to constrain side-handle adjustments.

4. When you're finished, click the Done button.

   The adjustment is applied to the clip.

Apply Transformation button

A Click the Apply Transformation button to enable the on-screen controls.

B Drag from the corner to maintain the clip's aspect ratio.

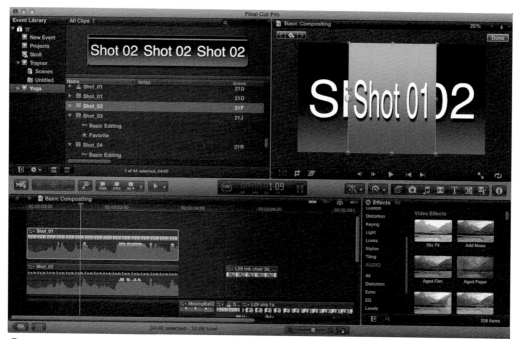

C Drag from one of the side handles to squeeze or stretch the image horizontally.

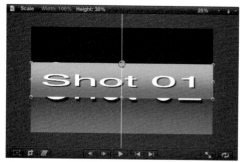

D Drag from the top or bottom handle to stretch the image vertically.

To change the position of a clip in the Viewer:

1. Select the clip in the Timeline.

2. In the Viewer, right-click and choose Transform from the shortcut menu **E**.

   The transformation controls appear in the Viewer.

3. Drag anywhere in the body of the object to move it to a new position **F**.

4. When you're finished, click Done.

   The transformation is applied to the clip.

To change the rotation of a clip in the Viewer:

1. Select the clip in the Timeline.

2. In the Viewer, click the Apply Transformation button, or press Shift-T **G**.

   The transformation controls appear in the Viewer.

E Right-click anywhere in the Viewer and choose Transform to enable the on-screen controls.

F Drag anywhere in the body of the object to reposition it.

G Press Shift-T to enable the transformation on-screen controls.

Rotate handle

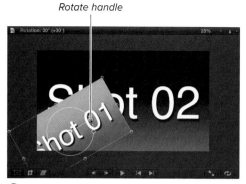

Drag the Rotate handle to rotate the image.

3. Drag the Rotate handle to rotate the clip .

TIP The farther from the center point you move your mouse, the more precise your rotation adjustments will be.

TIP Hold Shift to constrain rotation movements to only horizontal or only vertical (depending on the direction of mouse movement).

‣ Hold Shift to constrain rotation movements to 45° increments.

4. When you're finished, click Done.

The transformation is applied to the clip.

Manage Layer Order

Remember that whichever clip is higher up in the Timeline will obscure the clips beneath it .

At any point, you can rearrange the clips vertically in the Timeline to change the display order in the Viewer.

You must use connected clips to perform compositing, but you don't need to put all the clips above the primary storyline. As long as the clip in the primary storyline is not completely obscuring what's below it, you can connect clips beneath the primary storyline too .

Clips on higher tracks obscure the clips beneath them.

You can connect clips beneath the primary storyline too!

To transform a clip numerically:

1. Select the clip in the Timeline.

2. Open the Video Inspector **K**.

3. In the Transform category, adjust the Position, Rotation, Scale, or Anchor parameters.

   This allows you to maintain precision, which can be important for accurately matching the settings of two or more clips.

To reset transform settings:

- In the Video Inspector, click the Reset button in the Transform section.

  All transformation settings are returned to their defaults.

Controlling Zoom Level

As you do more transformations and other compositing tasks, you may find yourself wanting to zoom out on the Viewer so you can see where the edge of an object when it is offscreen.

To zoom out on the Viewer:

- *Do one of the following*:

  ▶ Click the Zoom menu at the top of the Viewer, and choose a smaller number **L**.

  ▶ Click on the Viewer window to make it active, then press Command – (minus).

TIP The minimum zoom level is **12 percent** (which you can only get to using the keyboard shortcut). If you have moved an object too far offscreen and you can't see or grab it, open the Video Inspector for that clip and reset the transformation controls to restore the clip's Position parameter to its default value.

Reset button

K The Video Inspector has numerical controls for all transformation settings.

L Set the Viewer zoom level so you can see objects outside the viewable area.

Animating Transformations

You can animate all of these transformations so they change over time. For more about animating transformations, see Chapter 21, "Keyframing Effects."

Spatial Conformations

Final Cut Pro automatically scales clips that do not natively match the project frame size. You can select how the object is resized:

- The Fit option scales the clip so its larger dimension is no larger than the corresponding dimension in the project ⓜ.

- The Fill option scales the clip so its smaller dimension matches the corresponding dimension in the project ⓝ.

- None leaves the clip at its native size, regardless of how much it exceeds the visible area in the Viewer ⓞ.

ⓜ Fit scales the clip, ensuring that the entire image fits within the project dimensions.

ⓝ Fit scales the clip so it fills the frame, even if some of the object exceeds the visible area in the Viewer.

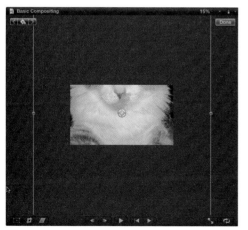

ⓞ None sets the clip to 100 percent scale. In this example, the image size is much larger than the project size, so the bounding box greatly exceeds the visible area.

To change the spatial conform settings:

1. Select the clip in the Timeline, and open the Video Inspector 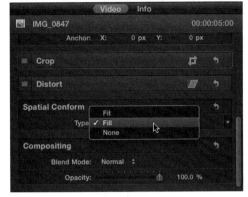.

2. In the Spatial Conform section, choose a setting from the pop-up menu.

   The Spatial Conform settings are updated.

TIP Spatial conforming does not change the Scale slider in the Transform section, so you can continue to scale the "conformed" object.

Ⓟ The Spatial Conform section allows you to choose Fit, Fill, or None.

Apply Crop button

A Click the Apply Crop button to enable the on-screen controls.

Trim button

B Choose Trim mode from the choices in the upper left.

C Cropping in Trim mode shows exactly what you will get. Empty space is left in the areas you crop out.

Crop Effects

While transformations allow you to scale, move, and rotate a clip, you need to switch to a different mode to reframe, or *crop*, the image. In fact, the cropping mode has three different submodes: Trim, Crop-Fit, and Ken Burns.

Trim Mode

Trim mode works the same way the Crop tool worked in previous versions of Final Cut Pro.

In Trim mode, you drag the edges of the clip, dynamically hiding part of the image from view as you drag. The clip gets smaller because you've cropped off one or more of the edges. If no clip is behind the cropped clip, that area will show black.

The advantage to using the Trim mode is that it's WYSIWYG; the Viewer shows you exactly what your finished output will look like as you crop the image.

The disadvantage is that the word *Trim* already has two completely different meanings related to video editing. Did we really need a third?

To crop a clip using Trim mode:

1. Select a clip in the Timeline.

2. In the Viewer, click the Apply Crop button **A**.

   The crop controls appear on the clip.

3. Click the Trim button at the top of the Viewer to make sure you're in Trim mode **B**.

4. Drag the handles on the edge of the clip to limit the visible area of the clip **C**.

continues on next page

TIP Press Shift while dragging to constrain the crop to the aspect ratio of the original clip.

TIP Once you begin cropping, you can click in the middle of the cropped area and drag it to reframe the selection **D**.

5. When you're done cropping, click the Done button in the upper-right corner of the Viewer.

Crop-Fit Mode

Crop-Fit mode is less WYSIWYG than Trim mode, but some users might find it more intuitive. In Crop-Fit mode, you can always see the whole image you're cropping, and you just draw a little box around the part of the image you want to keep.

When you click the Done button, the selected part of the image is automatically scaled up to fill the screen. Unless you're working with very high-resolution footage, this scaling can reveal artifacts or make your video look out of focus, so beware of how much you crop the image. The smaller the box you draw, the more scaling that will be required.

To crop a clip using Crop-Fit mode:

1. Select a clip in the Timeline.

2. Right-click anywhere in the Viewer, and choose Crop from the shortcut menu **E**.

   The crop controls appear on the clip.

3. Click the Crop button at the top of the Viewer to make sure you're in Crop-Fit mode **F**.

   A frame appears on top of the image. The area inside the frame is your cropped selection.

D While cropping, you can click the crop selection and drag it to a new position.

E Right-click the Viewer and choose Crop to enable the crop on-screen controls.

Crop button

F Click the Crop button to switch to Crop-Fit mode.

Done button

G The outline of the frame indicates the area that will be visible when you click Done.

H When you confirm the edit by clicking Done, the selected area is scaled up to fill the Viewer.

I Press Shift-C to show the on-screen controls.

4. Drag the frame and adjust its boundaries to identify the specific area you want to select **G**.

TIP Press Option while dragging to crop around the center of the selection.

5. When you're done cropping, click the Done button in the upper-right corner of the Viewer **H**.

The cropped area is scaled up to fill the screen.

Ken Burns Mode

This mode is just like Crop-Fit mode, except there are two boxes. You select a starting frame and an ending frame, and Ken Burns automatically animates your video between the two frames over the duration of the clip—instantly elevating your production to an Emmy Award-type documentary from the 1990s.

To crop a clip using Ken Burns mode:

1. Select a clip in the Timeline.

2. In the Viewer, press Shift-C.

The crop controls appear on the clip **I**.

3. Click the Ken Burns button at the top of the Viewer to make sure you're in Ken Burns mode.

A red box and a green box appear on the image. The green box indicates your starting frame, and the red box indicates your ending frame.

continues on next page

4. Drag the green frame and adjust its boundaries to identify the specific area you want to select for the starting frame .

5. Drag the red frame and adjust its boundaries to identify the specific area you want to select for the ending frame **(K)**.

6. When you're done cropping, click the Preview button to see the animation play **(L)**.

TIP You can reverse the beginning and end frames by clicking the Swap button.

7. Click the Done button in the upper-right corner of the Viewer to confirm your work.

The animation is automatically applied to the clip.

TIP If you later change the duration of a clip with a Ken Burns effect applied, the animation will be updated so it always begins on the first frame and ends on the last frame of the clip.

(J) Position the green box to identify the desired starting frame.

(K) Position the red box to identify the desired ending frame.

Preview Animation button

Swap button

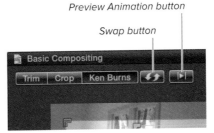

(L) In Ken Burns mode, there are two frames: a green "starting" frame and a red "ending" frame. When you're done cropping, click the Preview button to see the animation play.

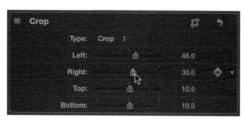

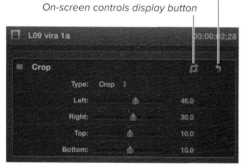

M The Video Inspector contains numerical controls for the Crop settings.

N Choose a crop type from the pop-up menu, and adjust the sliders to crop the image.

Reset button

On-screen controls display button

O Turn on and off the on-screen controls by clicking the blue Crop icon. This is the same as clicking the Apply Crop button in the Viewer.

Cropping from the Inspector

You can also perform Trim and Crop-Fit cropping effects from the Inspector. This allows you to crop your clip using specific numeric values.

To crop numerically:

1. Select a clip in the Timeline, and open the Video Inspector M.

2. In the Crop section, choose the type of cropping you want to apply from the Type pop-up menu N.

TIP Although you can select Ken Burns from the Type pop-up, there are no numeric controls for that type.

3. Adjust the Left, Right, Top, and Bottom sliders to create the cropping effect you desire.

TIP If you plan to crop in the Inspector using Crop-Fit mode, click the Crop icon in the Crop header area to enable the on-screen controls O. Otherwise, the on-screen feedback may be very confusing.

To reset crop settings:

-   In the Crop section of the Video Inspector, click the Reset button.

    All crop settings (Trim, Crop, and Ken Burns) are all reset to their defaults.

Animating Crop Effects

Although the Ken Burns effect is a built-in type of animation, the other two types of crop effects can be animated as well. For more about animating crop effects, see "Keyframing in the Viewer" in Chapter 21.

Distortion

If you want to modify the shape of your clip so the four corners are independently moved from their original positions, you can use Distort mode.

Distorting can create simulated 3D effects, or you can use it to create unusual shapes and unnatural-looking images. Try it! It's fun.

To distort a clip in the Viewer:

1. Select the clip in the Timeline.

2. In the Viewer, click the Apply Distortion button, or press Shift-Command-D **A**.

   The Distort controls appear in the Viewer.

3. Click any of the corner points, and drag them to a new location **B**.

4. When you're finished, click Done.

Apply Distort button

A Click the Apply Distortion button to enable the Distort on-screen controls.

B Distort the image by dragging the corner points to new locations.

Click to expand the distort group

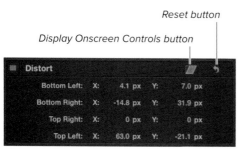

C The Video Inspector has a Distort category that is collapsed by default. Move your mouse over the header, and click Show.

Reset button

Display Onscreen Controls button

D The Inspector has settings to specify the coordinates of the four corner points numerically.

To distort a clip numerically:

1. Select the clip in the Timeline, and open the Video Inspector **C**.

2. Click the Show button that appears when you move your mouse over the Distort header.

   The Distort parameters appear **D**.

   TIP You can turn on the on-screen controls in the Viewer by clicking the Display Onscreen Controls button in the Inspector.

3. Enter precise coordinate values for the four corner points of the selected clip.

   TIP You can switch between Transform, Crop, and Distort modes before ever clicking the Done button.

To reset the Distort settings:

- In the Distort section of the Video Inspector, click the Reset button.

  All Distort settings are reset to their defaults.

Animating Distortions

You can animate distortions so they change over time. For more about animating distortions, see "Keyframing in the Viewer" in Chapter 21.

Compositing Effects

Although virtually all the techniques described in this chapter fall under the category of compositing, Final Cut Pro has a section of controls in the Video Inspector called Compositing. This section deals with the transparency and blend mode of the selected object.

Opacity

Any clip can be made partially or completely transparent. Transparency (called *opacity* in Final Cut Pro) can be controlled either in the Video Inspector or in the Timeline, if you turn on display of the Video Animation Editor.

Because it's a common effect to fade clips in and out, there is a special control in the Video Animation Editor specifically designed to perform such fades.

To adjust clip opacity in the Video Inspector:

1. Select a clip in the Timeline, and open the Video Inspector 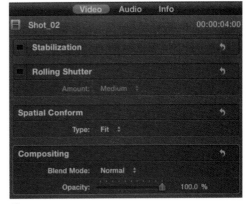.

2. Scroll to the Compositing section, and expand it if necessary.

3. Adjust the Opacity slider.

   The lower the opacity, the more transparent the clip will become 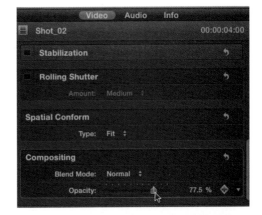. If nothing is beneath the clip in the Timeline, lowering the opacity makes the clip appear to fade out.

A The Inspector has a Compositing section where you can set a clip's opacity.

B The lower the Opacity slider is positioned, the more transparent the image.

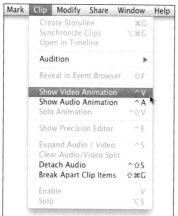

C Enable
the Video
Animation
Editor in the
Clip menu.

To adjust clip opacity in the Timeline:

1. Select the clip in the Timeline.

2. To open the Video Animation Editor, *do one of the following*:

   ▸ Choose Clip > Show Video Animation **C**.

   ▸ Click the clip's Action menu, and choose Show Video Animation **D**.

   ▸ Press Control-V.

   The Video Animation Editor appears above the clip **E**.

continues on next page

Click to open the Action menu.

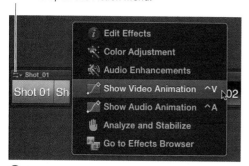

D Open it from the clip Action menu (or press Control-V).

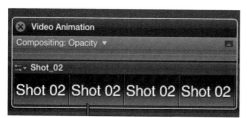

E The Video Animation Editor opens above the clip.

3. Double-click the Opacity bar in the Video Animation Editor 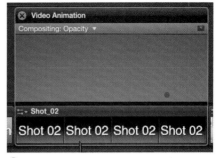.

The Opacity graph expands.

4. Drag the Opacity line down to the desired level **G**.

5. Optionally, Option-click the Opacity line to add keyframes to the line **H**.

You must add at least two keyframes to create a change over time.

TIP Double-click the Opacity graph to collapse it again. You will still be able to see the keyframes and move them in time **I**.

F Double-click the Opacity bar to expand it so you can make changes to it.

G Drag the Opacity line down to make the clip more transparent.

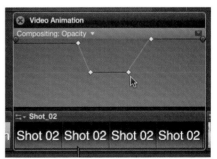

H Option-click the Opacity line to add keyframes.

I When the graph is collapsed, you can still see Opacity keyframes and move them in time.

Fade In handle   Fade Out handle

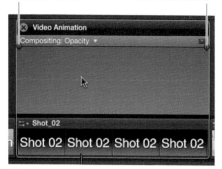

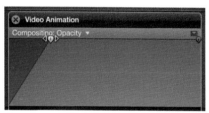

J Opacity graphs in the Video Animation Editor have a built-in Fade In handle and Fade Out handle.

K Drag the Fade In and Fade Out handles to add a fade-in or fade-out to the clip. Here a fade-in is applied.

To fade in and fade out a clip:

1. Perform steps 1 through 3 of the previous task **J**.

2. Drag the Fade In or Fade Out handle from the left or right edge of the Opacity bar in the Video Animation Editor **K**.

   A fade effect is added to the beginning or end of the clip.

3. Click the Close box to hide the Video Animation Editor, or press Control-V.

TIP You can also use Cross Dissolve transition effects to perform a fade-in or fade-out effect. For more on using transition effects, see Chapter 18, "Transition Effects."

For more on using the Video Animation Editor, see "Keyframing in the Timeline" in Chapter 21.

Blend Modes

In addition to opacity, every clip can have a blend mode assigned that will control the way it interacts with any clips beneath it in the Timeline.

Blend modes offer a wide range of creative looks and unusual interactions between clips. Often, combining a blend mode with a reduced Opacity setting can create especially interesting results.

In most cases, you may find it useful to experiment with different blend modes before settling on one. In some cases, you will get different results depending on which clip is on top.

To assign a blend mode to a clip:

1. Select a clip in the Timeline that is above another clip, and open the Video Inspector.

2. Scroll down to the Compositing section of the Video Inspector, and expand it if necessary .

3. Click the Blend Mode pop-up menu, and select from one of the choices **M**.

TIP The Blend Mode pop-up menu is arranged in groups to help you predict the results: The first group tends to make the resulting image darker, the modes in the second group make the image lighter, and so on **N**.

4. Repeat step 3 until you find a look you are satisfied with.

L Blend modes are found in the Compositing section of the Video Inspector.

M Select a blend mode from the pop-up menu.

N Some sample blend modes: Darken, Difference, and Linear Light.

Video Effects

Part of the fun of playing with a program like Final Cut Pro is the ability to modify the look and feel of your video clips. Sometimes, this is about fixing or repairing mistakes made in production. At other times, it's about purely aesthetic exploration.

Final Cut Pro includes dozens of filters to apply to your video. You can use these filters to create subtle, naturalistic effects (such as blurs or light flares), and you can use them to create wholly unnatural effects (such as kaleidoscopes or overlapping background squares).

Many filters can simply be applied and left alone. Others have a variety of settings you can employ to customize the effect and better integrate the results into your particular program.

You can also add multiple effects to a clip and control the order in which they are applied. Applying multiple filters exponentially expands the flexibility and creativity available to you.

The Effects Browser

Video filters are found in the Effects Browser. There are eight categories of video effects: Basics, Blur, Distortion, Keying, Light, Looks, Stylize, and Tiling. Take some time to explore and preview the different effects.

Some, such as those found in the Looks category and some of the effects in the Basics group, are essentially color correction presets and are discussed in more detail in Chapter 15, "Color Correction."

To open the Effects Browser:

- Click the Effects Browser icon, or press Command-5.

  The Effects Browser opens **Ⓐ**.

The Effects Browser displays all the effects available to you (including third-party plug-ins if you have any installed). Each effect is displayed as a thumbnail preview and with a descriptive name.

The Browser has two parts: the stack, where the list of effects is displayed, and a sidebar containing category names.

You can find specific effects either by searching for a particular name or by browsing through the various categories.

To find specific video effects:

- *Do one of the following*:
  - ▸ Type the name of the effect you're looking for in the search field at the bottom of the Effects Browser **Ⓑ**.

The stack is filtered to show only effects containing the letters in the search field.

TIP Clear the search field by clicking the circled X at the right edge of the field or by pressing Escape.

Effects Browser icon

Ⓐ Click the Effects Browser icon to open the Effects Browser.

Search field   *Clear search field*

Ⓑ Search for a specific effect by typing in the search field.

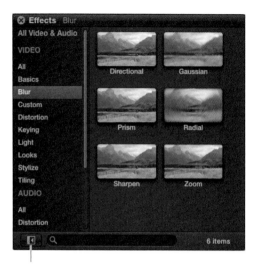

Hide/Show Sidebar button

C Click a category in the sidebar to filter the list. Hide or show the sidebar by clicking the Show/Hide Sidebar button in the lower-left corner of the Effects Browser.

D Skim across Effects icons to see a preview, or hover over the icon and press the Spacebar to play.

E Drag an effect to any clip to apply the effect to that clip.

▶ Click one of the category names in the sidebar on the left side of the Effects Browser, and scroll through the main stack area on the right **C**.

The stack is filtered by category.

Previewing Effects

You can preview what each effect looks like prior to adding it to your project. This enables you to experiment with a variety of effects quickly.

TIP You must select a specific clip in the Timeline in order to see a preview.

To preview an effect:

■ Select a clip in the Timeline, and then *do one of the following*:

▶ Hover your pointer over a transition icon in the Effects Browser to skim across the effect preview **D**.

▶ Position your pointer over an effects icon, and press the Spacebar.

The Viewer loops a sample of the effect applied to the selected clip.

TIP Click different effects icons while previewing to view different previews dynamically.

To apply an effect:

1. Select a clip in the Timeline to which you want to apply the effect, and then *do one of the following*:

▶ In the Effects Browser, double-click an effect.

▶ Drag the effect from the Effects Browser to the clip in the Timeline **E**.

The effect is applied to the clip.

Modifying Effects

Once you have applied effects to a clip, many effects have parameters you can modify to customize the result and tailor it to work with your particular shot.

To modify parameters in the Inspector:

1. Select the clip in the Timeline with an effect applied.

2. Open the Video Inspector by *doing one of the following*:

   ▸ Click the Inspector button in the tool-bar, and click Video at the top of the Inspector.

   ▸ Choose Edit Effects from the clip's Action menu.

   ▸ Press Command-4 .

3. In the Effects category, identify the effect you want to modify and select from items from pop-up menus, drag sliders, and click checkboxes as desired.

Ⓐ When effects are applied to a clip, their controls appear in the Effects category of the Video Inspector.

Effect Order Matters

You can apply multiple effects to a single clip, or even apply multiple instances of the same effect to a single clip. When you do this, the order in which you apply the effects has an impact on what the results will look like.

Effects are rendered in the order in which they appear in the Video Inspector. If you apply a Black & White effect after adding a colored Frame effect, the colors in the frame are going to be displayed as gray . If, however, you apply the Frame effect second, the clip will still be desaturated, but the frame will retain its custom colors .

Effects at the top of the list are applied before the effects below them.

B The order in which you apply effects impacts the way in which the results are displayed. In this example, the Black & White filter is applied after the Frame filter.

C In this example, the Black & White filter is applied before the Frame filter. Notice that while the video is desaturated, the frame retains its color.

To reorder effects:

- In the Effects category of the Video Inspector, drag the name of the effect above or below the other effects in the list **D**.

  The filters are reordered.

To disable an effect:

- In the Effects section of the Video Inspector, click the blue activation checkbox to the left of the effect name **E**.

  The blue checkbox turns black and the effect is disabled.

To reset an effect:

- Click the Reset button to the right of the effect name.

  The effect is reset to its default settings.

To reset all effects:

- Click the Reset All Effects button to the right of the Effects section header.

  All effects are reset to their default settings.

To delete an effect:

- In the Effects section of the Video Inspector, click the name of the effect, and press Delete.

D Reorder effects by dragging them by their name in the Video Inspector.

Reset All Effects button

Activation checkbox   *Reset Effect button*

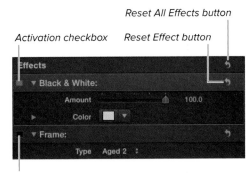

Disabled Activation checkbox

E To disable an effect without deleting it, simply click the big blue activation checkbox.

Color Correction

No matter how well your source footage was shot, there's always room to clean up and adjust the look of it in post. Whether you're trying to fix a poorly exposed shot, trying to match clips to make them look like they were shot in the same location, or altering the color and contrast as a storytelling technique, manipulating the appearance of your footage is a significant part of the post-production process.

Final Cut Pro has a unique color correction workflow that combines automatic color balancing (based on analysis), color matching across shots, and an unconventional new interface called the *Color Board* that allows you to make manual adjustments to color, saturation, and contrast.

There are also a large number of prebuilt "looks" that you can apply to your shots in a single step. Some of these are video effects, and some are presets in the Color Board.

Color Balance

One of the key aspects of the optional footage analysis in Final Cut Pro is a determination of the relative contrast and color temperature of your source footage.

By finding the lightest and darkest parts of the shot in each of the color channels, the software can automatically *stretch* the contrast to give a shot a sharper, cleaner look. This also serves to neutralize a shot's white balance, removing unwanted color casts or erroneous hue shifts (caused by incorrect camera settings or poor lighting environments). This magic is called *color balance*, and it's built into every clip in FCP.

Still, any automatic correction is bound to have limited usefulness, and this is no exception. There will always be shots where the Color Balance setting makes it look worse or removes a particular look that you spent hours on set perfecting. Fortunately, you can easily try the automatic correction and, if it's not to your liking, disable it.

Clip Analysis

To take advantage of the automatic color balancing, your clips must be analyzed. This can be done when importing clips, or it can be done later.

The Color Balance setting in the Video Inspector indicates whether the selected clip has been analyzed 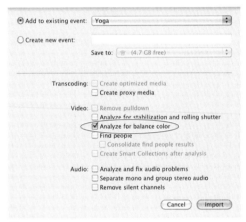.

To analyze files during import:

- In the Video section of the Import Files dialog, select the "Analyze for balance color" checkbox .

A To see whether a clip has been analyzed, check the Color section of the Video Inspector.

B When importing footage, select the "Analyze for balance color" checkbox.

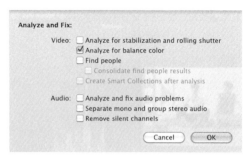

C Analyze already-imported clips by opening the Analyze and Fix dialog.

D Choose Balance Color from the Auto Enhancements menu. If color is currently balanced, the menu item will display a check mark (as shown here).

Activation checkbox

E In the Video Inspector, enable Color Balance by clicking the activation checkbox.

To analyze files after import:

1. In the Event Browser, select the clip or clips you want to analyze, and *do one of the following*:

   ▸ Choose Modify > Analyze and Fix.

   ▸ Right-click the selected clips, and choose Analyze and Fix from the shortcut menu.

   The Analyze and Fix dialog opens **C**.

2. In the Video section, select the "Analyze for balance color" checkbox, and click OK.

   The analysis begins in the background.

TIP To learn about how to monitor background-processing tasks, see Chapter 1, "Introduction."

To balance a shot's color:

■ Select the clip, and *do one of the following*:

   ▸ Click the Auto Enhancements menu in the toolbar, and choose Balance Color.

   A check mark will appear next to the menu item when Balance Color is enabled **D**.

   ▸ Press Option-Command-B.

   ▸ Open the Video Inspector, and in the Color section, click the activation checkbox next to Balance Color **E**.

   The image's color is "balanced."

To disable Color Balance:

- Select the clip, and *do one of the following*:

  ▸ Click the Auto Enhancements menu in the toolbar, and choose Balance Color .

    The checkbox will disappear.

  ▸ Press Option-Command-B.

  ▸ Open the Video Inspector, and in the Color section, click the blue activation checkbox next to Balance Color to deselect it .

  The Color Balance effect is removed.

F Turn off Color Balance in the Auto Enhancements menu.

G Or click the blue activation checkbox to deselect it.

A Position the playhead over the frame in the clip you want to match.

B The Match Color window is where you set the matching shot.

Match Color

One of the most common color correction tasks is to change the look of one shot to match that of another shot. This can help make a sequence seem more coherent or provide a subtle but essential clue to a viewer that two scenes take place in the same setting (even if they were filmed in completely different locations).

To match a shot's color:

1. Select the clip in the Timeline, and open the Video Inspector.

2. Position the playhead over the clip on a representative frame **A**.

   This will be the frame you will use to judge the new color settings.

3. *Do one of the following*:

   ▸ In the Color section of the Inspector, click the Choose button in the Match Color parameters.

   ▸ In the Auto Enhancements menu in the toolbar, choose Match Color.

   ▸ Press Option-Command-M.

   The Match Color window opens. The Viewer shows a two-up display with the current shot on the right and a black frame on the left **B**.

   continues on next page

4. Skim through the project until you find the frame you want to copy the color settings from **C**.

The skimmed clips appear on the left side of the Viewer.

5. When you find a frame you want to match, click in the Timeline.

The right side of the Viewer updates to show how your clip will look with the new color settings applied **D**.

6. When you're satisfied with the new look, click the Apply Match button in the Match Color window.

The color settings are applied to the clip.

TIP You can also copy color settings from an Event Browser clip.

To remove Match Color settings:

- Click the blue activation checkbox for the Match Color parameter in the Color section of the Video Inspector.

  The Match Color effect is disabled. You can reenable it, and it will remember its last settings, or you can click Choose again to select a new match color.

C Skim in the project to find the frame to which you want to match the color of your clip. The clip you want to change appears on the right side; the clip you are matching to appears on the left.

D When you find the frame you want to match, click. The right side of the viewer updates to show you how your matched shot will look.

The Effects Browser contains a variety of looks
(and also some "basics") that are essentially preset
color correction settings.

Preset Color Correction

Using the Color Balance and Match Color
settings can improve the look of your
shots, but they're pretty limited in terms of
applying creative and dramatic visual style.

Of course, you can use the manual color
correction tools to create an unlimited variety of looks and styles, but that takes some
time and skill.

In between the auto settings and full-man-
ual control are the variety of preset color
correction settings that are like fully baked
"looks" you can apply with a single click.

There are two different types of color
settings that fall in this category: effects
and presets.

Color Effects

The Effects Browser contains many video
effects that are nothing more than color
correction settings. This includes all of the
effects in the Looks category and many of
the effects in the Basics category. Many
of these effects have adjustable parameters you can use to further customize the
results Ⓐ.

For more on applying and modifying
effects such as these, see Chapter 14,
"Video Effects."

Presets

The other group of one-click settings is the preset list in the Color Board window. These presets modify the controls in the Color Board; so if you want to customize one after you've applied it, follow the instructions in the "Manual Color Correction" section of this chapter.

You can also save your own presets to this list. If you use the Color Board to create a look or a style that you want to reuse later, you can save them to the Preset list.

TIP Saved presets retain settings made in all three Color Board panes: Color, Saturation, and Exposure.

To apply a preset Color Board setting:

1. Select a clip in the Timeline, and open the Video Inspector.

2. In the Color section of the Inspector, click the Show Correction button at the right edge of the Correction 1 parameter **B**.

   The Color Board opens.

3. Click the gear icon in the lower-right corner of the Color Board **C**.

   The Color Board presets list appears **D**.

4. Select a preset from the pop-up menu.

   The preset is applied to your clip **E**.

Show Correction button

B Open the Video Inspector for your clip, and click the Show Correction button.

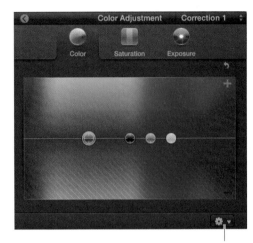

Preset corrections pop-up menu

C The Color Board opens in all its glory.

D Click the Gear icon to see a list of preset corrections.

To save a Color Board setting:

1. Adjust the Color Board settings based on the instructions in the following "Manual Color Correction" section.

2. Click the gear icon in the lower-right corner of the Color Board.

   The Color Board preset list appears **F**.

3. Choose Save Preset.

   The Save Preset dialog appears.

4. Type a name into the Save Preset dialog, and click OK **G**.

   The settings are saved to the list as a preset **H**.

E Apply a preset, and the settings are applied in the Color Board, affecting the selected clip.

F Open the Preset Correction menu, and choose Save Preset.

G Enter a name in the Save Preset dialog.

H The saved preset is added to the pop-up menu.

Manual Color Correction

All those automatic settings and preset corrections are fun and easy to employ, but the real power of color correction lies in making manual adjustments in the Color Board.

The Color Board has three panes: Color, Saturation, and Exposure. All three follow the same basic rules and workflow: There are four *pucks* in each pane. The pucks represent the settings for the shadows, midtones, highlights, and a global setting. By dragging the pucks, you assign a value to that range of the image 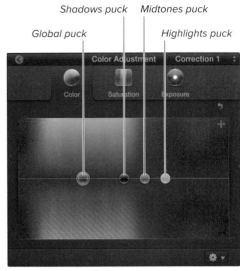.

For example, to add yellow to the highlights, drag the Highlights puck toward the yellow section of the Color pane. Similarly, to remove saturation from the shadows, drag the Shadows puck downward in the Saturation pane.

Dividing the image into these three ranges of brightness provides a surprising amount of precise control over the image, allowing you to perform different adjustments to each range simultaneously.

It's important to understand what portion of the image each puck affects. In fact, all three pucks have some impact on the whole image, but each puck's influence is heavily weighted in different ways.

In figure **B**, the blue line represents the Shadows puck, which has significant influence over the darkest areas of the image, and the influence tapers off in the brighter areas. The Highlights puck is represented by the green line, which has minimal influence over the darkest areas

Shadows puck *Midtones puck*

Global puck *Highlights puck*

A Each puck controls the color for a range of brightness in the selected shot.

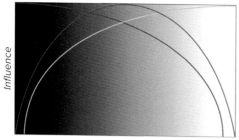

Influence

Brightness value

B This graph shows how the three main pucks affect an overlapping range of brightness. Red: Midtones, Blue: Shadows, and Green: Highlights.

but great influence over the bright areas. The Midtones puck (shown in red) affects the middle of the graph the most, and its effect tapers off toward both the brightest and darkest parts of the image.

The important things to take away from this is to understand that all three pucks will affect the whole image and that their influences overlap.

You can (and likely will) adjust multiple pucks simultaneously in each pane. The art and craft of color correction often involves dragging one of the pucks in one direction and tempering the effect by dragging another of the pucks in an opposing direction.

For example, you might drag the Shadows puck toward Cyan but drag the Midtones puck toward Red (which will remove Cyan). In this way, you carefully limit the cyan adjustment to just the darkest shadows.

Adjusting Contrast

It is wise to adjust your exposure before making any changes to the color of your image. Our eyes are much more sensitive to slight changes in *contrast* (the difference between the light and dark areas of the image). Often, fixing the contrast may make color changes unnecessary.

In general, nearly every image can benefit from *stretching* the contrast—that is, making the dark sections darker and making the light sections lighter. If you go too far, you risk losing detail in the highlights and shadows of your image. But if you stretch contrast properly, it has the effect of wiping a layer of grime off the screen.

To adjust the contrast:

1. Select a clip in the Timeline, and open the Video Inspector; then, *do one of the following*:

   ▸ In the Color section, click the Show Correction button next to Correction 1 .

   TIP If any corrections have been applied, the Show Correction button appears in color (as shown in Ⓒ).

   ▸ In the Auto Enhancement menu in the toolbar, choose Show Color Board Ⓓ.

   ▸ In the Timeline clip's Adjustment pop-up menu, choose Color Adjustment Ⓔ.

   ▸ Press Command-6.

Show Correction button

Ⓒ There are many ways to open the Color Board. For one, you can click the Show Correction button in the Video Inspector.

Ⓓ Here's another way: choose Show Color Board from the Auto Enhancement menu.

Click to open the Adjustment pop-up menu.

Ⓔ Two more ways to open the Color Board: choose Color Adjustment in the Time clip's Adjustment pop-up menu, or just press Command-6.

Exposure button

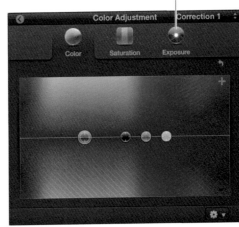

Ⓕ In the Color Board, click the Exposure button.

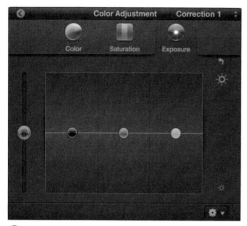

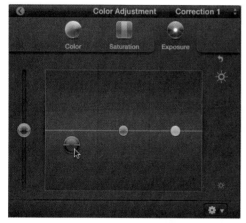

G The Exposure pane contains four pucks:
Shadows, Midtones, Highlights, and Global.

H Begin by setting the black levels.

The Color Board opens **F**.

2. Click the Exposure button to open the Exposure pane **G**.

3. Drag the Shadows puck down until the darkest areas of your image appear black **H**.

   There is great latitude here in terms of the look you desire. You must decide how much detail you want to retain in the shadows.

4. Drag the Highlights puck up until the brightest areas of your image appear white **I**.

continues on next page

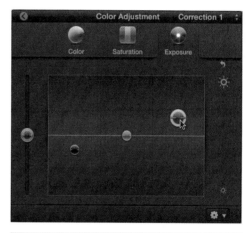

I Next, set the white levels.

Again, use your own discretion. You don't want to make skin tones (like those shown in ❶) or a yellow wall appear pure white, but if there's anything in the image that can be brightened without losing too much detail, go for it!

5. Drag the Midtones puck up or down to control the overall tone of the image ❶.

6. Optionally, you may want to drag the Global puck up or down to make a broad adjustment to the entire clip ❶.

TIP Remember to move your playhead around a bit within the clip while you are making corrections. Beware of making one frame look perfect at the expense of the rest of the shot.

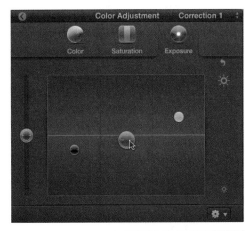

❶ If necessary, adjust the midtones. In this example, they have been raised slightly to give the overall image a brighter tone.

❶ The corrected version (on the right) looks like a layer of grime has been wiped off the screen.

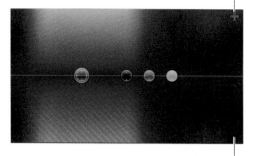

Add color

Subtract color

L Drag above the line to add a color, and drag below the line to subtract a color.

Show Correction button

M Click the Show Correction button to open the Color Board.

Adjusting Color

Once your contrast is looking good, you can begin adjusting the color and saturation of your image.

The Color pane of the Color Board works differently from the Exposure pane. You can drag each of the pucks anywhere at all on the board. Drag above the middle line to add a color, and drag below the middle line to remove a color **L**.

The color displayed in the board indicates the color you are affecting in the image. Dragging farther away from the centerline in either direction (up or down) adds or subtracts more of the color.

Unlike with exposure, there's no "correct" order in which to adjust the pucks in the Color pane. It really depends on the image you're correcting and what you're trying to achieve.

TIP Make tiny adjustments. Good color correction is subtle.

To adjust the color:

1. Select a clip in the Timeline, and open the Video Inspector; then *do one of the following*:

   ▸ In the Color section, click the Show Correction button next to Correction 1 **M**.

   ▸ In the Auto Adjustment menu in the toolbar, choose Show Color Board.

   ▸ In the Timeline clip's Adjustment pop-up menu, choose Color Adjustment.

   ▸ Press Command-6.

   The Color Board opens.

continues on next page

2. Click the Color button to open the Color pane 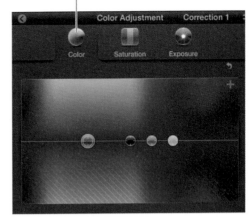.

3. Drag the Shadows, Midtones, and Highlights pucks to adjust the color to create your desired effect .

When a puck is selected, the info area below the board shows the numerical value of the color setting **P**.

TIP Remember, small adjustments go a long way!

TIP Remember to move your playhead around a bit within the clip while you are making corrections. Beware of making one frame look perfect at the expense of the rest of the shot.

4. Optionally, you may want to drag the Global puck to add a tint to the entire clip.

Color button

N In the Color Board, click the Color button to open the Color pane.

O In the Color pane, you can drag any of the pucks anywhere on the board.

P For whichever puck is selected, the window shows the numerical value for the applied setting.

Never Forget the Color Wheel

Unfortunately, Apple eschewed centuries of tradition and a great deal of useful information when it abandoned the color wheel in Final Cut Pro 7 for the Color Board in Final Cut Pro X. But the physics of color haven't changed.

It's very important to understand that subtracting one color has the same effect as adding its complementary color, and vice versa. When you remove red, you're adding cyan. When you remove cyan, you're adding red.

If you look at the way the colors are arranged on a traditional color wheel, you can see how the axes of color are arranged and how dragging away from one color inherently adds another **Q**.

In the Color Board, this relationship is not clear. You can inadvertently add one color by subtracting too much of another. The colors drawn on the board don't give any clue to this. Dragging up is pretty intuitive; drag toward the color you want, and you add that color. But when you drag down, you're subtracting, which means you're adding the complementary color **R**.

So, study your color wheel, and you'll understand why removing yellow adds blue, removing green adds magenta, and so on.

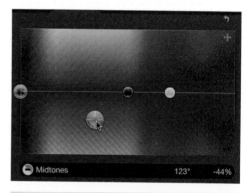

Midtones   123°   -44%

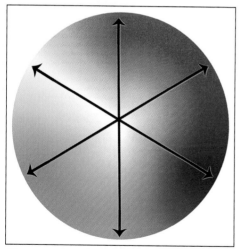

Q A color wheel illustrates how the farther you move away from one color, the more you move toward its complementary color. Also, the farther away from the center, the more saturated the added color.

R Dragging down is the same as dragging up on a different color. For example, in this example, the midtones are set to subtract green, which is equivalent to adding magenta.

Adjusting Saturation

Color and saturation are tied together very closely. In fact, adding more color by dragging one of the pucks in the Color pane toward the top or bottom of the Color Board does effectively increase the saturation of that color.

However, sometimes you want to adjust the overall saturation of the image. The Saturation pane facilitates this and allows you to also limit your adjustments to the shadows, midtones, or highlights.

To adjust the saturation:

1. Select a clip in the Timeline, and open the Color Board.

2. Click the Saturation button to open the Saturation pane .

3. Drag the Shadows, Midtones, and Highlights pucks up to add saturation to that range of the image, or drag them down to remove saturation from that range 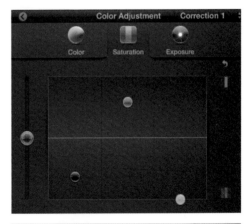.

4. Optionally, you may want to drag the Global puck up or down to raise or lower the saturation for the whole clip.

Saturation button

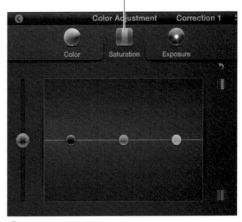

Ⓢ Click the Saturation button to open the Saturation pane.

Ⓣ Drag the pucks to increase or decrease saturation in the specified brightness range. In this example, the shadows and highlights have been desaturated, while the midtone saturation has been boosted.

Return to Video Inspector button

(U) To return to the Video Inspector, click the button in the upper-left corner of the Color Board, or press Command-6.

Reset button

(V) To reset a specific pane, click the Reset button for that pane.

(W) To reset all panes in the Color Board, click the Reset button for the correction in the Video Inspector.

To close the Color Board:

- Click the Return to Video Inspector button in the upper left of the Color Board, or press Command-6 (U).

To reset one pane of the Color Board:

- Click the Reset button for the pane you want to reset (V).

   The pucks in that pane are reset to their default positions.

To reset all panes of the Color Board:

1. Close the Color Board.

2. In the Color section of the Video Inspector, click the Reset button for the correction you want to reset (W).

   All panes of the Color Board are reset to their default (neutral) settings.

Secondary Color Correction

All of the techniques described thus far are what considered *primary* color correction. This has nothing to do with the idea of *primary colors* (that is, red, green, and blue). Rather, primary correction refers to adjustments that affect the entirely of an image.

In contrast, *secondary* correction refers to changes that are limited to a portion of the image, such as the sky, a character's skin, or an area of the frame masked by a shape. The term *secondary* refers to the fact that these corrections are typically done after primary corrections have been made.

By masking certain areas of the frame, you can apply different corrections to the different parts of the scene; you can make the sky bluer, the grass greener, and the skin tones skin-tonier. In fact, major motion pictures employ this technique on every frame of every movie. There's no reason that Andrew Garfield's skin should get the same adjustment as Judy Greer's. And neither should get the same look as the Swamp Thing does! Using secondaries, actors can be tweaked to make them look their best—and now, in Final Cut Pro, you can bestow your own actors with the same indulgence.

You can employ as many corrections as you want, and each one can be limited using a color mask, shape masks, or both.

Add Correction button

Ⓐ Click the Add Correction button to add a new color correction setting.

Add Color Mask button

Ⓑ Click the Add Color Mask button.

Ⓒ A color mask item is added to the correction in the Inspector.

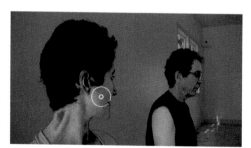

Ⓓ Click and drag in the Viewer on the range of color you want to select. Areas outside the selection appear in black-and-white. In this example, the skin tones are being selected.

Color Masks

You create color masks by choosing a specific range of colors in the image, such as the blue of the sky, or the color of a person's skin. Once that area has been identified, you can make adjustments using the three panes of the Color Board, and those corrections will be limited to that selected area.

To create a color mask:

1. Select a clip in the Timeline, and open the Video Inspector.

2. Click the Add Correction button to add a new correction Ⓐ.

   A new correction is added to the Color section of the Inspector.

   TIP This step presumes you're using Correction 1 to perform whatever primary color adjustments your shot requires.

3. Click the Add Color Mask button for Correction 2 Ⓑ.

   A mask row is added to the correction, and the pointer changes to an eyedropper (once you hover over the Viewer) Ⓒ.

4. Click the color you want to select, and optionally drag to select a range of color Ⓓ.

   A circle appears under the pointer to show the range of colors selected. Any similar colors throughout the image are automatically selected, and the rest of the image is temporarily displayed in black-and-white.

   When you release the mouse, it appears that your selection has been lost, but it has not; it's just that you haven't made any changes in the Color Board yet, so you can't see any change in the Viewer.

continues on next page

TIP You can Shift-click with the eyedropper to add colors to your selection.

5. Click the Show Correction button for Correction 2 ⓔ.

   The Color Board opens.

6. Make adjustments in the Color Board as described in the earlier "Manual Color Correction" section ⓕ.

   The adjustments are limited to the color range selected ⓖ.

7. Return to the Video Inspector, and adjust the Mask Softness slider ⓗ.

TIP You can also redefine the selected color by repeating step **4** after you've made the corrections in step **6**.

To delete a color mask:

■ Click the mask name in the Color section of the Video Inspector, and press Delete.

   The color mask is deleted. If you had any corrections applied, they will now be applied to the entire image.

ⓔ Click the Show Correction button to open the Color Board for Correction 2.

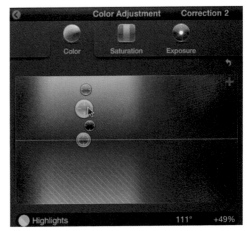

ⓕ Make adjustments in the Color Board. In this example, we're going to turn the yoginis into Martians.

ⓖ The changes are limited to the selected area in the image—in this case, the skin tones.

ⓗ Optionally soften the selection using the Mask Softness slider in the Color section of the Video Inspector.

Add Correction button

I Click the Add Correction button to add a new correction.

Add Shape Mask button

J Click the Add Shape Mask button to add a new shape mask.

Rotation handle

Center point handle   *Control points*

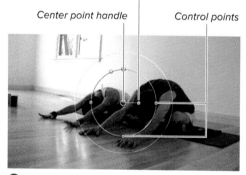

K The shape mask appears in the Viewer.

Shape Masks

In addition to color masks, you can identify a portion of the image using a simple shape (oval or rectangle). The idea is the same as with the color mask—identify an area in the image, and the corrections you apply are limited to that selected area.

TIP You can create multiple shapes in the same correction to color correct a noncontiguous selection.

To add a shape mask:

1. Select a clip in the Timeline, and open the Video Inspector.

2. Click the Add Correction button to add a new correction **I**.

   A new correction is added to the Color section of the Inspector.

3. Click the Add Shape Mask button for the new correction **J**.

   A shape appears in the Viewer **K**.

continues on next page

4. In the Viewer, move the mask by dragging in the center point, resize it by dragging any of the four control points, and rotate it by dragging the rotation handle ⓛ.

   The mask is customized to your liking.

5. Click the Show Correction button for the correction.

   The Color Board opens.

6. Make necessary adjustments to any of the three panes ⓜ.

   The corrections are limited to the area specified by the mask ⓝ.

ⓛ Drag the shape handles to resize and rotate it, and drag the center point handle the mask to move it around.

ⓜ Make whatever changes are desired in the Color Board.

ⓝ The changes are reflected only in the masked area of the Viewer.

Roundness handle

O Drag the Roundness handle to make your shape more square.

Softness handle

P Drag the outer ring to control the softness of the mask.

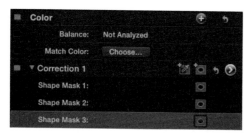

Q Add as many shape masks as you want. They will all use the same correction settings.

To convert a mask from an oval to a rectangle:

- Drag the roundness handle to the left to make the shape more square, and drag it to the right to make the shape more round **O**.

To control mask softness:

- Drag the outer ring around the mask to control the softness **P**.

  The farther away the outer ring is from the inner ring, the softer the edge of the mask.

To add additional shape masks:

- Click the Add Shape Mask button for the correction **Q**.

To hide the mask on-screen controls:

- Click the Toggle Shape Mask On-Screen Controls button for the mask whose controls you want to hide ⓡ.

  The on-screen controls for that mask are hidden in the Viewer.

To delete a shape mask:

- Select the shape mask under the correction in the Color section of the Video Inspector, and press Delete.

  The mask is deleted.

TIP If you have made adjustments in the Color Board for that correction and you delete the last mask, the correction will be applied to the entire image.

Combining Masks

You can combine color masks and shape masks in the same correction. This allows you to select the intersection of the masks, which can be extremely useful in terms of limiting your selection effectively.

For example, if you were trying to select an actor's face but didn't want the correction to affect their hand that was also visible in the shot, you could use a color mask to select the skin tones (which would select both the face and the hand), then add a shape mask around the face, excluding the hand from the effects of the correction.

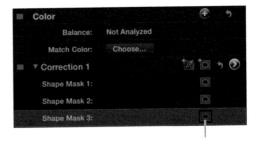

Show/Hide On-Screen Controls button

ⓡ Hide or show the on-screen controls by clicking the Toggle Shape Mask On-Screen Controls button for the mask in question.

S Add a color mask to identify a range of color.

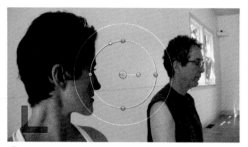

T Add a shape mask to limit what part of the color mask is used.

U Corrections applied will be limited to the intersection of both color and shape masks. In this case, now only one of the actors is from Mars.

To combine a color mask and a shape mask in one correction:

1. Add a color mask as described in the task on page 345 S.

2. Add a shape mask as described in the task on page 347 T.

3. Adjust the shape mask to overlap the portion of the color mask you want to include in the selection U.

   The resulting correction will affect only those areas selected by *both* masks.

Inside vs. Outside

Whenever you add masks to limit the effect of a correction, you have the option to apply different color settings to the area inside the mask and the area outside the mask.

By default, changes you make in the Color Board affect only the inside of the masked area, but you can make corrections to the outside as well. The result is two completely separate sets of Color Board settings, saved in a single correction.

This allows you to use one mask to create two corrections. For example, if you create a shape mask around the sky in a landscape shot, you can use the inside of the mask to increase the contrast and the depth of the blue sky, and you can use the outside of the mask to add a golden hue to the land.

To make corrections to the outside of a masked area:

1. Create a correction using a color or shape mask (or both) as described in the previous tasks .

2. Click the Show Correction button (or press Command-6) to open the Color Board.

3. Make the corrections as desired to the area inside the mask.

4. In the bottom of the Color Board window, click the Outside Mask button .

   The Color Board is reset to neutral settings.

5. Make corrections to any of the three panes in the Color Board.

   The settings are applied to the area outside the mask 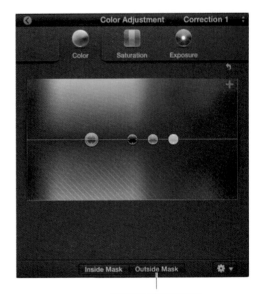.

6. Click the Inside Mask button in the Color Board to make more changes to the correction inside the mask.

   You can continue to switch between the inside and outside masks, making changes to both. Each set of changes is saved independently within the same correction.

V Add a color mask or a shape mask to your image. In this example, the color of the grass is being intensified and sharpened using a shape mask.

Outside Mask button

W Click the Outside Mask button at the bottom of the Color Board window.

X A separate set of corrections is applied to the outside area.

Video Scopes

Video scopes can be helpful when color correcting your images. They provide an objective perspective on the color and contrast values of your video. When looking at a video with a greenish tint, your eyes quickly get used to the color cast and your brain automatically corrects for the error.

Using scopes can help you see such errors, and also can allow you to compare multiple images in a more objective way.

There are three scopes: Histogram, Vectorscope, and Waveform monitor.

- *Histogram* plots the pixels of the image on a two-dimensional graph where the left side shows darker pixels and the right side shows lighter pixels. The more pixels of a particular color, the higher the bump in the graph.

  The Histogram is helpful in determining how the brightness of an image (or of its individual channels) is distributed. This indicates overall contrast as well as potentially identifying if the image is over- or under-exposed.

continues on next page

Ⓐ An example of a Histogram.

- *Vectorscope* plots the pixels of the image on a graph where the more saturated the color, the farther away it appears from the center point, and the hue determines the angle .

  The Vectorscope is helpful in determining if the image has a color cast or other type of hue-related problems. It can also show you how saturated an image is, as well as indicate the accuracy of specific colors, such as fleshtones.

- *Waveform Monitor* plots the pixels of the image on a graph where the vertical axis indicates the brightness of the pixels (higher is lighter) and the horizontal axis represents the horizontal placement in the image 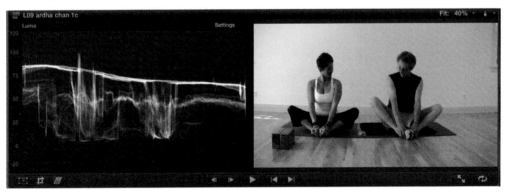.

  The Waveform Monitor can help you quickly identify the overall contrast level of an image, a well as identify specifically what areas might be under- or over-exposed.

B An example of a Vectorscope.

C An example of a Waveform Monitor.

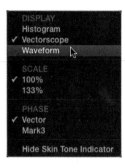

D Choose Show Video Scopes from the Viewer Display Options menu or press Command-7.

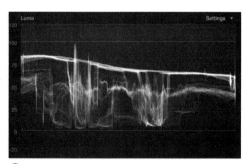

E Choose a scope from the Display section of the Settings pop-up menu.

F The display changes to show the scope of your choice.

To display Video Scopes:

- Click the Viewer Display Options menu and choose Show Video Scopes or press Command-7 **D**.

  The Viewer is split in half, and the left side displays one of three mathematical representations of the color and lightness values that comprise your video image.

  Once the scopes are showing, you can choose among any of the three types of scopes, and for each of the three, there are additional settings available.

To switch between Video Scopes:

1. Right-click anywhere on the scopes, or click the Settings pop-up menu **E**.

2. From the Display section of the pop-up menu choose the scope you wish to display **F**.

To select specific scope view settings:

1. Right-click anywhere on the scopes, or click the Settings pop-up menu **G** **H** **I**.

2. Select the channels you want to display, or change other settings as desired, based on the specific scope.

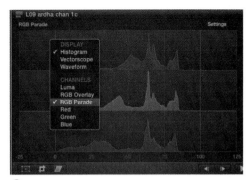

G The Histogram allows you to select a variety of different channels or channel combinations.

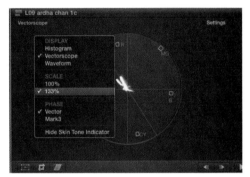

H The Vectorscope allows you to zoom in on the scope, change the phase of the display, and hide or show the Skin Tones indicator.

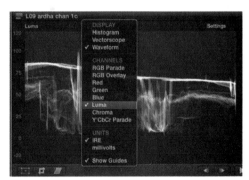

I The Waveform Monitor allows you to select a variety of different channels or channel combinations, change the scale between IRE and millivolts, and hide or show guides.

16

Compound Clips

Final Cut Pro puts great emphasis on keeping the interface clean and simplified and on trying to keep your workflow similarly streamlined. As you build bigger and more complex projects, you can take advantage of *compound clips* to keep your Timeline from becoming unwieldy. As you'll see in the coming pages, compound clips offer a variety of other benefits as well.

In This Chapter

Using Compound Clips

A compound clip is simply a single clip object that represents multiple items .

Note that previous versions of FCP referred to this as a *sub-sequence* or a *nested sequence*, and the command used to create such an object was Nest Items.

Here are some common examples of compound clips:

- A foreign-language interview with connected subtitles

A The three selected clips in the top image are replaced by the single compound clip in the bottom.

B An interview with connected subtitles is a good candidate to be turned into a compound clip.

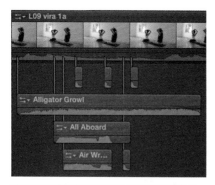

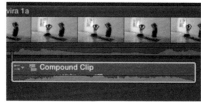

C By combining the two video clips, title, and background generator into a compound clip, you can adjust the whole group as a single object.

D By combining all of the sound effects in the top image into one compound clip (as shown in the bottom image), you can move the group all at once and adjust a single level that makes the entire group louder or quieter.

- A group of clips arranged into a split screen that you want to edit as if it were a single item **C**
- A collection of overlapping sound effects whose levels you want to adjust all at once **D**

Once you convert the group of objects into a single compound clip, you can edit the new clip as if it were a single piece of media.

At any point you can delve inside the compound clip and modify its contents or break apart the compound clip, replacing it with the individual clips it comprises.

As the previous examples imply, compound clips can be used for a variety of purposes, including reducing visual clutter on the screen, allowing you to modify multiple objects at once, and overriding the order in which certain effects are rendered.

This chapter will describe each of these workflows and how using compound clips can improve your efficiency and effectiveness as an editor.

Making Compound Clips

Any collection of clips, either in the Timeline or in the Event Browser, can be made into a compound clip. In either case, the result is a new project-like object that can be edited as if it were a single clip.

Making Compound Clips in the Timeline

When made into a compound clip, clips in the Timeline will retain their relative positions, as well as any effects that may be applied to them. If there are gaps in your selection, those gaps will appear in the compound clip  **A**.

The compound clip will replace the individual items in the Timeline.

With rare exceptions, a project will look identical playing in the Viewer before and after creating a compound clip. Only the representation of the clips in the Timeline changes.

TIP You can create a compound clip that contains other compound clips! Just don't try to make a compound clip that contains itself!

To create a compound clip in the Timeline:

1. Select the clips you want to combine **B**.

2. Choose File > New Compound Clip, or press Option-G.

   The clips are replaced by a single compound clip **C**.

A The three clips in the top image are replaced by the single compound clip in the bottom.

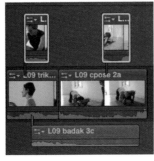

B You must select whole clips, but the clips don't have to be adjacent to each other.

C The newly created compound clip shows thumbnails that represent the combined contents.

Making Compound Clips in the Event Browser

Unlike what happens in the Timeline, a compound clip in the Event Browser does not replace the clips selected when it was created. The compound clip you create in the Event Browser contains copies of those individual clips.

Sort Order Matters

Compound clips created in the Event Browser contain the selected objects arranged in the order in which they were sorted when the compound clip was created **D** **E**. With the Event Browser in Filmstrip view, clips will be arranged in the order in which they are selected.

No gaps will ever be added inside the compound clip.

D In this example, the Event Browser is set to sort in reverse alphabetical order.

E The compound clip contains the clips in the order in which they were sorted in the Event Browser when the compound clip was created.

To create a compound clip in the Event Browser:

1. Select the clips you want to combine **F**.

2. Choose File > New Compound Clip, or press Option-G.

   The Compound Clip sheet opens.

3. Name the compound clip, and set the starting timecode, Video Properties and Audio and Render properties settings **G**.

4. Click OK.

   A new compound clip is added to the current event in the Event Browser **H**.

Custom Compound Clip Settings

Compound clips are no different from other projects, and all projects have properties that determine the frame size, frame rate, and so on. (For more about Project Properties, see "Changing Project Properties" in Chapter 5, "Projects.")

When creating a compound clip in the Event Browser, you have the option of matching the project properties for the compound clip to those of the first clip in the selection. This is almost always what you want, since it's desirable to have your project settings match your clip settings. However, you can manually create different properties if you need to do so.

The most likely reason to customize these settings would be if the first clip in your selection was not similar to the rest of the footage you planned to use. For example, the first item in the selection might be 720p, while the rest of your footage is 1080i. Or the first item in the selection might be a still image of a custom size. If you based the compound clip's properties on that still image, all the other video clips you add might appear stretched or distorted.

F Make a compound clip out of related shots, either as a quick rough edit or as a collection of shots to watch all at once.

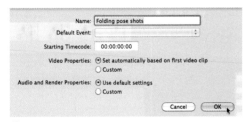

G Name the compound clip something that'll help you remember what's inside.

Compound clip icon

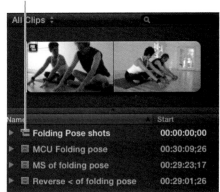

H The compound clip appears in the browser beside the other shots. Note the custom icon.

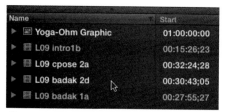

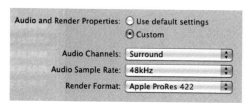

I When combining clips with different settings, you may want to customize the compound clip settings. Note that the first clip in this example is a graphic.

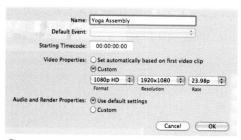

J When you click Custom, three pop-up menus appear.

K The Format pop-up menu contains presets. Choosing one automatically sets the other two pop-up menus.

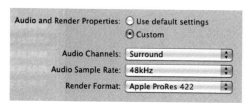

Audio and Render Properties: ○ Use default settings
                               ⊙ Custom
              Audio Channels: Surround
           Audio Sample Rate: 48kHz
              Render Format: Apple ProRes 422

L Audio and Render settings become customizable when you enable the Custom choice.

To customize compound clip settings:

1. Select items in the Event Browser, and choose File > New Compound Clip **I**.

   The Compound Clip sheet appears.

2. In the Video Properties setting, click Custom **J**.

   The Custom Video Properties settings appear.

3. Select a preset from the Format pop-up menu **K**.

   The Resolution and Rate pop-ups change automatically based on the format you select.

4. To override the format presets, set a specific frame size and frame rate from the individual pop-up menus.

5. In the Audio and Render Properties setting, click Custom.

   The Custom Audio and Render Properties settings appear **L**.

6. Select an Audio Channels, Audio Sample Rate, and Render Format setting from each of the corresponding pop-up menus.

7. Name the compound clip, and click OK **M**.

   The custom compound clip is created and appears in the Event Browser.

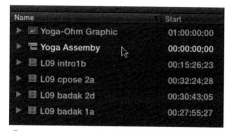

M When you create a compound clip in the Event Browser, the new item appears beside the other items.

Viewing and Editing the Contents of a Compound Clip

Creating compound clips is *nondestructive*, so you can always go back and edit the individual components of the compound clip or even break apart the compound clip into its constituent parts, restoring the original clip layout in the Timeline.

Because compound clips are essentially projects, FCP displays their contents in a Timeline.

There, you can edit the contents of the compound clip just like any other project. You can add and delete clips, trim edit points, and apply effects, transitions, titles, audio clips, and so on.

Any changes you make inside the compound clip are automatically reflected in the *parent* project (the project that contains the compound clip object).

TIP Let's be clear: Changes you make to compound clips located in the Timeline will *not* be reflected in the parent compound clip (if one exists) in the Event Browser.

To view and edit the contents of a compound clip:

1. *Do one of the following*:
    ▸ Double-click the filmstrip area of your compound clip in the Timeline.
    ▸ Click the Compound Clip icon **A**.
    ▸ Select the compound clip, and choose Clip > Open In Timeline.

    A new Timeline opens displaying the contents of the compound clip **B**.

2. Make any edits to the project in the Timeline **C**.

Compound Clip icon

A Click the Compound Clip icon (to the left of the clip name) to open it into its own Timeline.

Timeline navigation buttons

Path shows parents of currently open Timeline

Name of current project

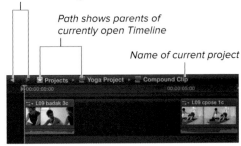

B When viewed in its own Timeline, a compound clip looks and acts just like any other project. The path at the top of the Timeline shows the project that contained the compound clip.

C In this example, the first clip is lengthened, and an audio clip has been attached.

D The changes made inside the compound clip Timeline are automatically reflected in the parent project.

E To break apart a compound clip, select it and press Shift-Command-G.

F The compound clip is replaced by the items that were inside it. In this example, the audio in the parent project was moved out of the way to make room for the audio added inside the compound clip.

3. Click the Timeline History Back button (see again **B**), or press Command-[.

   The previously open Timeline reappears **D**.

4. Play around the compound clip.

   The changes you made in step 2 are automatically updated in the parent project.

Note that you can also use these same steps to view and edit the contents of a compound clip created in the Event Browser. However, step 3 will simply reveal the previously open Timeline, which will not necessarily contain the compound clip you just edited.

Breaking Apart Compound Clips

For compound clips used in a project, you can, at any point, revert the clip to its constituent parts in the Timeline. Any effects or modifications made to the compound clip as a whole will be lost.

To break apart a compound clip:

1. Select the compound clip in the Timeline.

2. Choose Clip > Break Apart Clip Items, or press Shift-Command-G **E**.

   The compound clip is replaced by the individual clips that it comprised **F**.

Editing with Compound Clips

The primary use for creating compound clips is to treat the group of clips they represent as a single unit. You can edit, move, trim, apply effects to, and do anything else to a compound clip that you might do to an individual media clip.

The most basic thing you can do to a compound clip is to edit it in a project just like any other piece of source footage. This includes adding it to a Timeline, moving it around in a Timeline, and even trimming it in the Timeline.

To edit with a compound clip:

- Select the compound clip in the Timeline, and move or trim it .

    The compound clip behaves like any other piece of source footage.

One important limitation to understand is that the duration of a compound clip is limited by the number of frames within it: You can shorten the compound clip in the parent project, but you cannot lengthen it without first adding additional frames inside the compound clip **B**.

Also, if you do change the duration of the items within a compound clip, the parent project will not automatically update to reflect that duration change. If you remove frames, black frames will be played where no media exists. If you add frames, you must manually extend the compound clip in the parent project to see those added frames. This is clarified further in the following two tasks.

A You can pretty much forget that a compound clip contains multiple items and treat it just like a regular clip if you want.

B You can shorten a compound clip in the parent project, but you can't lengthen it without first going inside and adding frames.

G In this example, the compound clip is five seconds and seven frames long.

D As the first clip is lengthened by 1:17, the overall duration of the project is lengthened, but the hash marks indicate the locked duration based on what was set in the parent project, so those frames at the end will not be seen.

E In the parent project, the overall clip remains the same length.

F Because new footage was added inside the compound clip, you can now ripple it to make it longer. The clip maxes out (as indicated by the red trim edge) after adding 1:17 frames.

To lengthen a compound clip:

1. Select the compound clip in the parent project and press Control-D to display the duration in the Current Frame indicator **G**.

TIP Once the Duration field is showing in the Current Time indicator, you can type a new number to change the duration.

2. Double-click the compound clip to open it into its own Timeline.

3. Trim one or more of the clips to add frames to any of the edits in the compound clip **D**.

    Frames are added, increasing the total duration of the compound clip.

    The hash marks indicate the section of the compound clip that is in use in the parent project.

4. Click the Timeline History Back button to navigate back to the parent project **E**.

    The parent project is opened, and the compound clip still retains its original duration. The added frames are not visible in the parent project.

5. Ripple the right edge of the compound clip **F**.

    Additional frames are available for trimming, allowing you to incorporate the added frames.

To shorten a compound clip:

- Ripple the edge of the compound clip in the parent project **G**.

As you can see, shortening a compound clip is far easier than lengthening one!

However, it's important to understand that if you do shorten the duration of the *contents* of the compound clip, you must manually update the object in the parent project to avoid seeing black frames.

To update a compound clip's duration after removing frames from within it:

1. Select the compound clip in the parent project and press Control-D to observe its duration in the Current Frame indicator **H**.

2. Double-click the compound clip to open it into its own Timeline.

3. Trim one or more of the clips to remove frames from any of the edits in the compound clip **I**.

   The frames are removed, shortening the duration of the compound clip.

4. Click the Timeline History Back button, or press Command-[.

   The Timeline shows the parent project. The duration of the compound clip has not changed **J**.

5. Play over the compound clip.

   Black frames appear at the end of the compound clip.

6. Ripple the right edge of the compound clip **K**.

   Once you modify the duration of the compound clip, its duration will be limited by the total number of frames inside.

G To shorten a Compound clip, just trim it in the parent project.

H In this case, the compound clip begins with a duration of five seconds and seven frames.

I One of the clips within the compound clip is trimmed by 1:07.

J Back in the parent project, the duration is still 5:07, and the end of the clip shows black frames.

K Once you ripple the clip to be shorter than the new number of frames inside the compound clip, that shorter length becomes the maximum length of the clip in the parent project.

(A) The effect is applied separately to each of the three clips. To make changes, you'd have to open all three clips' Info windows and make the changes three times.

(B) By combining the clips into a single compound clip, changes made once will update all the clips at once.

(C) Trying to perform an animated effect across multiple clips is especially challenging.

Advanced Uses for Compound Clips

This idea of treating a compound clip like an individual piece of footage can be exploited in a variety of other powerful ways and allow you to accomplish tasks that would otherwise be impossible or at least very tedious.

Applying an Effect to Multiple Clips

For example, if you wanted to apply an Aged Film effect to a group of three clips, you could select all three clips in the Timeline and double-click the effect **(A)**.

However, if you then wanted to modify the settings of that filter, you would have to select each affected clip individually and match the settings for each of the clips.

If, instead, before applying the filter, you made a compound clip out of the three clips, you would have only one set of controls that would apply to all three clips **(B)**.

That way, you can continue to experiment with different settings with the confidence that the all three clips will always have identical settings applied.

To take it a step even further, if you wanted to *keyframe* that Aged Film filter so the amount of grain increased gradually over the course of the three shots, it would be extremely difficult to do manually, because you'd have to make sure the setting at the end of the first clip matched the setting at the beginning of the second clip, and so on **(C)**.

If you ever wanted to trim one of the edits, you'd have to go back and redo all the filter settings on multiple clips.

If, however, you applied a single Aged Film filter to a compound clip, you could keyframe right across the clip boundaries, creating a smooth gradual effect .

For more on applying effects, see "To apply an effect" in Chapter 14, "Video Effects." For more on keyframing, see Chapter 21, "Animating Effects."

To apply a single effect to a group of clips:

1. Select the group of clips in the Timeline to which you want to apply the effect **E**.

2. Press Option-G to create a compound clip **F**.

   The clips are replaced by a single compound clip.

3. Select the compound clip in the Timeline.

4. Press Command-5 to open the Effects Browser **G**.

5. Double-click the effect of your choice to apply it to the compound clip **H**.

   The effect is applied to the compound clip.

D Animating a single clip, on the other hand, is relatively simple.

E Select the clips to which you want to apply the effect.

F Press Option-G to convert the clips into a compound clip.

H The orange render bar in the time ruler indicates that the effect has been applied to the compound clip.

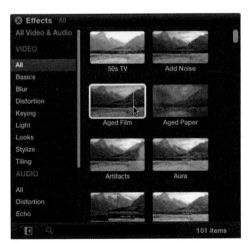

G Open the Effects Browser.

I Three clips are arranged into a split-screen composition. For the clips to all appear on-screen at once, they must overlap the same frames in the Timeline, as shown.

J The group is flattened into a compound clip, but the composition remains the same. The thumbnails for the compound clip show the composition.

Applying Complex Transformations

Another way you can take advantage of compound clips to perform a task that would be otherwise impossible (or at least very difficult) is to transform a group of clips as a single object.

Because the compound clip acts as a single entity, you can scale, rotate, move, and perform other transformations to the group of items all at once.

To transform a group of objects as one:

1. Arrange multiple clips into a composition **I**.

2. Select the group of clips in the Timeline, and choose File > New Compound Clip or press Option-G.

   A single Compound Clip object replaces the clips **J**.

continues on next page

3. Select the compound clip, and click the Apply Transformations button, Crop button, or Distort button.

4. Apply the desired transformations to the compound clip **K**.

5. Click Done to close the Transformation window.

Adjusting Audio Levels for Multiple Clips

One benefit of compound clips specific to audio clips is the ability to modify the audio level of multiple clips simultaneously; you can even fade the group of clips in and out as a single object.

To treat a group of audio clips as a single item:

1. Select the group of connected audio clips in the Timeline **L**.

2. Choose File > Create New Compound Clip, or press Option-G.

A single compound clip replaces the group of clips in the Timeline **M**.

3. Modify the audio levels and fade settings of the compound clip **N**.

The changes are applied to the group of clips.

Click Done to accept the transformation.

K Now you can manipulate the group of objects as if it were a single object. In this example, the group of clips has been distorted to simulate a 3D look. Doing this with the three individual clips would have been possible but hardly worth the effort.

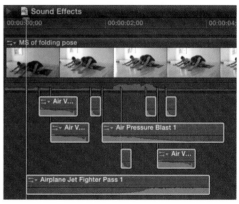

L When you build a complex sound effect, it may include many separate audio clips.

N Level and fade adjustments apply to the combined result of all the individual items.

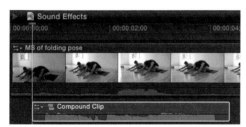

M By combining the separate elements into a single compound clip, you can manipulate the group of sound effects as if they were a single item.

 You can identify the order in which effects are rendered by observing their arrangement in the video pane of the Info window.

 Because transformations are applied after filters, this image shows the blur effect being abruptly cropped.

TIP Remember, you can still make changes to the levels of the individual audio elements. The results will be the combination of the level set inside the compound clip Timeline and the settings applied to the compound clip itself.

For more about modifying audio levels, applying fades and other audio effects, see Chapter 12, "Audio Effects."

Controlling Render Order

Another benefit of compound clips is that they allow you to override the order in which certain effects are rendered.

Ordinarily, filters are applied to a clip first, and transformation effects are applied second. This means the transformation is being applied to the filtered clip **O**.

TIP The order in which effects are rendered is easy to remember because the controls appear in the Inspector in the order in which they are applied.

So, for example, if you apply a Blur filter to a clip and crop the edge of that clip, the blur effect is cut off abruptly at the edge of where the crop has been applied **P**.

If you wanted the blur to affect the cropped edge, you would need the cropping to happen first and the blurring to happen second.

That means you must crop the clip first and then apply the blur effect to the cropped image. This can be accomplished only using compound clips.

To override the default order of render operations:

1. Apply the desired transformation to the clip  **Q**.

2. Select the clip in the Timeline, and choose File > New Compound Clip (or press Option-G).

   The clip is converted into a compound clip **R**.

> **TIP** There's no reason you can't make a single object into a compound clip.

3. Double-click the effect in the Effects Browser to apply it to the compound clip.

   The filter is applied to the transformed version of the clip **S**.

This concept can be employed in a variety of similar cases where you want to override the default order of operations.

Another example would be if you wanted to create an effect where an object was scaled around one anchor point and rotated around a different anchor point. You could apply the scale to the individual clip and the rotation to a compound clip containing the individual clip. The possibilities are limitless!

Q In this example, the clip is cropped to show just the two yogis.

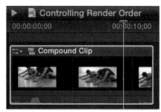

R In the Timeline, convert the cropped clip into a compound clip.

S The blur effect is applied to the precropped clip. Both the active pixels and the black ones are blurred, creating this nice, soft-edged blur.

Timing Effects

Final Cut Pro X has a wide range of tools and techniques for altering the playback speed of your video (called *retiming*). You can speed things up, slow things down, freeze on a specific frame, play in reverse, and perform *ramp* speed effects, where the speed of a clip speeds up or slows down over time.

There are also a few one-click timing effects such as Instant Replay and Rewind, which apply preset speed changes quickly and easily.

You can also customize the playback speed of your clips in a variety of ways. Finally, you can modify settings such as the rendering quality of timing effects as well as how and when audio should change pitch when a clip's speed has been changed.

Understanding Speed and Duration

One important concept that you must understand when beginning to experiment with timing effects is that the duration of a clip and its playback speed are fundamentally connected.

For example, if a 10-second clip of a sprinter running a 100m dash is played back at 2x normal speed, it's going to take the runner only 5 seconds to cross the finish line. If, instead, you play the clip at 25 percent speed, she's going to take a glacial 40 seconds to finish.

If you want to keep the slowed-down clip to ten seconds, you'll have to do some additional editing to choose whether you'll see her leaving the starting gate or crossing the finish line (or some section in between).

When you retime a clip, FCP's Timeline will automatically adjust the surrounding shots to make room for the new clip length.

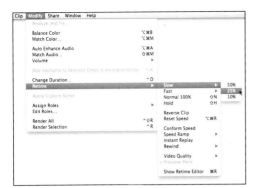

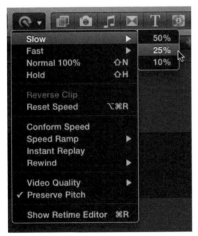

A The Retime submenu in the Modify menu contains all the retiming tools in FCP.

B The Retime menu in the toolbar (accessed by clicking the Retime button) offers duplicates of the commands in the Modify menu.

C When a timing effect is applied to a clip, the Retime Editor appears above that clip indicating the current speed.

Constant Timing Changes

Basic timing changes are those where the speed of a clip is uniformly retimed, so the whole clip plays at a faster or slower speed than normal. These changes are called *constant* timing changes, because although the clip's speed is altered, it remains at a constant speed throughout its duration.

Slow Motion

Perhaps the most common and basic of all timing effects is the *slow-motion* effect where a scene plays back at a slower-than-normal frame rate. Playing video at a reduced speed produces a compelling (and often comic) effect that allows the viewer to see the action of the shot in more detail than regular playback could ever allow.

FCP has preset slow-motion settings of 50 percent, 25 percent, and 10 percent. You can also modify the timing manually to set any speed between 99 percent and 1 percent. To apply a custom speed, see "Custom Timing Changes" later in this chapter.

To play a clip at a preset slow-motion speed:

- Select a clip in the Timeline, and *do one of the following*:
  - ▶ Choose Modify > Retime > Slow, and select one of the preset speeds A.
  - ▶ Click the Timing pop-up menu in the toolbar, choose Slow, and select one of the preset speeds B.

The Retime Editor appears above the clip, and the slow-motion preset is applied C.

Fast Motion

The opposite of the slow-motion effect is the fast-motion effect where a clip plays back faster than in real time. This is how you'd make your ten-second sprinter suddenly appear superhuman.

FCP has preset fast-motion settings of 2x, 4x, 8x, and 20x. You can also modify the timing manually to set the clip to virtually any fast speed until the clip is only one frame long. (Remember, speeding up a clip automatically shortens its duration.) To apply a custom speed, see "Custom Timing Changes" later in this chapter.

To play a clip at a preset fast-motion speed:

- Select a clip in the Timeline, and *do one of the following*:
  - ▸ Choose Modify > Retime > Fast, and select one of the preset speeds ⓓ.
  - ▸ Click the Timing pop-up menu in the toolbar, choose Fast, and select one of the preset speeds ⓔ.

  The Retime Editor appears above the clip, and the fast-motion preset is applied ⓕ.

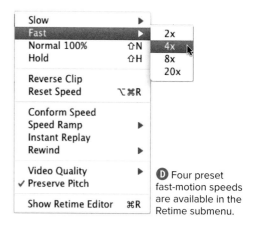

ⓓ Four preset fast-motion speeds are available in the Retime submenu.

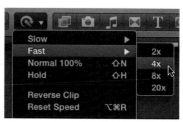

ⓔ If the Retime submenu is too far away, use the identical controls in the toolbar.

ⓕ When a clip is sped up, its duration gets shorter.

Current speed indicator   *Preset Speed pop-up*

Close button   *Retime handle*

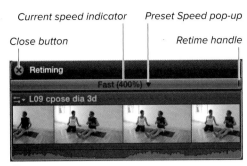

G The Retime Editor appears above the clip.

H Green indicates normal (100 percent) speed.

I Blue indicates fast-motion speed.

J Orange indicates slow-motion speed.

Custom Timing Changes

Although the preset speed settings are quick to apply, sometimes you want to play your clip at a speed somewhere in between the preset values.

To assign a custom speed to a clip, you must open the clip's Retime Editor.

As demonstrated in the previous tasks, applying a preset speed change automatically opens the Retime Editor, but you can also open it manually, without first applying a preset timing effect.

To open the Retime Editor:

- Select a clip, and *do one of the following*:

  ▸ Press Command-R.

  ▸ Choose Modify > Retime > Show Retime Editor.

  ▸ Click the Retime pop-up menu in the toolbar, and choose Show Retime Editor.

  The Retime Editor appears above the clip **G**.

The Retime Editor appears in different colors depending on the current playback speed of the clip:

- Green indicates that the clip is set to 100 percent (or normal) speed **H**.

- Blue indicates that the clip is set to a speed faster than 100 percent **I**.

- Orange indicates that the clip is set to a speed slower than 100 percent **J**.

To apply a custom speed:

1. Open the Retime Editor (if it's not already showing).

2. Drag the Retime handle at the right edge of the Retime Editor to the right to slow down the clip, and drag it to the left to speed up the clip 🄚.

   As you drag, the Current Speed indicator displays the current clip speed 🄛.

   The longer the clip gets, the slower it will play back. The shorter it gets, the faster it will play.

🄚 As you position your mouse over the Retime handle, it lights up.

🄛 As you drag the Retime handle, the current speed is displayed in the colored bar.

Optimal Slow-Motion Speeds

You already know that when you slow a clip down, the clip gets longer. But what that means from a technical standpoint is that the software must generate new frames out of thin air.

Think about it: If a 100-frame clip was slowed down to 200 frames, where did those new frames come from? FCP *interpolates* them from the surrounding frames.

The slower you set the clip to play, the more frames must be created, and the overall image quality will decline.

You can apply different settings for how the software generates those new frames (discussed in "Speed Settings" later in this chapter), but no matter which video quality setting you select, you can help the software along by choosing speeds with a uniform number of interpolated frames.

For example, if you retime a clip to exactly 50 percent, every other frame will be a "fake" frame, and playback will appear relatively smooth and uniform.

If, instead, you set the speed to 40 percent, then the number and placement of the "fake" frames is uneven, and you may notice some strobing or stuttering that will result in a lower-quality effect 🄜.

So, for best results, stick with the preset slow-motion speeds of 50 percent, 25 percent, or 10 percent, or the custom speed of 33 percent.

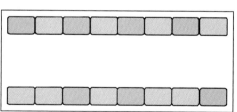

🄜 Green frames represent original frames from the camera, and orange frames are the ones generated by the software. In the top figure, speed is set to 50 percent, and every other frame is computer-generated. In the lower figure, at 40 percent the interpolated frames are distributed less uniformly.

Preset Speeds pop-up

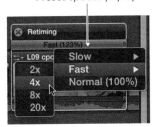

N Click the Preset Speeds pop-up, and select a new speed for the clip.

O Reset a clip to normal speed by pressing Shift-N.

P The Preset Speeds pop-up in the Retime Editor contains an option for 100 percent.

TIP Once you've modified a clip's playback speed, you can still edit the clip's duration by dragging the edge of the thumbnail area (or by using the Trim tool). The number of frames in the clip will change, but the timing will remain set to the speed indicated in the Retime Editor.

To return to a preset speed:

1. Open the Retime Editor.

2. Click the Preset Speeds pop-up menu, and choose one of the preset speeds **N**.

   The clip is retimed to your chosen preset speed.

TIP You can also just apply a new speed setting from the Retime submenu or the Retime menu in the toolbar.

Resetting Speed to Normal

As you experiment with retiming clips, you may find the need to return the clip to normal 100 percent playback. You can drag the Retime Editor manually until the speed reaches exactly 100 percent, but it might be easier to use the FCP command specifically for that purpose.

To reset a clip to normal speed:

- Select the clip in the Timeline, and *do one of the following*:

  ▶ Choose Modify > Retime > Normal 100%.

  ▶ Press Shift-N.

  ▶ Click the Retime pop-up menu in the toolbar, and choose Normal 100% **O**.

- If the Retime Editor is showing, click the Preset Speeds pop-up menu, and choose Normal 100% **P**.

  The clip is reset to 100 percent speed.

Hiding the Retime Editor

The Retime Editor allows you to customize your timing effects, and as you'll learn in the coming sections, it also allows you to divide a clip into multiple segments to perform more complex timing effects.

However, once you're done adjusting the timing of your shots, you may want to hide the Retime Editor to keep your Timeline view clean or to use that section of the Timeline for keyframing. (To learn more about keyframing, see Chapter 21, "Animating Effects.")

Hiding the Retime Editor does not disable any timing effects you may have applied. It just temporarily hides the controls you use to modify them.

To hide the Retime Editor:

- Select the clip (or clips), and *do one of the following*:

  ▸ Press Command-R.

  ▸ Click the Close button in the upper left of the Retime Editor **O**.

  ▸ Click the Retime pop-up menu in the toolbar, and choose Hide Retime Editor.

  The Retime Editor is hidden from view.

Close button

O Hide the Retime Editor by clicking the Close button or pressing Command-R.

A Position the playhead over the last frame in the clip. The filmstrip graphic on the right side of the Viewer indicates that you're on the last frame of the project.

B A speed segment is added to represent the freeze frame. Freeze frames are indicated in red and marked as "0%" in the Retime Editor.

Freeze Frames

Another common retiming effect is to create a *freeze frame*: a few seconds of playback where the video holds (or *freezes*) on a single frame as if it were a photograph.

This technique is frequently employed at the end of a movie, suspending the action indefinitely as the movie fades out. Other times, a freeze frame occurs in the middle of a scene to emphasize a certain moment, and then playback resumes from where it left off.

FCP makes both of these techniques very easy to do.

To create a freeze frame at the end of a shot:

1. Select the clip you want to freeze, and position the playhead on the last frame of the shot **A**.

> **TIP** Press the Down Arrow key and then the Left Arrow key to navigate to the last frame of a shot.

2. *Do one of the following*:
   ▸ Press Shift-H.
   ▸ Choose Modify > Retime > Hold.
   ▸ Click the Retime pop-up menu in the toolbar, and then choose Hold.

   A two-second freeze frame speed segment is added to the end of the shot. If it's not already showing, the Retime Editor appears above the clip **B**.

To create a freeze frame in the middle of a shot:

1. Select a clip, and position the playhead on the frame you want to freeze **C**.

2. *Do one of the following*:

   ▸ Press Shift-H.

   ▸ Choose Modify > Retime > Hold.

   ▸ Click the Retime pop-up menu in the toolbar, and then choose Hold.

   A two-second freeze frame is added in the middle of the clip. The clip resumes normal playback after the freeze ends **D**.

While the two-second default freeze frame might be useful in some cases, most of the time you'll probably want to change the duration to whatever is appropriate for the project at hand.

To change the duration of a freeze frame:

1. Create a freeze frame using one of the techniques described earlier **E**.

2. In the Retime Editor, drag the Retime handle at the right edge of the freeze frame bar to the left to shorten the duration, and drag it right to lengthen the duration **F**.

   The frozen section changes duration.

C Position the playhead over the frame you want to freeze.

D A freeze frame segment is added to the clip at the selected frame.

E Once you've created a freeze frame, you may want to customize its duration.

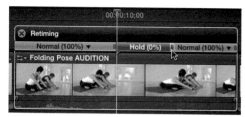

F Drag the Retime handle to change the duration of the freeze frame.

A Ramp to 0% breaks your clip into four speed segments, each with a slower speed. The exact speeds will depend on the original duration of your clip.

Speed Ramp Effects

In addition to creating constant speed changes, you can also make a clip's playback speed change over time. This creates an effect where the clip's speed appears to *ramp* up or ramp down, getting faster or slower over the course of the clip.

To do this, FCP breaks the clip into four *speed segments* and assigns a different speed value to each, adjusting each subsequent speed to make the clip appear to be slowing down or speeding up over time.

TIP You can apply a speed ramp to an individual speed segment, restricting the clip's speed change to that limited range.

FCP offers two speed ramp commands: Ramp to 0% and Ramp from 0%. Ramp to 0% sets each subsequent speed segment to play at a slower rate. Ramp from 0% sets each subsequent speed segment to play at a faster rate.

Once you've created speed segments within a clip, you can customize their individual playback rates manually (including setting an individual segment to ramp to or from 0 percent), creating a wide range of custom and unique timing effects.

Note that applying a ramp effect to a clip will replace any existing speed effects or speed segments currently applied to that clip.

To set a clip to ramp to 0 percent:

- Select a clip, and choose Modify > Retime > Speed Ramp > To 0%.

  The clip is broken into four speed segments, and each is assigned a diminishing speed value **A**.

  Playing the clip will result in the playback appearing to slow down to a stop.

To set a clip to ramp from 0 percent:

- Select a clip, and choose Modify > Retime > Speed Ramp > From 0%.

  The clip is broken into four speed segments, and each is assigned an increasing speed value **B**.

  Playing the clip will result in the playback beginning in very slow motion and increasing gradually to regular speed.

To select a speed segment:

- Click the blank area of the Retime Editor above a clip (don't click the speed value or the Preset Speeds pop-up) **C**.

TIP It may help to zoom in on the Timeline in order to select the range.

The range of the clip controlled by that speed segment is selected.

To modify a speed segment's playback rate:

- *Do one of the following*:
  - Click the Preset Speeds pop-up for the segment you want to modify, and choose an option from the menu **D**.
  - Drag the Retime handle at the right edge of the Retime Editor for each speed segment to the right to slow the clip down, or drag it to the left to speed it up **E**.
  - Select the speed segment, and choose a setting from the Retime menu.

B Ramp from 0% also breaks your clip into four speed segments, but this time each segment is set to faster speed than the last.

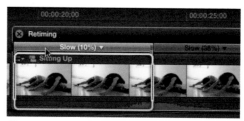

C The freeze frame changes length to match the value you selected.

D Each speed segment has its own Preset Speeds pop-up that you can use to control the speed of that segment.

E You can drag the Retime handle to change the speed of any segment individually.

F Choose Change End Source Frame from the Preset Speeds pop-up.

G The right edge of the Retime Editor turns into a filmstrip icon.

H A check mark to the left of a Change End Source Frame menu item indicates that it is active. Choose the item again to disable it.

Modifying a Speed Segment

You can also change the duration of a segment without changing its speed. This adds or removes frames from the segment, taking them away from or adding them to the adjacent segment.

This is equivalent to *rolling* an edit point, but you're simply rolling where one speed segment ends and the next one begins.

You always modify the *end* of a segment, although by definition you are also adjusting the beginning of the next segment. You cannot adjust the Change End Source Frame setting on the last segment in a clip.

To change where a speed segment ends:

1. Click the Preset Speeds pop-up for the segment you want to change, and choose Change End Source Frame **F**.

   A filmstrip icon appears at the edge of the speed segment **G**.

2. Drag the filmstrip icon left or right to choose a new ending frame for the speed segment.

   TIP As you drag, the Viewer updates to show the current end frame.

   When you have successfully chosen the new end frame, click the Preset Speeds pop-up again, and select Change End Source Frame again **H**.

   The speed segment is adjusted.

Reverse Playback

Another special effect that falls in the timing category is reverse playback, where the video plays backward. Video can be played in reverse at any speed, and you can change the speed at which a clip plays before or after assigning it to play in reverse.

To set a clip (or group of clips) to play backward:

- Select the clip (or clips), and choose Modify > Retime > Reverse Clip.

  The clip is set to play in reverse. If the Retime Editor is not showing, it appears above the clip .

TIP The Reverse Clip command works only on whole clips. To play a segment of a clip in reverse, use the Rewind command described in the next section.

A When you set a clip to play in reverse, the Retime Editor appears and shows a pattern of left-facing arrows. The color of the bar still reflects whether the clip is playing in fast motion (orange), in slow motion (blue), or at its normal speed (green) as shown here.

Ⓐ Select the range of the clip you want to rewind.

Ⓑ Choose the speed at which you want the rewound section to play: 1x (normal speed), 2x, or 4x.

Rewound section (at -2x) *Remainder of clip*

Original selected range *Section that will replay at normal speed*

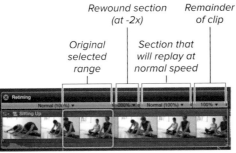

Ⓒ Rewind adds three speed segments: one for the section playing backward, one for the section that plays forward to get back to the frame where the original clip resumes, and one for the remainder of the clip.

Rewind and Instant Replay

Two special retiming commands apply commonly used but complex-to-create speed effects in a single step.

Rewind

Rewind applies a timing effect where the selected range of a clip is played backward (at one of three speeds) and then playback resumes through the end of the clip.

Rewind always makes the resulting clip significantly longer: Not only does it add time to show the selected section in reverse, but then it plays forward again, replaying the selected section and then continuing with whatever frames remain in the clip.

To rewind a clip:

1. Use the Range Select tool (R) to select the section of the clip you want to rewind **Ⓐ**.

2. Click the Retime pop-up menu in the toolbar, choose Rewind, and then select 1x, 2x, or 4x to determine at what speed the rewound section should play **Ⓑ**.

> **TIP** Once you've created the rewound segment, you can customize its speed manually.

Three new speed segments are added to the clip: one for the rewound section, one for the area where the clip is replayed in forward motion, and one for the area between the replayed section and the end of the clip **Ⓒ**.

Instant Replay

Instant Replay adds a speed segment that repeats the selected clip (or range of a clip) at the current playback speed.

Like Rewind, Instant Replay makes the clip longer by adding a section equal in length to the selected range.

Although by default Instant Replay plays the repeated section at regular speed, it's very easy to slow it down after the fact to create a slow-motion instant replay.

To perform an instant replay:

1. Use the Range Select tool to select the portion of the clip you want to replay **D**.

2. Click the Retime pop-up menu in the toolbar, and choose Instant Replay.

   A speed segment is added to the clip, repeating the selected section **E**.

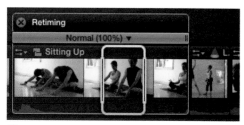

D Select the range of the clip you want to play as an instant replay.

Selected section repeated

Originally selected range *Remainder of clip*

E Instant Reply adds two speed segments: a one-frame segment rewinding the clip to the beginning of the selected range and a second segment replaying the selected range at the speed previously selected.

F Set the speed of the replay segment to 50 percent using the Preset Speeds pop-up.

How Instant Replay Works

If you zoom in and closely examine a clip after Instant Replay has been applied, you'll see a one-frame speed segment between the end of the selected range and the new replayed version. This one frame is how the clip is rewound to the first frame so it can play forward again **G**. Because it's only one frame long, you don't notice any reverse playback occur.

One-frame segment rewinding clip to first frame of selected range

G Instant Reply adds two speed segments: a one-frame segment rewinding the clip to the beginning of the selected range and a second segment replaying the selected range at the speed previously selected.

To create a slow-motion instant replay:

1. Complete steps 1 and 2 in the previous section.

2. Click the Adjust Speed menu on the newly created speed segment, and choose Slow > 50% (or whatever speed you prefer) **F**.

   The instant replay plays in slow motion.

Conform Speed

If you have clips in your sequence with differing frame rates, FCP converts the frame rate on-the-fly to make sure all clips play back in real time. However, you can override that setting and instruct FCP to play clips at the project frame rate regardless of the rate at which it was originally shot.

This means that a 5-second clip at 30fps will become 6 seconds long in a 25fps project, playing at 75 percent speed.

Similarly, shots filmed at 60fps can be put in a 30fps project and set to play at 50 percent speed without requiring any interpolation or rendering, which means they will be as visually sharp as footage that came straight from the camera, except they will play in slow motion.

For professional cameras that can record at higher frame rates, this feature enables you to add such clips to your project, preserving the high-quality slow motion created in the camera.

To force a clip to play at the project frame rate:

- Select the clip, and choose Modify > Retime > Conform Speed.

  The Retime Editor appears, and the clip is retimed to play at the project frame rate .

(A) A clip that was filmed at a higher frame rate will play in slow motion when conformed in a lower-frame rate project.

A Select one or more clips from which you want to remove all retiming effects.

C The clips are reset to play at 100 percent forward.

B Choose Reset Speed, or press Option-Command-R.

Removing All Timing Effects

At any point you can remove all timing effects from a clip, resetting it to its default. This will remove any speed segments, remove any timing changes applied to those segments, and reset playback to forward-play if Reverse Playback had been applied.

To remove all timing effects from a clip:

- Select a clip (or clips), and *do one of the following* **A**:

  ▸ Choose Modify > Retime > Reset Speed.

  ▸ Click the Retime pop-up menu in the toolbar, and choose Reset Speed **B**.

  ▸ Press Option-Command-R.

  Any timing effects applied to the clip are removed, resetting it to play forward at 100 percent **C**.

Retiming Settings

You can use two settings to control the way timing effects are applied. Video Quality allows you to set the interpolation method FCP uses when generating new frames for slow-motion effects. Preserve Pitch controls whether audio pitch is altered when a clip is sped up or slowed down.

Video Quality

When a clip or clip segment is assigned to play in slow motion, new intermediate frames must be generated to create the effect. FCP offers three choices for how such frames are rendered:

- **Normal** duplicates adjacent frames. This option doesn't require any rendering but results in a stuttery, steppy visual effect.

- **Frame Blending** creates intermediate frames by cross dissolving between the surrounding frames. This requires rendering, but it creates a smoother-looking slow-motion effect than the Normal method does. Frame Blending can result in an undesirable softness or blurriness, especially at lower speeds where more artificial frames are required.

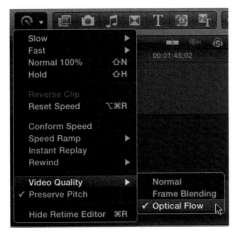

A Click the Retime pop-up menu in the toolbar, and choose one of the three Video Quality options.

B While a clip is being analyzed for Optical Flow, text is displayed in the Viewer.

- **Optical Flow** uses a more sophisticated interpolation method where the clip is analyzed and the directional movement of objects within the frame is identified. Although it takes more time (the clip first must be analyzed, and the speed effect then must be rendered), Optical Flow can result in sharper and more accurate intermediate frames than Frame Blending. However, if there is too much movement in the frame—as happens with camera movement or very complex scenes—Optical Flow may produce undesirable artifacts.

Note that playing back a slow-motion clip prior to rendering will always play in the Normal, frame duplication method.

To set the rendering quality for slow-motion effects:

- Choose Modify > Retime > Video Quality, and choose one of the three settings, or click the Retime pop-up menu in the toolbar, and choose one of the three Video Quality options **A**.

The video-rendering quality is set based on your selection.

If you choose Optical Flow, a message will appear in the Viewer indicating that the clip is being analyzed **B**.

To observe the progress of Optical Flow analysis:

1. Click the Background Tasks indicator in the Current Frame indicator **C**.

   The Background Tasks window opens.

2. Expand the Transcoding and Analysis category **D**.

   The progress of the Optical Flow analysis is displayed.

Preserve Pitch

By default, FCP maintains audio pitch when a clip has been retimed. However, you may want to disable this setting to allow the audio pitch to shift up as a clip is sped up and to shift down as a clip is slowed down.

Turning off this setting creates a more obvious (and often comic) speed effect.

To disable audio pitch preservation:

- Choose Modify > Retime > Preserve Pitch, or click the Retime pop-up menu in the toolbar and choose Preserve Pitch **E**.

   Pitch preservation is disabled. When this setting is on, a check mark appears next to the command in the menu.

Background Tasks indicator

C Click the Render Clock to open the Background Tasks window.

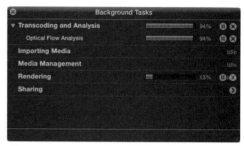

D The Background Tasks window shows the progress of all background rendering tasks.

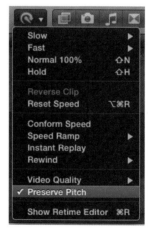

E Turn off Preserve Pitch to have the audio get higher when sped up or lower when slowed down. The only indicator of whether this setting is on or off is in the Retime submenu or the Retime pop-up menu in the toolbar.

Transition Effects

In most projects, the majority of your shots will transition from one clip to the next using a *cut*, where one clip abruptly stops and the next abruptly starts. This common convention works great in many situations.

Sometimes, however, you want a different type of transition between shots. Often this is to create a more gradual change from one shot to the next (typically using a *dissolve*), and sometimes it's to create a more dramatic shift, signaling to the viewer that the two adjacent shots should not be viewed in combination but rather that they are of two wholly different sections. This is where wipes, page-curls, zoom-blurs, and other more visually striking transition effects come into play.

Fortunately, adding and modifying such transitions in Final Cut Pro is easy and intuitive. This chapter will cover all aspects of working with such transition effects.

In This Chapter

Adding Cross Dissolves

The most basic type of transition effect is a *cross dissolve* (sometimes called just *dissolve*) where one shot fades out at the same time another fades in.

Because cross dissolves are so common, Final Cut Pro makes it extremely easy to add them to any edit in your project, using one of two methods: Available Media or Full Overlap (see the sidebar "Two Ways to Handle Transitions" for a full explanation).

To add a dissolve to an edit:

1. Click the edit to select it **A**.

   The edit is highlighted in yellow.

2. Choose Edit > Add Cross Dissolve, or press Command-T.

   A cross dissolve effect is added to the edit **B**.

To add a dissolve to the beginning and end of a clip:

1. Click the clip to select it **C**.

2. Choose Edit > Add Cross Dissolve, or press Command-T.

   A cross dissolve effect is added both to the edit at the beginning and to the edit at the end of the selected clip **D**.

> **TIP** You can also right-click any clip and choose **Add Cross Dissolve** from the shortcut menu. Dissolves will be added to the beginning and ending of the clip.

A Click either side of the edit to select it.

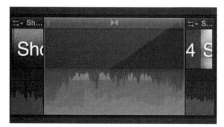

B The cut is converted into a dissolve.

C Select a clip rather than an edit.

D And dissolves are added to both sides.

Two Ways to Handle Transitions

Final Cut Pro 7 and iMovie handle the way transitions are added to a project differently. Final Cut Pro X supports both methods, so it's important to understand how they differ from each other and why you'd want to choose one over the other.

The issue revolves around which frames are used during the transition effect. A cut edit has no duration; one shot ends, the next begins. But with a transition effect, there is a period of time where one shot is ending and the next is starting.

Whenever you add a transition effect, you begin with an existing cut, and presumably you chose the ending frames of the outgoing shot and the starting frames of the incoming shot deliberately. But when you add the transition effect, more frames are needed to fill out the duration of the effect; a one-second dissolve requires a half-second worth of frames to fade out the outgoing shot and a half-second of fade-in frames for the incoming shot.

In prior versions of FCP, those extra frames were taken from the unused frames (aka *handles*) in your source media—frames after your chosen Out point and before your chosen In point **E**.

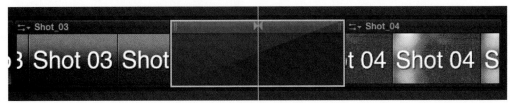

E "Final Cut Pro–style" transitions do not change the clip length.

This could cause issues because there might be a mistake, a camera shake, or something else in those frames that you don't want to include in your project. However, this method ensures that your clips maintain their existing duration and that those deliberate In and Out points you set remain at the center point of the transition.

In iMovie, the two clips are each shortened by a half-second, so no extra frames are required. This ensures no unexpected frames are used, but because the frames at the very beginning and very ending of the transition effect are barely visible, those "important frames" you chose as the original edit point are now mostly hidden. Also, changing the duration of the shots can impact the "flow" of the scene **F**.

F "iMovie-style" transitions shorten the durations of both clips.

Final Cut Pro X gives you the option of using the Final Cut Pro 7 way (called *Available Media*) or the iMovie way (called *Full Overlap*).

To choose how transitions are applied:

1. Open the Preferences window by choosing Final Cut Pro > Preferences or pressing Command-, (comma).

2. Click the Editing icon to open the Editing pane 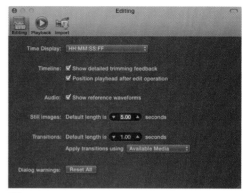.

3. In the Transitions category, click the "Apply transitions using" pop-up menu .

4. Then *do one of the following:*

   ‣ To select the Final Cut Pro 7 way of doing things, choose Available Media.

   ‣ To choose the iMovie way of doing things, choose Full Overlap.

G Open the Editing pane of Final Cut Pro preferences.

H Choose which style of transitions you prefer.

Ⓐ Click the Transitions icon to open the Transitions Browser.

Using the Transitions Browser

Cross dissolves are useful for communicating time passage, location changes, or shifts in emotional state within a story, but sometimes you want to employ something a little more disruptive. Final Cut Pro comes with a collection of nearly 100 transition effects you can use to draw your audience's attention away from the content of the footage and instead to the construction of the movie.

Sometimes such interruption is important. For example, in a safety training video, you may want to ensure that viewers disengage from a compelling dramatic reenactment before presenting them with a list of important safety tips. In such a case, a really obnoxious or goofy transition might produce just the desired effect.

Final Cut Pro's myriad transition effects can be previewed, selected, and applied to your project from the Transitions Browser.

To view the Transitions Browser:

- Click the Transitions Browser icon Ⓐ.

  The Transitions Browser opens.

The Transitions Browser displays all the effects available to you including third-party plug-ins if you have any installed. Each effect is displayed with an illustrative thumbnail image and a descriptive name.

The Transitions Browser has two parts: the stack where the list of effects is displayed and a sidebar containing category names.

You can find specific transition effects either by searching for a particular name or by browsing through the various categories of effects.

To find specific transition effects:

■ *Do one of the following*:

▶ Type the name of the effect you're looking for in the search field at the bottom of the Transitions Browser **B**.

The stack is filtered to show only transition effects containing the letters in the search field.

TIP Clear the search field by clicking the circled X at the right edge of the field or by pressing Escape.

▶ Click one of the category names in the sidebar on the left side of the Transitions Browser, and scroll through the main stack area on the right **C**.

The stack is filtered by category.

TIP Hide or show the sidebar by clicking the Show/Hide Sidebar button in the lower-left corner of the Transitions Browser.

Previewing Transition Effects

You can preview what each effect looks like prior to adding it to your project. This enables you to experiment with a variety of effects quickly.

To preview a transition effect:

■ *Do one of the following*:

▶ Hover your pointer over a transition icon in the Transitions Browser to skim across the effect preview **D**.

▶ Position your pointer over a transition icon, and press the Spacebar.

The Viewer loops a sample of the transition effect.

TIP Click different transition icons while previewing to view different effects previews dynamically.

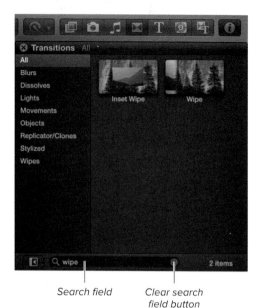

Search field   Clear search field button

B Search for a specific transition effect by typing in the search field.

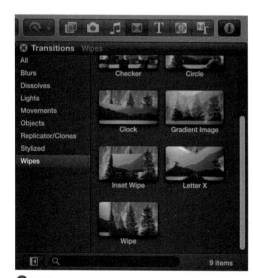

C Click a category in the sidebar to filter the list.

D Skim across transition icons to see a preview or hover over the icon, and press the Spacebar to play.

E If an edit is selected, double-clicking a transition icon will apply it to that edit.

F If a clip is selected, double-clicking a transition icon will apply it to the head and tail of the clip.

G You can also drag and drop a transition effect to an edit in the primary storyline.

Adding a Transition Effect to the Primary Storyline

Once you've settled on which transition effect you want to use, you can add it to an edit in your primary storyline in one of two ways.

To add a transition effect:

- *Do one of the following*:
  - ▸ Select an edit in the primary storyline, and double-click a transition icon in the Transitions Browser.

    The transition effect is added to the selected edit **E**.
  - ▸ Select a clip in the primary storyline, and double-click a transition icon in the Transitions Browser.

    The transition effect is added to the head and tail of the selected clip **F**.
  - ▸ Drag and drop the transition icon from the Transitions Browser to an edit point in the primary storyline **G**.

Transition Effects and Connected Clips

You cannot apply a transition effect to connected clips unless they are embedded in a secondary storyline. If you want to add such an effect to an edit that's not in the primary storyline, you must first create a secondary storyline containing the connected clip (or clips) to which you want to add the transition effect. Fortunately, it does this automatically anytime you attempt to apply a transition effect to a connected clip.

To add a transition effect between two connected clips:

1. Select the edit between two adjacent connected clips. **H**

2. Press Command-T.

   The clip or clips are converted into a secondary storyline and the transition is applied. **I**

TIP Be sure to select the clip inside the secondary storyline and not the storyline itself.

To add a transition effect to the beginning and end of a connected clip:

- Select the connected clip and press Command-T.

  The clip is converted into a secondary storyline and the transition effect is added to the head and tail of the clip **J**.

- Drag and drop the transition icon from the Transitions Browser to the desired edit point.

H Select the edit between two clips.

I By pressing the Command-T shortcut, a secondary storyline is automatically created and the transition is added.

J Once a clip is in the secondary storyline you can apply transitions to it just like to clips in the primary storyline.

To delete a transition, select it so it's highlighted with a yellow box.

Press Delete to remove the transition effect.

Removing a Transition Effect

Transition effects are best used in moderation, so after you've had a good time adding different ones to every edit in your project, you'll want to know how to remove them.

To remove a transition effect:

1. Click the transition effect in the Timeline to select it ⓚ.

2. Press Delete.

   The transition effect is removed, and the edit is restored to a regular cut ⓛ.

Note that if your "Apply transitions using" setting is set to Full Overlap, deleting a transition effect will not restore the clips to their original durations.

TIP You can also press Command-X to remove a transition and copy it to the clipboard and then select another edit point and press Command-V to paste it to that new location.

Replacing an Existing Transition Effect

Once you've applied a transition effect to an edit, you can swap out the specific effect for another without first removing the old effect.

To replace one transition effect with another:

- Select a transition effect in the timeline, and *do one of the following* :

  - ▶ Double-click a different transition effect in the Transitions Browser.

  - ▶ Drag and drop a new transition effect from the Transitions Browser onto the existing transition in the Timeline .

  The new effect replaces the old one, maintaining the duration established in the Timeline.

M Select a transition in the Timeline and double-click a different item in the Transitions Browser to replace one effect with another.

N Drag and drop one transition right on top of an existing one to replace the effect but maintain the existing duration.

Modifying Transition Effect Settings

You can modify any transition's duration, which can have a significant impact on how the transition effect is experienced by the viewer. For example, a three-frame dissolve (often called a *soft cut*) has a completely different meaning and effect on your audience than does a three-second *lap* dissolve, even though both use the same cross dissolve effect in the Timeline.

Additionally, many transitions have different settings and options you can adjust to customize an effect. This might be the number of bands in a Band Wipe, the center point of a ripple effect, or whether a Mosaic effect should employ the Classic, Wave, or Explode style.

By customizing these settings, you can make the effects in your project more distinctive and tailor them specifically to your project (by, for example, setting background colors to match colors used in your footage). This also allows you to use one general type of transition per project but with enough variation so it doesn't feel repetitive.

Changing Duration

You can modify a transition effect's duration in a variety of ways. In some cases, you may want to type in a specific duration as a number, and in other cases, you may want to drag a transition until it aligns with a particular frame in a clip.

To change a transition effect's duration numerically:

1. Select the transition in the Timeline.

2. Right-click the transition and choose Change Duration, or or select the transition and press Control-D and press Control-D .

TIP You can see the duration of the current selection displayed at the bottom of the Timeline window.

The Current Timecode indicator changes to the Duration field.

3. Type your desired transition as frames or timecode, and press Enter 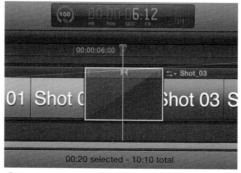.

The transition effect's duration is updated.

TIP When the Trim tool is selected, you can also use the trimming keys (< and >) to decrease or increase the duration of a selected transition one frame at a time.

To change a transition effect's duration visually:

1. Make sure "Show detailed trimming feedback" is enabled in the Editing preferences window .

Ⓐ Select a transition and press Control-D to modify its duration.

Ⓑ In this example, I typed *20* and then pressed Enter, shortening the transition to 20 frames.

Ⓒ Enable "Show detailed trimming feedback" in the Editing preferences.

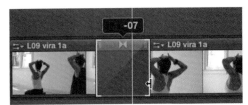

D Drag either edge of a transition effect to change its duration.

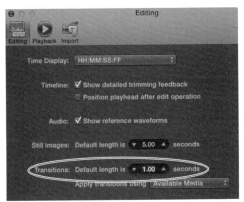

E The Viewer shows a two-up display of the new transition's beginning and end frames.

F The default transition length is set in the Editing preferences.

2. With the Select tool, drag either edge of the transition in the Timeline **D**.

The transition's duration changes by the number of frames you drag.

An Info window appears and shows how many frames you have added or removed from the transition's duration.

The Viewer displays the last frame of the outgoing clip before the transition starts and the first frame of the incoming clip after the transition ends **E**.

Note this is different from Final Cut Pro 7, which displayed the last used frame of the outgoing clip and the first used frame of the incoming shot.

Changing the Default Duration

By default, most transitions are exactly one second long. (There are a few theme-based transitions that default to a longer duration.) You can change this default if a particular show routinely requires shorter or longer transition effects.

To change the default transition effect duration:

1. Choose Final Cut Pro > Preferences.

2. Click the Editing icon to open the Editing pane **F**.

3. In the Transitions section, set the Default Length setting to your preferred value.

4. Close the Preferences window.

From that point forward, every new transition will be applied with the chosen duration. Existing transition effects in the Timeline will not be affected.

Changing Effect Controls

Not all transition effects have customizable settings, but many do. Examples include the width, color, and softness settings of the border on a Wipe effect; the curvature, color, and direction of a Page Curl; or the sample still images displayed in the Bulletin Board Pan transitions (described in more detail in a moment).

Transition effect controls can be displayed only after you have applied the effect to an edit in your project, so in many cases the only way to know what options may be available is to apply the transition to a sample edit before you commit to using the effect.

To modify Effect Controls:

1. Apply a transition effect to an edit in your project.
2. Select the transition in the Timeline .
3. Click the Show Inspector button, or press Command-4.

   The Inspector shows any parameters you can modify for the selected transition **H**.
4. Adjust the settings in the Inspector to your liking **I**.

TIP Be sure your playhead is parked over the transition effect in the Timeline to see the results of the changes you are making in the Inspector.

5. For best results, press Shift-? to play around with the edit to see how the effect looks while playing.

Note that some transitions don't have any modifiable settings and will display only the name of the transition in the Inspector.

G Select the transition you want to modify. It's also a good idea to make sure your playhead is parked over the transition.

H The Transition Inspector contains the parameters for the selected transition.

I As you change the parameter settings, you can watch the Viewer update in real time.

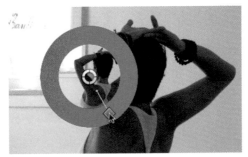

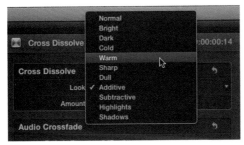

J Some effects have on-screen controls. This Circle Wipe, for instance, allows you to adjust the center point and the thickness of the border by dragging controls in the Viewer.

K Select a dissolve and position your playhead over it in the Timeline.

L In the Transition Inspector, choose one of the settings in the Look pop-up menu, and set the Amount slider to control how dramatic the effect.

TIP Some transitions (as well as other effects) have on-screen controls that allow you to manipulate certain parameters visually in the Viewer. The effect must be selected in the Timeline for these controls to be visible **J**.

Cross Dissolve "Looks"

One fun and powerful feature in Final Cut Pro is the cross dissolve Looks setting, which allows you to assign one of 11 different styles to any dissolve effect.

Furthermore, you can control how much or how little of the particular "look" you want to apply to the dissolve effect.

To change the cross dissolve look:

1. Select a Cross Dissolve effect in the Timeline, and position your playhead over it **K**.

2. Open the Inspector, and in the Cross Dissolve section, choose a setting from the Look pop-up menu. Choices include Normal, Bright, Dark, Cold, Warm, Sharp, Dull, Additive, Subtractive, Highlights, and Shadows **L**.

3. Set the Amount slider to control how much of the "look" to apply **M**.

4. Play around the edit to see the results of your changes.

M Always play around the transition to see how it looks in real time.

Choosing Sample Frames

Some theme-based transitions such as the Comic Book and Bulletin Board effects utilize frames from your project as graphic elements in the transition effect.

When such a transition is selected, new controls appear in the Timeline to allow you to choose the specific frames to be used.

To select sample frames:

1. Select the transition in the Timeline.

   A series of yellow flags appears in the Timeline around the transition effect.

   Each of these flags represents one of the sample frames used in the effect. The Viewer shows corresponding yellow highlights to identify where the selected frames will appear .

2. Be sure the playhead is over the transition effect, and drag each yellow flag to the specific frame in the Timeline you want to use .

   TIP Some of the sample images appear only briefly during the transition. You may need to shuttle through the transition to find a frame where the sample image is visible.

   The Viewer will update to show how the chosen frame will appear in the transition effect ℗.

3. Repeat step 3 for each of the remaining yellow flags.

4. Play around the edit to see the results of your changes.

Frame 1 will appear in this box.

The yellow flag indicates the displayed frame.

ℕ Some transition effects use other frames in the project as decorative elements. Yellow flags indicate which frames will be used.

◉ Drag the yellow flags to choose a new frame.

℗ Watch the Viewer to see the selected frame appear in one of the windows. Stop dragging when the desired frame is reached.

Trimming an Edit Under a Transition Effect

Just because you've applied a transition effect to an edit doesn't mean you can't ripple or roll the edit under the effect to change exactly which frames from the source clips are used.

You can ripple the outgoing clip, ripple the incoming clip, or roll the edit, and you can do all of these both in the Timeline and in the Precision Editor.

Note that trimming an edit will never affect the duration of the transition effect applied to that edit, unless your trim uses up all the available media in your source clips.

Rolling a Transition Effect

At the top of the transition effect there is a light gray bar that allows you to perform trimming effects on a transition-laden edit. You don't even need to use the Trim tool.

Rolling a transition moves the transition earlier or later in time by trimming the frames of the underlying clips. Rolling to the left will remove frames from the outgoing clip and, simultaneously, add the same number of frames to the incoming clip, effectively moving the transition effect earlier in time.

Rolling to the right performs the opposite, moving the transition effect later in time. For more on rolling edits, see Chapter 9, "Advanced Editing."

To roll an edit under a transition effect:

- *Do one of the following*:
  - ▶ Drag the inward-facing arrows icon **A** at the top center of the transition effect **B**.
  - ▶ Click the inward-facing arrows icon to select the edit, and press , (comma) to roll the edit to the left and press . (period) to roll the edit to the right.
  - ▶ Click the inward-facing arrows icon to select the edit, and type a time-code number (preceded by + or −) to roll the edit by a specific number of frames **C**.

  The transition effect moves to a new location in the Timeline.

Rippling Under a Transition Effect

Similar to rolling, you can ripple the clips underlying a transition effect. You can trim either the end of the outgoing clip or the beginning of the incoming clip. For more on ripple edits, see Chapter 9, "Advanced Editing."

To ripple the outgoing clip:

- *Do one of the following*:
  - ▶ Drag the Ripple Outgoing Trim handle at the top left of the transition effect **D**.
  - ▶ Click to the right of the left edge of the transition effect.

TIP Watch to make sure you see the Ripple Outgoing pointer (and not the Transition Resize pointer) before clicking. Otherwise, you'll change the transition's duration rather than rippling the edit.

Roll Transition handle

A The inward-facing arrows indicate the Roll Transition handle for the edit under the transition.

B As you drag, an Info window displays the number of frames.

C Select the Roll Transition handle to roll the edit from the keyboard.

Ripple Incoming Trim handle

Ripple Outgoing Trim handle

D Drag the Ripple Outgoing Trim handle to trim the outgoing clip.

ⓔ Select the Outgoing Trim handle to trim the outgoing clip from the keyboard.

ⓕ Select the Incoming Trim handle to trim the incoming clip from the keyboard.

▸ Click the Ripple Outgoing Trim handle to select the outgoing edit edge, and press , (comma) to shorten the outgoing clip and press . (period) to lengthen the outgoing clip **ⓔ**.

▸ Click the Outgoing Trim handle to select the edit, and type a timecode number (preceded by + or –) to ripple the outgoing clip by a specific number of frames.

The outgoing clip gets longer or shorter, and the transition effect maintains its duration.

To ripple the incoming clip:

■ *Do one of the following*:

▸ Drag the Incoming Trim handle at the top left of the transition effect.

▸ Click to the left of the right edge of the transition effect.

TIP Watch to make sure you see the Ripple Incoming pointer (and not the Transition Resize pointer) before clicking. Otherwise, you'll change the transition's duration rather than rippling the edit.

▸ Click the Incoming Trim handle to select the outgoing edit edge, and press , (comma) to lengthen the incoming clip and press . (period) to shorten the incoming clip **ⓕ**.

▸ Click the Incoming Trim handle to select the edit, and type a timecode number (preceded by + or –) to ripple the outgoing clip by a specific number of frames.

The incoming clip gets longer or shorter, and the transition effect maintains its duration.

Using the Precision Editor on an Edit with a Transition Effect Applied

You can also trim an edit using the Precision Editor even when a transition effect is applied to the clip. You can perform all the same trimming operations to the edit as you can when there is no transition effect, plus you can modify the transition effect's duration in the Precision Editor. For more on using the Precision Editor, see "Using the Precision Editor" in Chapter 9.

To open the Precision Editor on a transition:

- Do one of the following:
  - ▶ Select the transition effect in the Timeline, and press Control-E.
  - ▶ Double-click the inward-facing arrow icon or either of the Ripple handles on the top edge of the transition effect.
  - ▶ Right-click the transition effect, and choose Show Precision Editor from the shortcut menu **G**.

  The Precision Editor opens.

You can trim the edit using any of the methods described in the "Using the Precision Editor" section of Chapter 9.

To change a transition effect's duration in the Precision Editor:

- Drag either the left or right edge of the Transition icon in the center bar of the Precision Editor. Drag outward to make the transition effect longer, and drag inward to make the effect shorter **H**.

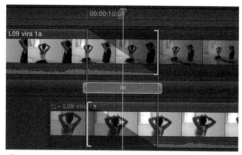

G Edits with transition effects applied can still be opened in the Precision Editor. The transition appears as a bar in the dividing bar.

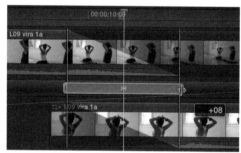

H Drag the edge of the transition bar to change the duration of the transition effect.

Audio Transitions

In addition to video transition effects, Final Cut Pro adds audio crossfades to create smooth transitions between adjacent audio clips. The good news is that these cross-fades are high quality and very customizable. The bad news is that Final Cut Pro adds them automatically whenever you add a video transition effect—which is desirable only some of the time. What's more, you can't easily add just an audio transition, for which there is ample need.

Fortunately, if you just keep track of a few things, you'll quickly learn how to make good use of audio transitions when you want them and how to avoid them when you don't.

Audio Transitions on the Primary Storyline

Clips on the primary storyline very frequently have both audio and video components. When these clips are collapsed (as they are by default), applying any video transition effect automatically adds an audio crossfade on the corresponding audio tracks. But it's not actually a transition effect; Final Cut Pro just overlaps the audio clips of the adjacent tracks and assigns a fade-out setting to the outgoing clip and a fade-in to the incoming clip.

You can control the fade type for both the incoming and outgoing fades in the Inspector, or you can expand the audio tracks and modify the overlapping audio with as much precision as you desire.

If you want to add a video transition effect without automatically overlapping your audio, you must expand the audio *prior to* applying the transition effect.

To modify the settings on an automatically applied audio crossfade:

1. Add a transition effect to an edit on the primary storyline **A**.

   The transition effect is added, and an automatic audio crossfade is applied.

   What's actually happened is that the corresponding audio has been over-lapped and fades have been applied.

2. Double-click the audio area for each of the clips affected by the transition **B**.

3. Select the transition effect in the Time-line, and open the Inspector **C**.

4. In the Audio Crossfade section, set the Fade In and Fade Out settings as desired.

For more on choosing Fade In and Fade Out settings, see the "Audio Fades" section of Chapter 11, "Audio Editing."

A When a transition is added to the primary storyline, it automatically adds a crossfade to the audio.

B When the audio is expanded, you can see the overlapping fades.

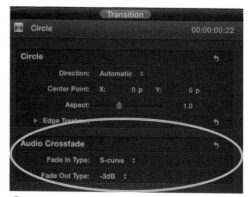

C The Transition Inspector contains settings to control the audio crossfade.

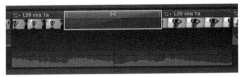

D Expand the audio tracks to separate the audio from the video.

E When expanded, transition effects do not affect the audio tracks.

To add a transition effect without affecting the corresponding audio:

1. Select the clips in the Timeline to which you plan to add the transition.

2. Choose Clip > Expand Audio/Video, or press Control-S.

   The audio clips are expanded **D**.

3. Select the video edit, and add the transition effect of your choice.

   The effect is added, but the audio clips remain unaffected **E**.

Audio Transitions on Connected Clips

If you want to create a crossfade between two connected clips, they must abut one another in the Timeline. Otherwise, any transitions you apply will fade a single audio clip up from or down to silence.

To add a transition to connected audio clips:

1. Select an edit point between the two audio clips in the Timeline 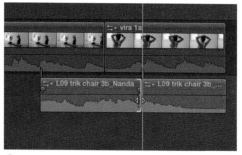.

2. Choose Edit > Add Cross Dissolve or press Command-T.

   The clips are converted into a secondary storyline and a transition effect is added between the two clips **G**.

   TIP You can also easily create a similar effect by just overlapping adjacent connected audio clips and applying fades to the overlapping edges **H**.

F Select an edit point between the two audio clips you want to transition between.

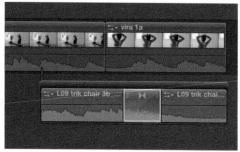

G Press Command-T to add an audio-only crossfade. A secondary storyline is automatically created.

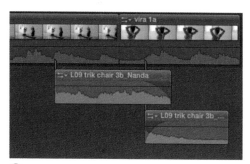

H You can also manually create a crossfade effect by overlapping two clips and adjusting their built-in fade settings.

19

Text and Titles

Nearly every project needs some bit of text—even if it's nothing more than an introductory title or some credits at the end. But text can be used in all sorts of other ways too.

Many projects require subtitles or *lower thirds* (text identifying an interview subject). Sometimes text can be used as a design element, as a way to communicate branding, or as a way of identifying the images on-screen.

Sometimes text is superimposed over video; other times it's displayed over a black screen. In some cases, you might create an interesting visual background, either by using one of Final Cut Pro's built-in *generators* or by applying effects to still images or video clips. And sometimes text just pops, fades, or scrolls on and off, but other times you may want a more expressive animated entrance and exit.

FCP has a plethora of prebuilt, animated titles to use in all of these situations, and employing them is as simple as dragging and dropping them.

The Titles Browser

You can find all of the titles that come with FCP neatly arranged in the Titles Browser. Like effects, transitions, and other items in the media browsers, the Titles Browser has a stack and a sidebar.

The stack shows previewable icons for each of the text objects, and the sidebar provides organizational categories and groups.

To show the Titles Browser:

- Click the Show Titles Browser button in the toolbar.

  The Titles Browser opens to the right of the Timeline .

A Click the Show Titles Browser button to open the Titles Browser.

To find specific titles:

- *Do one of the following*:

  ‣ Type the name of the title you're looking for in the search field at the bottom of the Titles Browser **B**.

    The stack is filtered to show only titles containing the letters in the search field.

TIP Clear the search field by clicking the circled X at the right edge of the field or by pressing Escape.

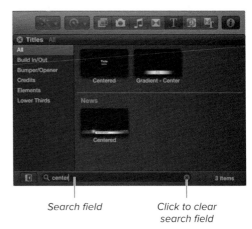

Search field   Click to clear
                      search field

B Search for a specific title effect by typing in the search field.

Show/Hide Sidebar button

C Click a category in the sidebar to filter the list.

D Skim across title icons to see a preview or hover over the icon, and press the Spacebar to play.

▸ Click one of the category names in the sidebar on the left side of the Titles Browser, and scroll through the main stack area on the right **C**.

The stack is filtered by category.

Previewing Titles

You can preview what each title looks like prior to adding it to your project. Remember, however, that you will be able to choose the font as well as modify a wide range of text style settings, enabling you to customize the title to a great degree.

To preview a title:

■ *Do one of the following*:

▸ Hover your pointer over a title icon in the Titles Browser to skim **D**.

▸ Position your pointer over a title icon, and press the Spacebar.

The Viewer loops a sample of the animated title.

TIP Click different title icons while previewing to view different previews dynamically.

Adding Titles to a Project

When you've decided which title you want to use, you can add it to the Timeline in one of two ways: You can add it as a regular clip to any storyline (so the text appears over black), or you can connect it to the primary storyline, superimposing the text over the background graphics or video in the storyline beneath it. This latter choice is the default behavior.

To connect a title to the primary storyline:

- Position the playhead at the frame in the project where you want the title to begin, and *do one of the following*:

  - ▸ Double-click the title in the Titles Browser.

  - ▸ Click the title in the Titles Browser to select it, and press Q.

  - ▸ Drag the title to the playhead position, and drop it above the primary storyline **E**.

  The title is added to the Timeline as a connected clip.

To add a title to the project as a regular clip:

- *Do one of the following*:

  - ▸ Drag the title into a storyline, and drop it between two clips to perform an insert edit **F**.

  - ▸ Drag the title into a storyline, and drop it on top of an existing clip to perform a replace edit **G**.

  - ▸ Press P to activate the Position tool, and drag the title anywhere in an existing storyline to perform an overwrite edit **H**.

  - ▸ Click the title in the Titles Browser, and press W, E, or D to perform an insert, append, or overwrite edit.

  The title is added to the project as if it were a normal video clip.

To learn more about the various edit types, see Chapter 7, "Basic Editing."

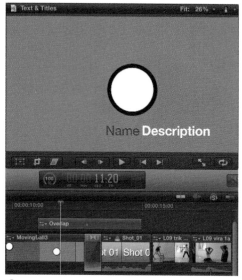

E Connect a title to the primary storyline, and it will be superimposed over the clips beneath it.

F Alternatively, a title can be treated just like a regular clip. It can be inserted between two shots.

G A title can replace an existing clip or gap.

H You can overwrite existing clips if you edit using the Position tool.

I When a title is selected in the Timeline, the text boxes become active in the Viewer.

J Double-click the text boxes to enter your own custom text.

Entering Title Text

Once you've added the title to your project, the first thing you're probably going to want to do is replace the sample text with the custom test required by your movie. Fortunately, in Final Cut Pro, you can enter your custom text directly in the Viewer.

To enter custom text in a title:

1. Click the title object in the Timeline to select it **I**.

   The text boxes become highlighted in the Viewer.

2. Position the playhead so you can see the title text on-screen in the Viewer.

3. In the Viewer, double-click a text box, and type your desired custom text **J**.

4. Repeat step 3 until all the text boxes have been customized.

TIP In some cases, the way the text object animates onto the screen means you won't be able to see all the text at one time. In such a case, repeat steps 2 and 3 until you've customized all the text.

5. When all the text is updated, deselect the title by clicking in a blank area of the Timeline, or press Shift-Command-A.

Modifying Titles

Most titles were created with specific design ideas in mind. The font, font size, color, and so on, were all preselected. The position of the text and even the duration of the title were preset to make it especially easy to drop the title into your project, enter your desired text, and go.

However, despite the availability of these presets, you can customize any of the titles in a variety of ways. You can choose your own fonts, styles, colors, and a variety of other attributes specific to the individual title effects.

These settings are controlled in the Inspector. You can modify title settings in two Inspector panes: the Title Inspector and the Text Inspector.

Changing Title Attributes

The Title Inspector contains different settings depending upon which title is selected. These may include the font and size for individual lines in a multiline title or the background color or attributes of a background effect. For the build in/build out category, the Title Inspector usually contains checkboxes to enable or disable the build-in or build-out effects.

Some titles have no title-specific attributes at all. When you select one of these titles, there will be no settings to adjust in the Title Inspector.

To change title-specific attributes:

1. Select the title in the Timeline, and park your playhead over it **A**.

2. Open the Inspector by clicking the I button in the toolbar or pressing Command-4.

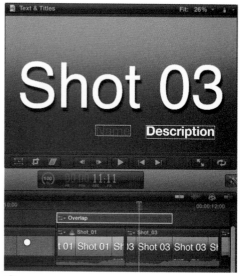

A Select the title you want to modify.

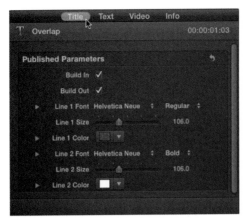

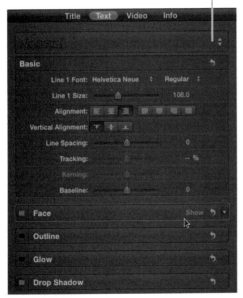

Text Title Preset drop-down menu

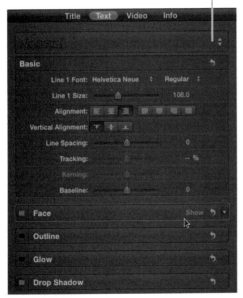

B In the Inspector, click the Title header to open the Title pane.

C The Text pane contains specific parameter fields to control optional Face, Outline, Glow, and Drop Shadow settings.

3. In the Inspector, click the Title header to open the Title pane (if it's not already showing) **B**.

4. Adjust the parameters to your heart's content.

5. Play around the title in the project to see the results of your work.

Changing Text Attributes

In addition to the title-specific attributes available in the Title Inspector, all titles also have a Text Inspector that controls the appearance of the text itself. The Text Inspector always contains the same settings, regardless of which title type you are modifying.

There are five categories of controls in the Text Inspector: Basic, Face, Outline, Glow, and Drop Shadow **C**.

Depending on the presets saved in the individual title, one or more of these settings will already have attributes assigned, but you can always override those defaults to customize the title.

To choose from a preset text style:

- Click the Preset Style pop-up menu at the top of the Text Inspector, and select a new text style from the list .

  Some styles contain both Basic and Style attributes. Others contain only Basic or only Style settings.

  The WYSIWYG pop-up menu gives you a preview of what attributes will be changed if you apply a particular preset.

To save the current text style as a preset:

1. Click the Preset Style pop-up menu at the top of the Text Inspector, and *do one of the following*:

   ▸ Choose Save Basic Attributes to save just the font, font size, alignment, and other attributes in the Basic category ⓔ.

   ▸ Choose Save Style Attributes to save the Face, Outline, Glow, and Drop Shadow settings.

   ▸ Choose Save All Basic+Style Attributes to save all the Inspector settings into a single preset.

   The Save Preset To Library window opens ⓕ.

ⓔ Save your own text preset styles by setting the parameters to your desired state, clicking the Preset Style pop-up menu, and choosing one of the Save Preset choices at the top of the menu.

ⓓ Click the Preset Style pop-up at the top of the Text pane to select from one of the preset text styles.

ⓕ Name your preset something descriptive and memorable.

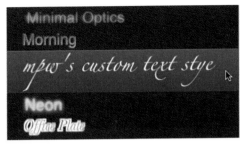

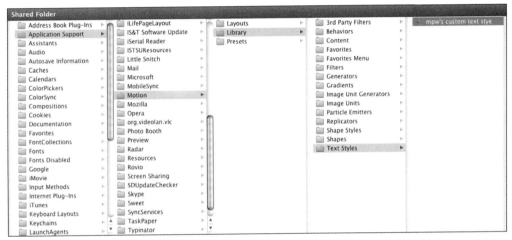

2. Type a name for your new preset, and click Save.

Your saved preset appears in the pop-up list **G**.

TIP Share saved text presets by sharing the file in the Finder **H**. Preset text styles are saved in **User** > **Library** > **Application Support** > **Motion** > **Library** > **Text Styles.**

G Once saved, your preset will appear in the Preset Style pop-up menu forevermore.

H Preset text styles are saved as files in the Finder so you can share them with your friends; you can delete them if you want them to go away forever.

To modify specific text style parameters:

1. In the Viewer, select the specific text you want to modify **I**.

> **TIP** You can set different text style attributes for individual text objects, or even individual letters within a text object.

2. To enable or disable specific Face, Outline, Glow, and/or Drop Shadow attributes, click the blue box to the left of the category header **J**.

3. Position your pointer over the header area, and when the *Show* text appears, click it to expand the category **K**.

> **TIP** You can also double-click the header to expand (or collapse) the attribute list.

I Select the specific text you want to modify. You can select a whole text box or just individual characters.

J The blue box enables or disables all the settings in that category.

K When the word *Show* appears, click it to expand the category of settings.

L Modify any of the settings you want to change.

M As you modify the settings, changes appear instantly in the Viewer. In this example, a yellow glow has been added to the word *Hero*.

N Control the speed of the title animation by shortening (to speed up) or lengthening (to slow down) the duration of the text object in the Timeline.

4. Modify any specific parameters to your liking **L**.

Changes update dynamically in the Viewer **M**.

Changing Animation Duration

Because the preset text effects have animations associated with them, different text effects have different default durations. When you add a text object to a project, it appears at its default duration.

You can speed up or slow down the animation effect by changing the overall duration of the text effect.

Note that you cannot apply retiming effects to titles.

To change the speed of a text object's animation:

- Using the Arrow pointer, drag the left or right edge of the title object in the Timeline **N**.

  Making the title object shorter will speed up the animation effect, and making the object longer will slow down the animation.

TIP You can trim the end of a title (to make it shorter by cutting off the end of the animation) by dragging the right edge with the Position tool.

Generators and Themes

Final Cut Pro comes with a collection of preexisting content such as solid-color backgrounds and various textures, shapes, and other elements that can be added to your projects like any other still image or video clip.

These clips are called *generators*. More generators are widely available from third-party developers, and new generators can be created in Motion and can be made to automatically appear inside Final Cut Pro.

Motion also contains a collection of *themed* titles and transitions, which employ a consistent look and feel.

Many beginning editors are tempted to add a diverse range of effects in a single project, which may seem fun during the editing process but subjects the viewer to a barrage of competing visual styles, which can distract or disengage them from the story.

By restricting your use of effects to those within a specific theme, you can ensure a consistent style for your project.

The Generators Browser

You can find all of the generators that come with Final Cut Pro listed by category in the Generators Browser. Like effects, titles, and other items in the media browsers, the Generators Browser has a stack and a sidebar.

The stack shows previewable icons for each of the generators, and the sidebar provides organizational categories and groups.

To show the Generators Browser:

- Click the Show Generators Browser button in the toolbar.

  The Generators Browser opens to the right of the Timeline **A**.

To find specific generators:

- *Do one of the following*:

  ▸ Type the name of the generator you're looking for in the search field at the bottom of the Generators Browser **B**.

  The stack is filtered to show only generators containing the letters in the search field.

TIP Clear the search field by clicking the circled X at the right edge of the field or by pressing Escape.

Show Generators Browser button

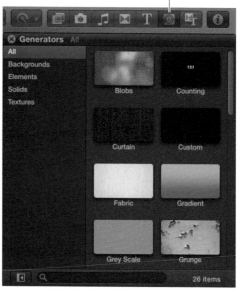

A Click the Show Generators Browser button to open the Generators Browser.

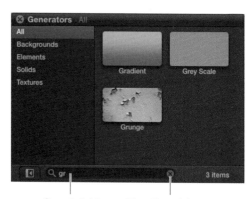

Search field   *Clear Search button*

B Search for a specific generator effect by typing in the search field.

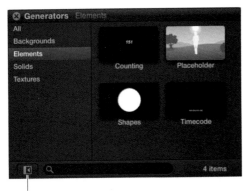

Show/Hide Sidebar button

C Click a category in the sidebar to filter the list.

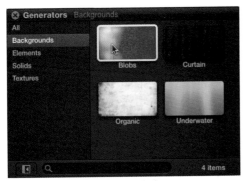

D Skim across icons to see a preview, or hover over the icon and press the Spacebar to play. Remember, many generators are not animated.

▶ Click one of the category names in the sidebar on the left side of the Generators Browser, and scroll through the main stack area on the right **C**.

The stack is filtered by category.

TIP Hide or show the sidebar by clicking the Show/Hide Sidebar button in the lower-left corner of the Generators Browser.

Previewing Generators

You can preview what each generator looks like prior to adding it to your project. Many generators are simply still images, so previewing them will just display a static frame. Others are animated, and the preview will display the animated effect.

Note that generators contain a variety of options or settings in the Inspector that significantly change the appearance of the generator. To explore these settings, you must add the generator to the project.

To preview a generator:

■ *Do one of the following*:

▶ Hover your pointer over an icon in the Generators Browser to skim **D**.

▶ Position your pointer over a generator icon, and press the Spacebar.

The Viewer loops a sample of the generators.

Adding Generators to a Project

When you've decided which generator you want to use, you can add it to the Timeline just like any other clip.

To add a generator to the project:

- *Do one of the following*:
  - ▸ Drag the generator into a storyline, and drop it between two clips to perform an insert edit **E**.
  - ▸ Double-click the generator to insert it at the playhead position.
  - ▸ Drag the generator into a storyline and drop it on top of an existing clip to perform a replace edit **F**.
  - ▸ Press P to activate the Position tool, and drag the generator anywhere in an existing storyline to perform an overwrite edit.
  - ▸ Click the generator in the Generators Browser, and press W, E, or D to perform an insert, append, or overwrite edit.

  The generator is added to the project in the chosen edit method **G**.

To learn more about the various edit types, see Chapter 7, "Basic Editing."

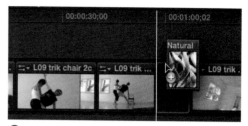

E Insert a generator between two shots using drag and drop, or double-click to insert it at the playhead position.

F A generator can replace an existing clip or gap.

G All generators are shown in brown in the Timeline, except the Placeholder generator, which appears in gray.

A Click the generator you want to modify to select it, and then park your playhead over it.

B In the Inspector, click the Generator header to open the Generators pane.

Changing Generator Attributes

A few generators contain a healthy selection of adjustable parameters, while many others contain few or none at all.

Some contain a pop-up menu that allows you to select different looks that are like a selection of completely different generators.

To change generator attributes:

1. Select the generator in the Timeline, and park your playhead over it A.

TIP You don't have to position the playhead over the generator, but otherwise you won't be able to see the results of changes you make in the Inspector.

2. Open the Inspector by clicking the I button in the toolbar or pressing Command-4.

3. In the Inspector, click the Generator header to open the Generator pane (if it's not already showing) B.

The Published Parameters section contains adjustable parameters for the selected generator.

continues on next page

4. Adjust the parameters to achieve the desired look .

5. Play around with the generator in the project to see the results of your work.

C Customize the generator as needed.

Using Themes

Themes are nothing more than collections of titles and transitions with common visual styles. They are added to a project in the same way as other transition effects and titles are.

To learn more about how to integrate transition effects, see Chapter 18, "Transitions." To learn more about how to use titles, see Chapter 19, "Text and Titles."

You can access all of the themed effects from within the Titles Browser and Transitions Browser, respectively, or you can view them grouped into their themed categories in the Themes Browser.

The Themes Browser

The Themes Browser is different from the other media browsers in that everything contained within it is also available in other browsers.

The difference is that in the Themes Browser the effects are grouped by style (listed in the sidebar), and when a style is selected, the stack shows lists of video transitions and titles consistent with that style.

You can preview the effects in the Themes Browser the same way you preview other titles, transitions, and other effects.

To show the Themes Browser:

- Click the Show Themes Browser button in the toolbar.

  The Themes Browser opens to the right of the Timeline **Ⓐ**.

To use the Themes Browser:

1. Click a theme from the list in the sidebar.

   The effects associated with that theme appear in the stack **Ⓑ**.

2. Scroll through the stack, and select the transition effects and titles you want to use in your project.

3. Add transitions and titles as described in Chapter 18, "Transitions," and in Chapter 19, "Text and Titles."

Show Themes Browser button

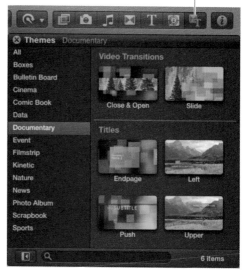

Ⓐ Click the Show Themes Browser button to open the Themes Browser.

Ⓑ Click a theme from the list in the sidebar, and the effects associated with that theme appear in the stack.

Animating Effects

There is an incredible wealth of video, audio, color correction, cropping, and other effects you can perform in FCP. But the real power of all these effects lies in the power to change them over time.

By animating effects, you can fly a title onto the screen, zoom in on a photograph, slowly fill a black-and-white image with color, subtly add reverb to the audio as a character walks deeper into a virtual cave, and perform many other cool effects.

Keyframing is the technique you use to animate effects in FCP. Keyframing simply means assigning a particular parameter value at a specific frame in time. A basic fade-in is a simple example. You specify on frame 1 that the picture will be at 0 percent opacity and that at frame 30 it will be at 100 percent. The software *interpolates* the difference (creates the in-between frames), and the result is an animated effect.

Keyframing in the Viewer

You can do keyframing in three parts of the FCP interface: the Viewer, the Inspector, and the Timeline.

In the Viewer, you can keyframe transformations (scale, rotation, position, and so on), cropping effects, and distortion effects. All three work the same way, utilizing on-screen keyframing controls that appear when you enable any of the three clip effects modes.

Note that the Ken Burns effect is a special case, in that it doesn't allow you to manually set specific keyframes. In Ken Burns mode, there are only two keyframes: one at the beginning of the shot and one at the end of the shot. Using the on-screen controls, you assign the beginning crop settings and the ending crop settings, and FCP automatically animates the clip accordingly.

To animate a transformation, crop, or distort effect:

1. Select a clip in the Timeline, and in the Viewer, click the Apply Transformation, Apply Crop, or Apply Distortion button **A**.

   The on-screen controls for the selected mode appear.

TIP If you choose Crop, you can click either Trim or Crop to select a cropping method.

Apply Transformation button

Apply Crop button

Apply Distortion button

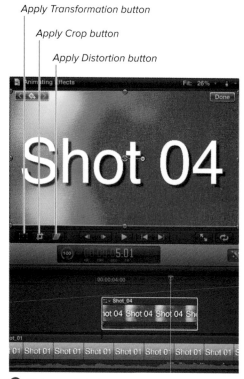

A Click one of the buttons to apply transformations, crops, or distortions. In this example, the Apply Transformations button has been clicked.

B Begin by placing the playhead on the frame where you want the effect to begin.

Add Keyframe button

C Click the Add Keyframe button in the upper-left corner of the Viewer.

D Adjust the clip in the Viewer to the starting position for the animation.

2. Position the playhead in the Timeline to the frame at which you want the animation to begin **B**.

3. In the Viewer, click the Add Keyframe button **C**.

   A keyframe is added at the current playhead position.

4. Adjust the clip in the Viewer using the Transformation, Crop, or Distort tool **D**.

TIP It's important to understand that setting a single keyframe does not create an animation. It's not until you set a second keyframe that any animation occurs.

continues on next page

5. In the Timeline, move the playhead to the frame where you want the animation to end (or change) **E**.

6. Click the Add Keyframe button in the upper-left corner of the Viewer.

A keyframe is added at the current playhead position.

TIP Keyframing in FCP X works differently from previous versions of Final Cut Pro: In FCP X, you must click the Add Keyframe button *prior to* adjusting the parameter settings.

7. In the Viewer, adjust the Transformation, Crop, or Distort settings as desired **F**.

8. Repeat steps 5–7 as many times as necessary to achieve the animation you desire.

TIP You can create as many keyframes as there are frames in your clip. But for the smoothest animation, set as few keyframes as you can, and spread them as far apart in time as possible.

9. Press / (Forward Slash) to play the clip and see the results of your work.

10. When you're happy with the results, click the Done button **G**.

Your animation is complete.

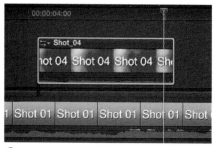

E Move the playhead to a different position.

Motion path

F Set the clip in the Viewer to the second position. In this case, because the center point has been changed, a motion path appears showing the movement the clip will make over time.

G When you're done adding keyframes, click the Done button.

H Click the Next Keyframe button to navigate to the next keyframe to the right of the current playhead position.

I If there are no more keyframes in one direction, the navigation buttons are dimmed.

Previous Keyframe button

J Click the Previous Keyframe button to navigate to the next keyframe to the left of the current playhead position.

Changing Existing Animations

Once you create an animation, you can easily go back and adjust, remove, or add keyframes to finesse or otherwise modify the overall effect.

To navigate between keyframes:

1. Select a clip in the Timeline, and in the Viewer, click the Apply Transform, Apply Crop, or Apply Distort button.

TIP A single clip can have separate Transform, Crop, and Distort animation settings. Be sure to enable the animation mode in which you want to modify the existing keyframes.

2. Click the Next Keyframe button to navigate to the next keyframe to the right of the current playhead position.

   The playhead moves to the frame containing the next keyframe **H**.

TIP If there are no more keyframes to the right, the Previous Keyframe button will be dimmed, and clicking it will have no effect **I**.

3. If desired, make any adjustments to the Transformation, Crop, or Distort settings.

   The keyframe is updated to store the new settings.

4. Click the Previous Keyframe button to navigate to the next keyframe to the left of the current playhead position **J**.

   The playhead moves to the frame containing the previous keyframe.

TIP If there are no more keyframes to the left, the Previous Keyframe button will be dimmed, and clicking it will have no effect.

To add a new keyframe to an existing animation:

1. Select a clip in the Timeline, and in the Viewer, click the Apply Transform, Apply Crop, or Apply Distort button **K**.

2. Move the playhead in the Timeline to a frame that doesn't contain an existing keyframe **L**.

> **TIP** If you're parked on a frame that already contains a keyframe, the Add Keyframe button turns into the orange Delete Keyframe button (see again **K**).

3. Click the Add Keyframe button.

   A new keyframe is added to the animation.

4. Make adjustments to the on-screen controls in the Viewer.

5. Repeat steps 2–4 as desired to add more keyframes.

6. When you're satisfied with your animation, click Done.

To remove a keyframe:

1. Select a clip in the Timeline, and in the Viewer, click the Apply Transform, Apply Crop, or Apply Distort button.

2. Use the Previous Keyframe or Next Keyframe button to navigate to the keyframe you want to remove.

   The Add Keyframe button turns orange to indicate you are currently parked on a keyframe **M**.

3. Click the Delete Keyframe button.

   The keyframe is deleted.

Delete Keyframe button

Apply Distortion button

K Animations can be stored in all three modes, Transform, Crop, and Distort. In this example, the Apply Distort button has been clicked.

Add Keyframe button

L Park on a frame where you want to add a new keyframe, and click the Add Keyframe button.

Delete Keyframe button

M When the playhead is on a frame where a keyframe exists, the Add Keyframe button turns into the orange Remove Keyframe button. Clicking it removes the keyframe.

 Open the Video Inspector for the clip you want to reset.

Reset parameter group

 Click the Reset button for the parameter set you want to reset. In this example, the Transform settings are being reset.

Resetting Clip Effects

You cannot reset the Transformation, Crop, or Distort effects in the Viewer to remove all keyframes. You must use the corresponding controls in the Inspector.

To remove all keyframes:

1. Select the clip you want to modify, and open the Video Inspector .

2. Click the Reset button for the category of effects for which you want to remove all keyframes (Transform, Crop, or Distort) .

   All keyframes within that control set are removed, and the parameters are reset to their default values.

Keyframing in the Inspector

Nearly every single parameter displayed in the Inspector can be animated. This includes built-in clip effects such as position, scale, opacity, and so on, as well as parameters for any filters or effects you add to a clip.

You can also keyframe parameters in the Audio Inspector, the Generator Inspector, the Title and Text Inspectors, and so on.

Pop-up menu and checkbox parameters cannot be keyframed (because it's often impossible to interpolate between fixed states), and there are certain other parameters that also can't be animated (such as the sliders that control image stabilization).

To identify whether a parameter can be animated:

- Move your pointer over the parameter in the Inspector.

  If an Add Keyframe button appears, the parameter can be animated ⓐ.

  If no Add Keyframe button appears, the parameter cannot be animated ⓑ.

Add Keyframe button

ⓐ If you roll your mouse over a parameter and an Add Keyframe button appears, the parameter can be animated.

ⓑ If no Add Keyframe button appears, the parameter cannot be animated.

C Open the Inspector in which you want to animate a parameter. In this example, the Generator Inspector has been opened.

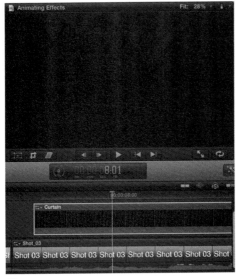

D Always start by positioning the playhead on the frame where you want the animation to begin.

E Click the Add Keyframe button in the Inspector for the parameter you want to animate.

To animate a parameter in the Inspector:

1. Select a clip, and open the Inspector **C**.

2. In the Timeline, position the playhead over the frame where you want the first keyframe to be added **D**.

3. In the Inspector, click the Add Keyframe button for the parameter you want to animate **E**.

   A keyframe is added at the current playhead position.

4. Adjust the slider, dial, color well, or other parameter control **F**.

continues on next page

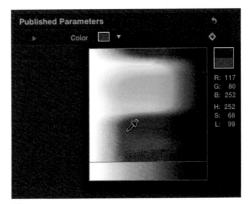

F Then, adjust the parameter control to the starting setting.

5. Move the Timeline playhead to a new frame 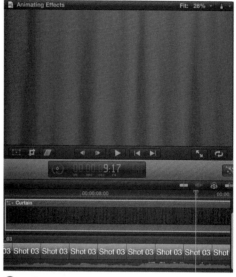.

6. In the Inspector, click the Add Keyframe button for the parameter you are animating ⒣.

A keyframe is added at the current playhead position.

TIP **Remember, you must click the Add Keyframe button before adjusting the parameter control.**

7. Adjust the parameter control to the new setting.

8. Repeat steps 5–7 as needed to create the desired effect.

9. Press / (Forward Slash) to play the clip and see the results of your work ⒤.

Ⓖ Then, move the playhead to a new position in time.

Ⓗ Click the Add Keyframe button again.

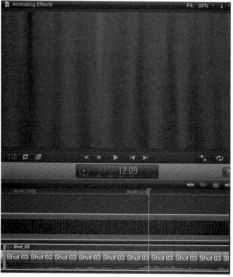

Ⓘ The parameter changes from one setting to the next over time.

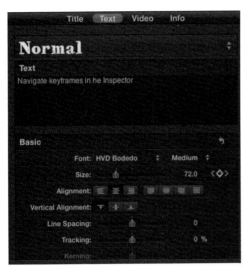

J Open the Inspector containing the parameter you want to modify.

Next Keyframe button

K Click the Next Keyframe button to move the playhead to the keyframe to the right of the current position.

L In no further keyframes exist to the right of the current playhead position, the Next Keyframe button appears dimmed.

Previous Keyframe button

M Click the Previous Keyframe button to move the playhead to the keyframe to the left of its current position.

Adjusting Existing Animations

Once a parameter has been animated, you can continue to modify the animation by changing keyframe values or by adding and removing keyframes.

To navigate between keyframes:

1. Select a clip in the Timeline, and open the Inspector containing the animated parameter **J**.

2. Click the Next Keyframe button to navigate to the next keyframe to the right of the current playhead position **K**.

   The playhead moves to the frame containing the next keyframe.

   TIP If there are no more keyframes to the right, the Previous Keyframe button disappears **L**.

3. If desired, make any additional adjustments to the parameter control.

   The keyframe is updated to store the new settings.

4. Click the Previous Keyframe button to navigate to the next keyframe to the left of the current playhead position **M**.

   The playhead moves to the frame containing the previous keyframe.

   TIP If there are no more keyframes to the left, the Previous Keyframe button disappears.

To add a new keyframe to an existing animation:

1. Select a clip in the Timeline, and open the Inspector containing the animated parameter.

2. Move the playhead in the Timeline to a frame that doesn't contain an existing keyframe.

3. Click the Add Keyframe button **N**.

   A new keyframe is added to the animation.

4. Make adjustments to the parameter control.

5. Repeat steps 2–4 as desired.

To remove a keyframe:

1. Select a clip in the Timeline, and open the Inspector that contains your existing animation.

2. Use the Previous Keyframe or Next Keyframe button to navigate to the keyframe you want to remove.

   The Add Keyframe button turns into the Delete Keyframe button to indicate that you are currently parked on a keyframe.

3. Click the Delete Keyframe button **O**.

   The keyframe is deleted.

To remove all keyframes:

1. Select the clip you want to modify, and open the Video Inspector.

2. Click the Parameter Menu button (the tiny arrow that appears at the right edge or the parameter bar when you mouse over a parameter).

3. Choose Reset Parameter from the pop-up menu **P**.

   The parameter is reset to its default values.

Add Keyframe button

N In the Inspector, click the Add Keyframe button to add a new keyframe at the current playhead position.

Delete Keyframe button

O When the playhead parked on an existing keyframe, the Add Keyframe button appears orange. Click it to delete the keyframe.

P Click the Parameter menu and choose Reset Parameter to remove all the keyframes and return the parameter to its default value.

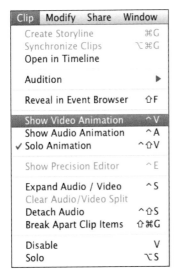

A Choose Show Video Animation from the Clip menu.

B Choose Show Video Animation from the Clip Action menu.

C The Video Animation Editor appears in the Timeline.

Keyframing in the Timeline

Although keyframing in the Viewer and the Inspector is easy to do, neither window allows you to observe an overview of your keyframes, seeing where they appear in time. By displaying keyframes in the Timeline, not only can you see such an overview, but you can also modify your keyframes' locations in time, thus speeding up or slowing down the speed at which effects animate.

Keyframes in the Timeline are displayed in a special animation editor that can be shown or hidden for each clip individually. Video keyframes are displayed in the Video Animation Editor, and audio keyframes are displayed in the Audio Animation Editor.

To show the Video Animation Editor:

- Select a clip in the Timeline, and *do one of the following*:
  - ► Choose Clip > Show Video Animation **A**.
  - ► Open the Clip Action menu, and choose Show Video Animation **B**.
  - ► Press Control-V.

  The Video Animation Editor appears above the selected clip **C**.

To show the Audio Animation Editor:

- Select a clip in the Timeline, and *do one of the following*:
  - ► Choose Clip > Show Audio Animation.
  - ► Open the Clip Action menu, and choose Show Audio Animation.
  - ► Press Control-A 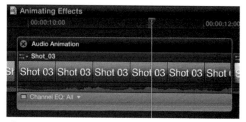.

  The Audio Animation Editor appears on the selected clip. The header appears above the clip, and the keyframe graphs appear below the clip.

TIP Because audio levels are keyframed directly on the audio waveform area of clips in the Timeline, the Audio Animation Editor displays keyframe graphs only when pan or audio effects settings have been applied to the selected clip.

Note that you can show only one animation editor—audio or video—at once. Showing the Audio Animation Editor while the Video Animation Editor is open automatically replaces the video editor with the audio editor, and vice versa.

To hide the animation editor:

- *Do one of the following*:
  - ► Click the Close button on the animation editor in the Timeline ⓔ.
  - ► Choose Clip > Hide Video Animation Editor (to close the Video Animation Editor) or Hide Audio Animation Editor (to close the Audio Animation Editor).

  The animation editor is hidden. Any existing keyframes remain applied to the clip.

ⓓ The Audio Animation Editor appears in the Timeline.

Close button

ⓔ Click the Close button to hide the animation editor.

Expand/Collapse Graph button

F Click the Expand/Collapse Graph button to expand the graph.

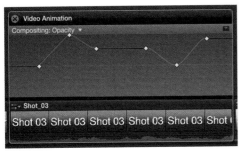

G When the graph is expanded, you can manipulate the keyframes more completely.

Controlling the Animation Editor View

The animation editors can display parameter graphs in a collapsed or an expanded view. When collapsed, you can see (and modify) where keyframes exist in time, but you can't see (or change) the parameter values.

In the expanded view, you can see both the keyframes' location in time as well as the relative parameter value, displayed as a two-dimensional graph.

Furthermore, in the Timeline you can optionally see the keyframes for multiple effects simultaneously. This allows you to coordinate the timing of complex effects requiring keyframes in two or more parameters.

When only one graph is showing, it's called Solo Animation mode, and you can select which parameter graph is displayed at any one time.

To expand or collapse keyframe graphs:

- Click the Expand/Collapse Graph button **F**.

TIP You can also double-click the parameter name to expand or collapse the graph.

The graph is expanded (if it was previously collapsed) **G** or collapsed (if it was previously expanded).

TIP Some graphs cannot be expanded. Usually these are graphs that refer to a parameter displayed in the Viewer, such as an effect's center point or a clip's Distort parameters.

To solo a parameter:

- Select the clip, and choose Clip > Solo Animation; or press Shift-Control-V 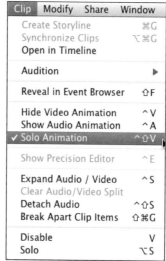.

  The animation editor is limited to display only one parameter at a time . Also, a check mark appears in the Clip menu next to the Solo Animation menu item.

To switch between soloed parameters:

1. Click the Parameter Graph pop-up menu to the right of the parameter name in the graph .

   A pop-up menu appears showing the names of all parameters that can be displayed.

2. Select one parameter from the pop-up menu.

   The selected parameter's graph replaces the current graph 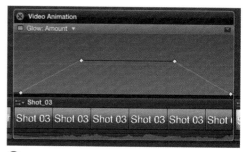.

H When Solo Animation is enabled, a check mark appears next to it in the Clip menu.

Parameter Graph pop-up menu

I Solo Animation restricts the view in the animation editor to a single parameter at a time.

J When Solo Animation is enabled, you can click the Parameter Graph pop-up menu to choose which parameter to display.

K The new parameter replaces the old one in the animation editor.

When Solo Animation is disabled, all active parameters are displayed simultaneously.

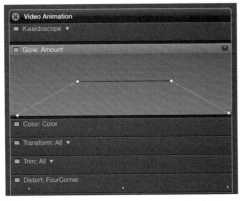

To manipulate individual keyframes, begin by expanding the graph.

Drag a keyframe horizontally to change its position in time or vertically to change the parameter value.

To show all parameter graphs:

- Select the clip, and choose Clip > Solo Animation; or press Shift-Control-V.

  The check mark is removed from the menu item, and the animation editor displays all parameter graphs simultaneously.

Adjusting Keyframes in the Animation Editor

Whether or not you're displaying one or more graph, you can modify the keyframes directly in the animation editor.

When a graph is collapsed, you can modify existing keyframes' positions in time, but you cannot add keyframes unless a keyframe is already present, and you cannot modify the parameter value or the interpolation method.

When a graph is expanded, you can add and remove keyframes, as well as modify their positions in time and the parameter value.

To modify keyframes:

1. Expand the keyframe graph in the animation editor.

2. Click an individual keyframe, and drag horizontally to reposition the keyframe in time or vertically to change the keyframe's parameter value.

   Note that you cannot change a keyframe's position in time and its parameter value simultaneously. You can do only one at a time. Once you begin to drag, you establish whether you are making a horizontal, time-based adjustment or a vertical, parameter value-based adjustment.

TIP Moving keyframes closer together speeds up the timing of the animation between those keyframes. Moving them farther apart from one another slows down the animated effect.

To add keyframes:

1. Expand the keyframe graph in the animation editor.

2. Option-click the parameter graph line **O**.

   A new keyframe is added at the frame where you clicked.

3. Adjust the keyframe's value and position in time as desired **P**.

TIP Many parameters also have built-in Fade In/Fade Out controls **Q**. Simply drag the fade control from the beginning or end of the graph to add a fade. For more detailed instructions, see Chapter 13, "Basic Compositing."

TIP You can also drag a line segment vertically to simultaneously increase or decrease the relative values of the two keyframes connected to that segment.

O Option-click the parameter graph line to add a new keyframe.

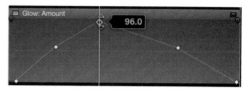

P Drag the new keyframe to your desired location.

Fade In handle   *Fade Out handle*

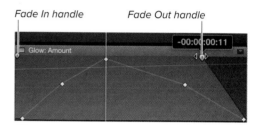

Q Drag the fade handles to create fade-in and fade-out effects for the selected parameter.

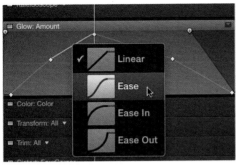

R Right-click any line segment, and select from one of the four interpolation methods.

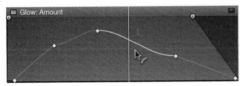

S The interpolation method is assigned to the line segment.

T Manually control a line segment's "ease" settings by dragging the segment left or right.

Controlling Keyframe Interpolation

You can control how FCP *interpolates* the values between keyframes, optionally creating a more organic-feeling change that simulates inertial forces in the real world. You can set different interpolation methods for the area between any two keyframes.

Choose from one of four interpolation methods:

- **Linear:** Parameter values shift abruptly from one value to the next.
- **Ease:** Values begin changing gradually and end changing gradually.
- **Ease In:** Values begin changing abruptly but end changing gradually.
- **Ease Out:** Values begin changing gradually but end changing abruptly.

By default, all parameters are set to Linear interpolation.

To choose the interpolation method:

1. Expand a graph containing two or more keyframes.
2. Right-click the line connecting any two keyframes.

   The Interpolation Method pop-up appears **R**.
3. Choose one of the four interpolation methods.

   The interpolation method is set for the specific graph line **S**.

TIP You can also add an ease effect to a line segment by dragging the curve horizontally. The pointer becomes the Adjust Curve pointer; dragging left makes the curve more linear, and dragging right makes the curve more "easy" **T**.

Creating Output: Sharing and Exporting

You've come this far. Now it's time to send your masterpiece out into the world.

Final Cut Pro has a variety of output options. This chapter walks you through FCP's output options and helps you decide which one will deliver what you need.

You'll learn how to use the Share window. With a few clicks you can set up automated export and delivery operations. FCP's Share feature can produce finished Blu-ray Discs and upload your day's work to YouTube. You can also use the movie export options to convert an FCP project or clip to another digital format for use in computer-based media.

You'll also learn how to amplify your output options by adding Apple's companion utility Compressor to your editing suite. Compressor is designed to offer more control and batch export options to FCP's feature set.

About the Share Window

Final Cut Pro's exporting options (called *sharing* in Final Cut Pro-speak) offer a variety of streamlined, automated ways to create and deliver output media files in a single operation. Some output options go further: The YouTube option, for example, generates a media file in the correct output format and then automatically logs into your YouTube account and uploads the file.

You access the Final Cut Pro exporting options using the Share menu. Selecting an output option opens the Share window. Share window options vary depending on which output option you select **A**.

The Share window offers streamlined output options in the upper part of the window; click the Show Details button to reveal a broader array of options.

TIP You can use the Share menu options to export a complete project only. To export a portion of your project, you could use Final Cut Pro's Send to Compressor option and set In and Out points in Compressor's Preview window. If you don't want to shell out $49.95 for a copy of Compressor 4, here's a work-around: Copy just the selected portion of your project into a new separate project and export that using the standard Share menu options.

TIP As part of its general streamlining and simplification trend, Final Cut Pro X restricts sharing output to one project at a time; Batch Export is no longer available. You'll need a copy of Compressor 4 ($49.95 at the Apple App Store) to output multiple files in a single operation. For more information, see "Sending to Compressor" later in this chapter.

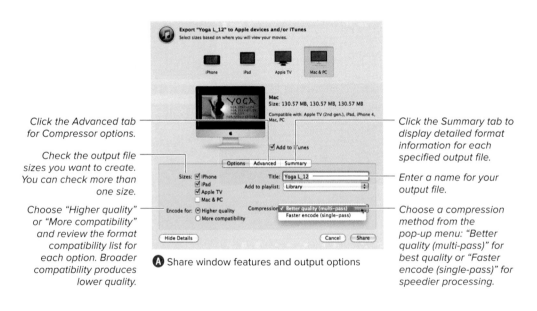

Click the Advanced tab for Compressor options.

Check the output file sizes you want to create. You can check more than one size.

Choose "Higher quality" or "More compatibility" and review the format compatibility list for each option. Broader compatibility produces lower quality.

Click the Summary tab to display detailed format information for each specified output file.

Enter a name for your output file.

Choose a compression method from the pop-up menu: "Better quality (multi-pass)" for best quality or "Faster encode (single-pass)" for speedier processing.

A Share window features and output options

Ⓐ Select the project, and choose Share > Media Browser.

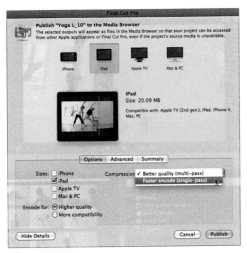

Ⓑ The Share window displays your output options. Click Show Details to open the bottom pane and view more-specific information on the size and quality of each export option.

Sending Projects to the Media Browser

Choosing Share > Media Browser is the correct export choice when you want to access a finished Final Cut Pro project in an Apple iLife or iWork app, such as Keynote or GarageBand. Once you've exported it, your Final Cut Pro project appears on the Media Browser tab that appears in all iLife and iWork applications.

To send a project to the Media Browser tab:

1. In the Project Library, select the project's icon, and choose Share > Media Browser **Ⓐ**.

   The Share window appears.

2. In the Share window, choose the destination Apple device where you're going to be using the exported movie. Click Show Details for more specific information on the size and quality of each export option **Ⓑ**. See "About the Share Window," earlier in this chapter, for details on your export options.

continues on next page

3. When you've set up your export options, click Publish **C**.

Final Cut Pro generates a movie file to your specifications. The exported movie will appear in the Media Browser tab of compatible Apple applications **D**.

C Click Publish to generate your exported movie file.

D The exported Final Cut Pro movie as it appears in GarageBand's Media Browser tab

Export Project for Playback on Another Apple Device

Choose Share > Apple Devices to generate a movie you can play back on an iPhone, iPad, iPod, or Apple TV. Choose Share > Apple Devices to export your Final Cut Pro movie to Apple's iTunes application. Use iTunes to transfer the exported movie file to your selected Apple device.

To export a project for playback on an Apple device:

1. In the Project Library, select the project's icon, and choose Share > Apple Devices.

   The Share window appears.

2. In the Share window, choose the Apple device where you're going to be playing the exported movie. Click Show Details for more-specific information on the size and quality of each export option **A**.

continues on next page

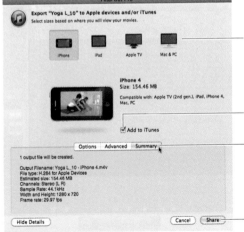

Click an icon to choose your destination Apple device.

Deselect the iTunes checkbox only if you don't want your movie to appear in iTunes.

Click the Share window's Summary tab to see detailed file format information for each export format option.

Click Share to generate your exported movie.

A The Share window displays little photos representing your output options. Click Show Details to reveal the bottom pane and view more-specific information on the size and quality of each export option.

3. When you've set up your export options, click Share.

Final Cut Pro generates a movie file to your specifications.

4. Click the Share Monitor button and open the Share Monitor utility to monitor your export's progress .

The exported movie appears in iTunes' Movie tab **C**.

B Click the Share Monitor button to open the Share Monitor utility and monitor your export's progress.

C The exported Final Cut Pro movie as it appears in iTunes' Movie tab

A Select
the project,
and choose
Share > DVD.

Creating DVDs

Final Cut Pro's Share menu features two disc output options—standard-definition DVD and high-definition Blu-ray Disc—plus the option to save either format as a *disc image*. A disc image is a computer file that can be burned as a disc or will behave like a DVD when mounted on your computer.

To export a project as a standard-definition DVD or disc image:

1. In the Project Library, select the project's icon, and choose Share > DVD **A**.

   The Share window appears.

2. In the Share window, choose a destination drive for your DVD or disc image from the pop-up menu. Use the Share window options to set up your DVD export preferences. Click the Summary tab to display more-specific information on the size and quality of your export settings **B**.

continues on next page

Choose your DVD drive to burn a DVD.
Choose your hard drive to build a disc image.

Choose Automatic to have Final Cut Pro base settings on the type of disc you insert.
Choose Single Layer to create a single-layer disc or disc image.
Choose Double Layer to create a double-layer disc image.

Choose a disc template for your DVD.

Enter a title for your DVD.

Choose Show Menu to display the DVD's main menu on startup.
Choose Play Movie to start playback on DVD startup.

Click to add a background graphic file to the menu.

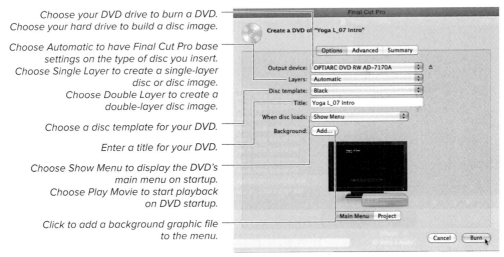

B Use the Share window options to set up your DVD export preferences.

3. When you've set up your DVD export
   options, click Burn.

   Final Cut Pro processes your project's
   video and audio as a DVD and prompts
   you to insert blank DVD media 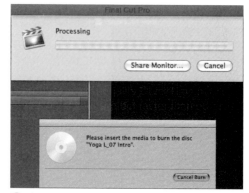. Once
   complete, the DVD will appear on the
   Share tab of the project's Inspector
   window . For details on how to display a project's Inspector window, see
   Chapter 5.

Please insert the media to burn the disc
"Yoga L_07 Intro".

Cancel Burn

C Insert a DVD when this prompt appears.

Properties	Sharing
Yoga L_07 Intro	00:02:19;23
August 11, 2011 10:13 AM	720p HD
1280x720	29.97p	Surround	48kHz
Burned DVD	
August 14, 2011 5:00 PM	

D The exported Final Cut Pro movie is burned
to a DVD and appears on the Share tab of the
project's Inspector window.

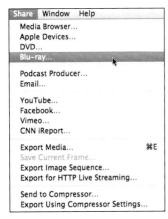

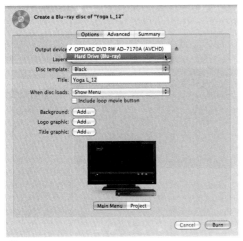

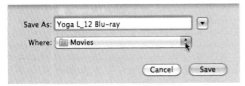

E Select the project, and choose Share > Blu-ray.

To export a project as a high-definition Blu-ray Disc or disc image:

1. In the Project Library, select the project's icon, and choose Share > Blu-ray **E**.

   The Share window appears.

2. In the Share window, choose a destination drive for your Blu-ray Disc or disc image from the pop-up menu. Each connected drive in the Output Device menu lists its output capabilities **F**.

3. Use the Share window options to set up your Blu-ray export preferences. See the previous task, "To export a project as a standard-definition DVD disc or disk image," for details on your output options.

4. When you've set up your Blu-ray Disc export options, click Next.

   Final Cut Pro asks you to select a destination for your disc image (if you've elected to create a Blu-ray disc image) and then processes your project's video and audio as a Blu-ray Disc or disc image **G**.

F The Share window displays your Blu-ray output options. The Output Device menu lists format capabilities of each connected drive. In this example, you'd need to generate a Blu-ray Disc image on the hard drive and transfer it to a drive capable of burning a Blu-ray Disc at a later date.

G If you're creating a Blu-ray disc image on your hard drive, Final Cut Pro will ask you to name the disc image file and select a location for saving it.

Sharing Your Projects on the Web

Final Cut Pro's Share menu offers a set of output options you can use to post your latest project on the Web in record time. The YouTube option, for example, generates a media file in the correct output format, automatically logs into your YouTube account, and uploads the file in a single operation.

The following task uses Vimeo, but all four of the third-party output options—YouTube, Facebook, Vimeo, and CNN iReport—operate in basically the same way.

Posting your movie on the Web is so easy, you might be tempted to upload your latest without viewing it first, but please—patience, Grasshopper.

To post a project directly to Vimeo:

1. In the Project Library, select the project's icon, and choose Share > Vimeo **A**.

   The Share window appears.

2. In the Share window, enter your Vimeo username and password, and then enter the title of the movie you're uploading plus any comments and tags. Click Show Details for more specific information on the size and quality of each export option **B**. See "About the Share Window" earlier in this chapter for details on your export options.

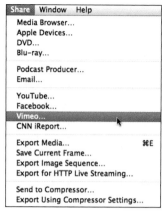

A Select the project, and choose Share > Vimeo.

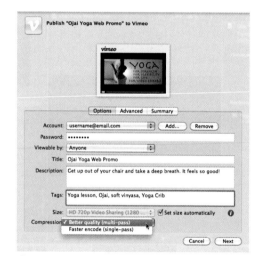

B Enter your Vimeo username and password and then title the movie you're uploading and add any comments and tags. Click Show Details to open the bottom pane and view more-specific information on the size and quality of each export option.

3. When you've set your export options, click Next.

Final Cut Pro generates a movie file to your specifications. Log in to your Vimeo account, and you'll see your uploaded movie posted **C**.

C The exported Final Cut Pro movie as it appears in Vimeo. Sometimes there's a short delay in posting unless you have a Plus or Pro (paid) Vimeo account.

Exporting Projects in a QuickTime Media Format

Choosing Share > Export Media gives you access to a broad selection of QuickTime-supported audio and video export file formats.

You can generate a QuickTime movie version of your project with video and audio.

You can export a movie file with video only (no audio) or as an audio file (with no video).

The Export Media feature can read FCP's *roles* data—tags you can attach to a clip to define its "role" (get it?) in your project. You can use the default roles to ID your audio clips as Dialogue, Effects, or Music and then use Export Media to organize and export your project dialogue, music, and effects tracks as separate files, also known as *media stems*. For more information, see "Export Project Audio" later in this chapter. You can also assign roles to video clips.

To export project video and/or audio in a QuickTime media format:

1. In the Project Library, select the project's icon **A** and choose Share > Export Media; or press Command-E.

   The Share window appears. This is your opportunity to review and confirm the export format settings.

Faster Movie Export

Using the Export Media option can produce a high-quality QuickTime movie version of your project faster than other Share options.

Choose Share > Export Media, and select the Current Settings option.

FCP will speed up the export process by copying your project's existing render files instead of regenerating them from scratch—and by using foreground processing, rather than the default background processing used by other Share options.

Foreground processing is faster, but it does tie up FCP while it generates your export file. Your decision.

A Select the project in the Project Library, and choose Share > Export Media.

2. In the Share window, specify any of the following export settings from the pop-up menus **B**:

- ▶ **Export:** Choose to include video and audio, video only, or audio only in your exported file. The Export pop-up menu also includes four roles export options. For details on using roles to sort and export your audio media, see "Export Project Audio" later in this chapter.

- ▶ **Video Codec:** Current Settings is the default setting, or choose a different export codec for your exported video. You can choose from a list of common FCP production video codecs including Apple ProRes.

- ▶ **Audio File Format:** Selecting Audio Only from the Export pop-up menu activates this pop-up menu. Choose an export file format for your project audio.

- ▶ **After Export:** Choose to review the exported file in QuickTime or Compressor or to do nothing.

continues on next page

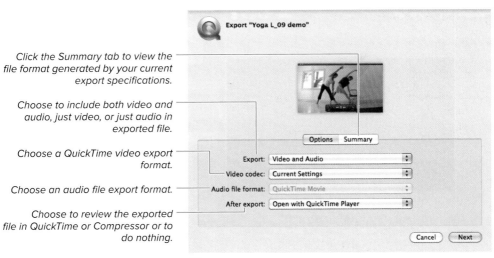

Click the Summary tab to view the file format generated by your current export specifications.

Choose to include both video and audio, just video, or just audio in exported file.

Choose a QuickTime video export format.

Choose an audio file export format.

Choose to review the exported file in QuickTime or Compressor or to do nothing.

B Specify export settings from the pop-up menus in the Share window.

3. When you've set up your movie export options, click Next.

FCP asks you to select a destination for your exported movie **C** and then processes your project's video and audio as a QuickTime movie **D**.

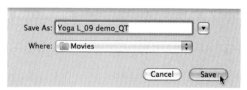

C Enter a name and select a destination for your exported movie file.

D The exported FCP movie as it appears in QuickTime.

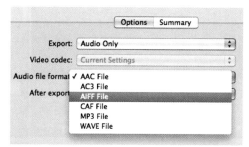

A Choose an audio file format from the Share window's "Audio file format" menu.

Export Project Audio

Use Share > Export Media to export just the audio from your project. Export Media offers a selection of high-quality and compressed audio file formats. If you need to work on your project audio outside FCP in a more professional and robust audio application, exporting your project audio is a good first step.

To export a project's audio:

1. In the Project Library, select the project's icon, and choose Share > Export Media.

   The Share window appears.

2. In the Share window's Export pop-up menu, choose Audio Only **A**.

   The "Audio file format" pop-up menu is activated.

3. Choose an audio file format from the "Audio file format" pop-up menu.

4. When you've set up your audio export options, click Next.

   FCP asks you to select a destination for your exported audio and then processes your project's audio and creates files in your specified format.

Exporting Project Audio as Media Stems

The latest version of FCP X offers roles, a clip-tagging scheme that makes it possible to sort the audio clips used in your project into dialogue, effects, and music tracks, or assign custom role name you can use to organize your production audio. Assigning role tags to your clips is covered in "About Roles" in Chapter 8.

In this section, you'll learn how to use Share > Export Media to export your Dialogue, Effects, or Music Role–tagged project audio clips as separate dialogue, music, and effects tracks files, also known as *media stems*. You can export stems in one multitrack QuickTime file or as separate audio files.

To export a project's audio as audio stems:

1. In the Project Library, select the project's icon, and choose Share > Export Media.

   The Share window appears.

2. In the Share window's Export pop-up menu, choose from the following media stem output presets:

   ▸ **Roles Multitrack QuickTime Movie:** Export all role-tagged clips in your project as one multitrack QuickTime movie file containing all roles, with each role segregated on a separate track.

   ▸ **Audio Roles Only As Separate Files** 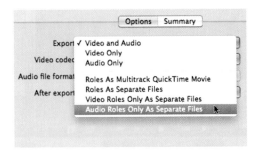**:** Export a separate audio file for each role type you select. For example, if you selected only audio clips tagged as Effects for export, this option would generate a single track the same duration as your project containing all clips marked Effects.

B Choose an audio stem export option from the Share window's Export pop-up menu. Choosing Audio Roles Only As Separate Files will generate a separate track for each audio role you specify. The track will contain all project audio clips with a matching role tag. The exported file will be the same duration as your project.

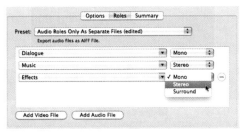

 On the Roles tab, specify Mono, Stereo, or Surround output for each audio stem.

TIP The following output presets apply only if you're exporting role-tagged video clips along with your audio, such as when you've role-tagged all your project's subtitle clips as Title and want to export them all in a single video file.

▸ **All Roles As Separate Files:** Export each video or audio role in your project as a separate video or audio file.

▸ **Video Roles Only As Separate Files:** Export each of the video roles in your project as a separate file.

The "Audio file format" pop-up menu is deactivated and the Roles button appears above the Export pop-up menu.

3. Specify AIFF or WAV as your export audio file format from the "Audio file format" pop-up menu.

4. Click the Roles button to confirm which role-tagged audio clips will be exported.

5. On the Roles tab, do any of the following:

▸ Click Add Audio File, and choose a role from the pop-up menu to add another role to your export operation.

▸ Click the Minus button next to a role to exclude it from your export operation.

▸ Specify Mono, Stereo, or Surround output for each audio stem **C**.

4. When you've set up your audio export options, click Next.

FCP asks you to select a destination for your exported audio stems and then processes your project's audio and creates files in your specified format.

TIP To check your audio stems, you can reimport them into your project and sync them up with your original project clips **D**. The Dialogue stem should contain just dialogue, the Music stem only music, and the Effects stem just effects. Of course, the accuracy of your stems' contents depends on the accuracy of your role tags. It's a good idea to check your exported audio stems before you hand them off to your post-audio specialist.

D To check your audio stems, you can reimport them into your project and sync them up with your original project clips. Each audio stem is a single clip the same duration as your original project.

A Position the Timeline playhead on the frame you want to export as a still, and choose Share > Save Current Frame.

B Choose a graphic file format from the Share window's Export menu.

C The exported Final Cut Pro still frame as it appears in the Finder

Export a Still Frame

Choose Share > Save Current Frame to export a still frame from your project.

To export a still frame:

1. In the Timeline, position the playhead on the frame you want to export as a still, and choose Share > Save Current Frame **A**.

    The Share window appears.

2. In the Share window, choose a graphic file format from the Export menu. Click the Summary tab for more specific information on the size and quality of each export option **B**.

3. When you've set up your graphic export options, click Next.

    Final Cut Pro asks you to select a destination for your exported still frame and then creates a file in your specified format **C**.

Sending Projects to Compressor

Final Cut Pro offers you the option of choosing the Share > Send to Compressor command to send your sequence directly to Compressor, skipping the rendering and exporting reference movie steps, because Compressor works directly with your source media files. The Send to Compressor route can produce a marginally cleaner encoded output file but takes much longer to compress. To save time, render your sequence first, and then export a reference movie that you can open and encode in Compressor.

Compressor is no longer included with Final Cut Pro; to use Compressor with Final Cut Pro X, you'll have to purchase a $49.95 copy of Compressor 4 from the Apple App Store. That said, there are a few other advantages to using Compressor with FCP:

- If you have a stack of different project files to export, Compressor allows you to queue multiple projects and process them in one operation.

- Send to Compressor allows you to change your project's frame size or specify custom dimensions on export Ⓐ.

- Exporting your project to Compressor is the only official way to export just a portion of your project; you mark In and Out points in Compressor before you process. Be sure to clear In and Out points after you export if you want to export the entire clip later.

You can also use the Compressor options located on the Share window's Advanced tab to set up background rendering or queue up multiple export operations.

TIP A complete list of QuickTime formats and codecs, plus a summary of format uses and characteristics, is available at the Apple Support site, at *http://support.apple.com/kb/HT3775*.

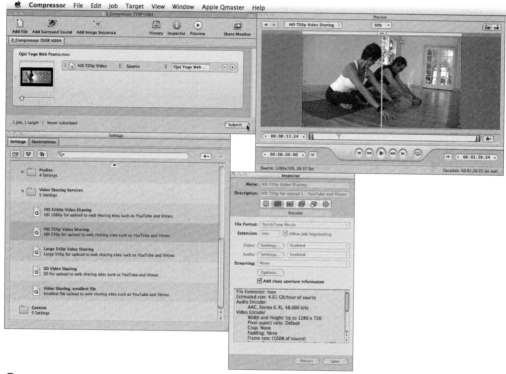

A Compressor allows you to change your exported project's frame size and specify custom dimensions.

To use Send to Compressor to export a project:

1. In the Project Library, select the project's icon, and choose Share > Send to Compressor **B**.

   If Compressor is present on your computer, the application launches, and your project appears in the Job window.

2. In the Compressor window, select or customize your export options, and then click Submit **C**.

Share   Window   Help

Media Browser...
Apple Devices...
DVD...
Blu-ray...

Podcast Producer...
Email...

YouTube...
Facebook...
Vimeo...
CNN iReport...

Export Media...   ⌘E
Save Current Frame...
Export Image Sequence...
Export for HTTP Live Streaming...

Send to Compressor...
Export Using Compressor Settings...

B Select the project in the Project Library, and choose Share > Send to Compressor.

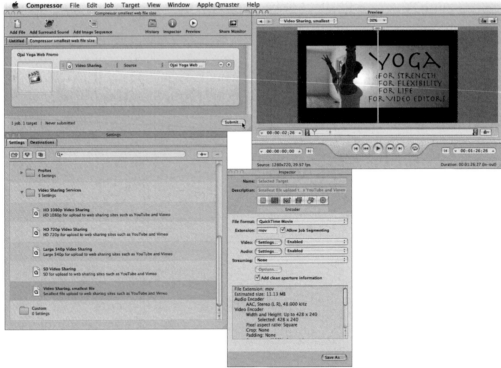

C In the Compressor window, select or customize your export options, and then click Submit.

D The processed file appears in the Finder

E Select the project in the Project Library, and choose a Share menu option.

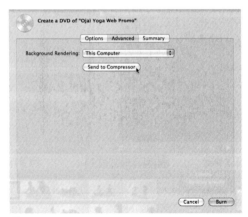

F In the Share window's Advanced tab, set rendering options, and click Send to Compressor.

Your exported project is processed in Compressor, and the finished file appears in the Finder **D**.

TIP To export just a portion of your project, mark In and Out points in Compressor's Preview window before you process the file.

To use Share window Compressor options to export a project:

1. In the Project Library, select the project's icon, and then choose a Share menu option **E**.

   The Share window appears.

2. In the Share window, click the Advanced tab. On the Advanced tab, set the rendering options, and click Send to Compressor **F**.

   If Compressor is present on your computer, the application launches, and your project appears in the job window.

   continues on next page

3. In the Compressor window, select or customize your export options, and then click Submit 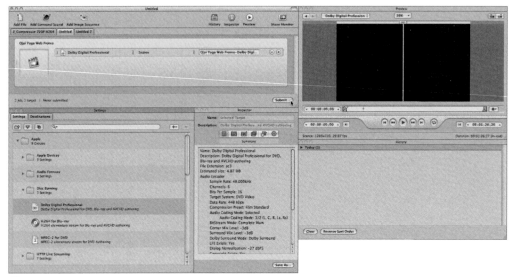.

Your exported project is processed in Compressor, and the finished file appears in the Finder.

TIP You can use these Share window Compressor options to export a project, but you might prefer to use the Compressor pathway available in the Share > Export Media option—processing is usually faster. See "Exporting Projects in a QuickTime Media Format," earlier in this chapter, for details.

G In the Compressor window, select or customize your export options, and then click Submit.

XML Export for Use in Third-Party Applications

For years, independent software developers have used FCP's XML and OMF "hooks" to develop custom interchange applications that make it possible to transfer a surprising amount of project data between FCP and other programs such as the Avid NLEs, Pro Tools, and After Effects.

FCP X introduced a completely new project structure, and its "flavor" of XML (called *Rich XML*) is not as interchangeable as you would hope for from an interchange application.

As we go to press, we're waiting on someone from the independent developer community to step up with an XML solution that will allow FCP 7 projects to be opened in FCP.

On the export side: At this time, there's no OMF/AAF export application capable of exporting FCP X project audio as discrete clips sorted into proper tracks—the kind of production audio export that postproduction audio professionals expect to receive.

The best place to check for updates on the XML exchange frontier is Apple's Final Cut Pro Resources page: *www.apple.com/finalcutpro/resources/*.

To export XML from Final Cut Pro:

1. In the Project Library, select the projects you want to export as XML files.

2. Choose File > Export XML.

3. In the file dialog, choose the destination folder where you want save these XML files, and then click Save.

Automatic Duck Update: Third-Party XML and OMF Interchange Applications to Continue?

Automatic Duck, the first company to create XML and OMF interchange tools for FCP, developed a suite of FCP plug-ins essential for editors working with FCP, Avid, Pro Tools, and After Effects.

At press time, Automatic Duck's line of FCP tools has gone missing, and Automatic Duck's founder has gone to work for Adobe. We hope for the Automatic Duck's return—those were some essential tools. Stay tuned.

Contact Automatic Duck for details at *www.automaticduck.com/products/*.

Index

metadata, 84–90
    creating new field for, 85
    defined, 34
    entering, 84
    examples of, 84
    value of, 91
metadata views, 86–90
Modify Marker window, 76, 77
Modulation audio filters, 293
Monitor Gain slider, 145
monitors, using two, 18, 21–22
mono tracks, 132
Motion application, 3, 433
motion path, 444
mouse, making selection with, 64
Move Project command, 106
Move Project to Trash command, 107
Move Referenced Events option, 112
movies. *See also* iMovie
    exporting clips/projects as, 15
    hardware required for making, 17
Movies folder, 103, 119, 124, 142
music files, importing, 139–140

N

naming
    compound clips, 362
    events, 33
    projects, 101, 110
navigation shortcuts, 183
nested sequences, 101, 358. *See also*
        compound clips
Nest Items command, 358
New Compound Clip command, 360, 363
New Event Name field, 112
New Folder button, 108
New Folder command, 96, 108
New Project window, 101, 151
New Smart Collection button, 95
noise, background, 288–289
nondestructive editing, 4, 40, 364
nonprogressive video, 60
notch filter, 290
numerical trimming, 223

O

Offline Clip icon, 42, 43
Offline Media warning, 127
OMF export applications, 485
one-click edits, 224–225
on-screen help, 8
Opacity slider, 314
Optical Flow option, 395–396
option-dragging, 37
OTS shots, 246
outgoing clips, 212, 215
Outgoing Trim handle, 415
Out point. *See* In and Out points
output options, 461–486
over-the-shoulder shots, 246
overwrite edits, 153, 156, 160, 205

P

Pan Amount slider, 275, 277, 279, 280
Pan Mode pop-up menu, 277
panning
    defined, 273
    presets, 279–280
    for stereo, 275–276
    for surround, 277
pan settings, 273–280
    presets for, 279–280
    purpose of, 273
    resetting, 279
    for stereo, 275–276
    stereo *vs.* surround, 273–274
    for surround, 277
Parameter Graph pop-up menu, 456
parent project, 364
Paste command, 179
pasting clips, 180–181
peak indicators, 264
peaking, 262
People search option, 93, 130–131
performance tips, 27–28
Photo Booth, 137–138
photos, importing, 137–138
Photoshop files, 15

HREE WAYS TO QUICKSTART

The ever popular Visual QuickStart Guide series is now available in three formats to help you "Get Up and Running in No Time!"

Visual **QuickStart Guide Books**

The best-selling Visual QuickStart Guide series is available in book and ebook (ePub and PDF) formats for people who prefer the classic learning experience.

eo **QuickStart**

eo QuickStarts offer the immediacy of streaming eo so you can quickly master a new application, k, or technology. Each Video QuickStart offers

Enhanced **Visual QuickStart Guide**

Available on your computer and tablet, Enhanced Visual QuickStart Guides combine the ebook with Video QuickStart instruction to bring you the best of both formats and the ultimate multimedia learning experience.

Visit us at: Peachpit.com/VQS

VISUAL QUICKSTART GUIDE

WATCH
READ
CREATE

Unlimited online access to all Peachpit,
Adobe Press, Apple Training and New
Riders videos and books, as well as conte
from other leading publishers including:
O'Reilly Media, Focal Press, Sams, Que,
Total Training, John Wiley & Sons, Course
Technology PTR, Class on Demand, VTC
and more.

No time commitment or contract
required! Sign up for one month or
a year. All for $19.99 a month

SIGN UP TODAY
peachpit.com/creativeedge